THE LEFT-HAND POSITION

Note that the thumb falls about opposite the joint of the second and third fingers. Keep the elbow in and the fingers curved.

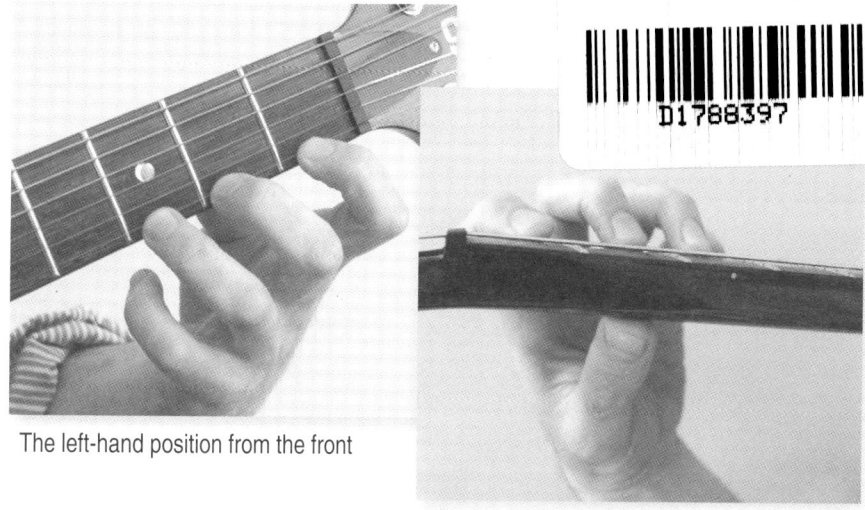

The left-hand position from the front

The left-hand position from the back

THE RIGHT-HAND POSITION

The pick is held firmly, but without squeezing it hard enough to cause tension in the right arm. The motion is a relaxed downward sweep of the wrist, not the entire arm. A downpick, or downstroke, is a downward motion toward the floor. An upstroke, is an upward motion away from the floor.

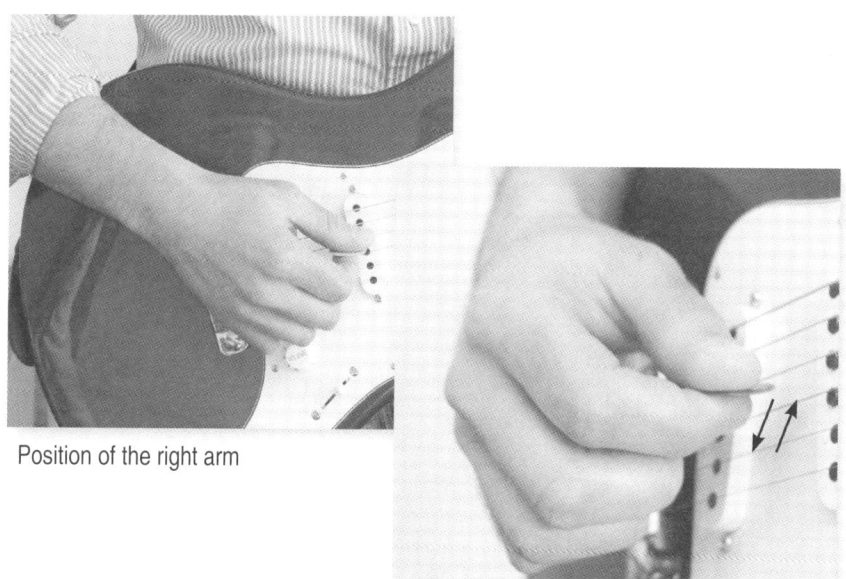

Position of the right arm

Motion of the pick

PLACING THE FINGER ON A STRING

When you place a left-hand finger on a string, make sure you press firmly and as close to the fret wire as you can without actually being right on it. This will ensure a clean, bright tone.

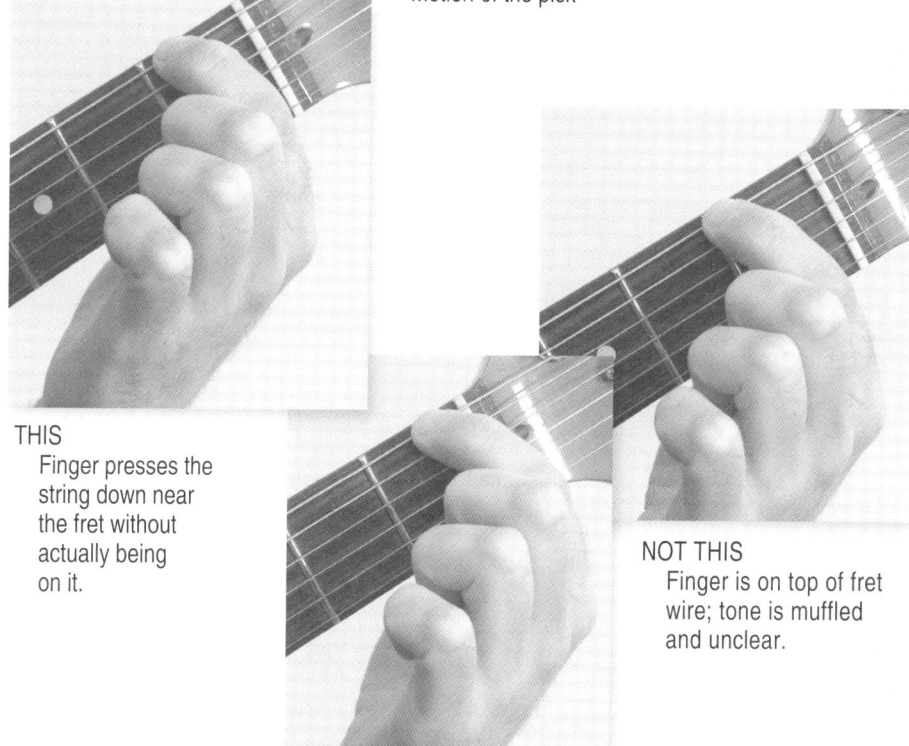

THIS
Finger presses the string down near the fret without actually being on it.

NOT THIS
Finger is on top of fret wire; tone is muffled and unclear.

NOT THIS
Finger is too far from fret wire; tone is "buzzy" and indefinite.

GETTING ACQUAINTED WITH MUSIC

Notes

Musical sounds are indicated by symbols called NOTES. Their time value is determined by their color (white or black) and by STEMS and FLAGS that may be attached to the NOTEHEADS.

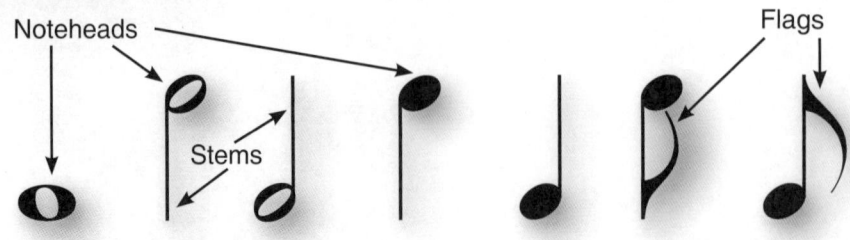

The Staff

The name and pitch of the notes are determined by the note's position on a graph, made of five horizontal lines and the spaces in between, called the STAFF. The notes are named after the first seven letters of the alphabet (A–G), repeated to embrace the entire range of musical sound.

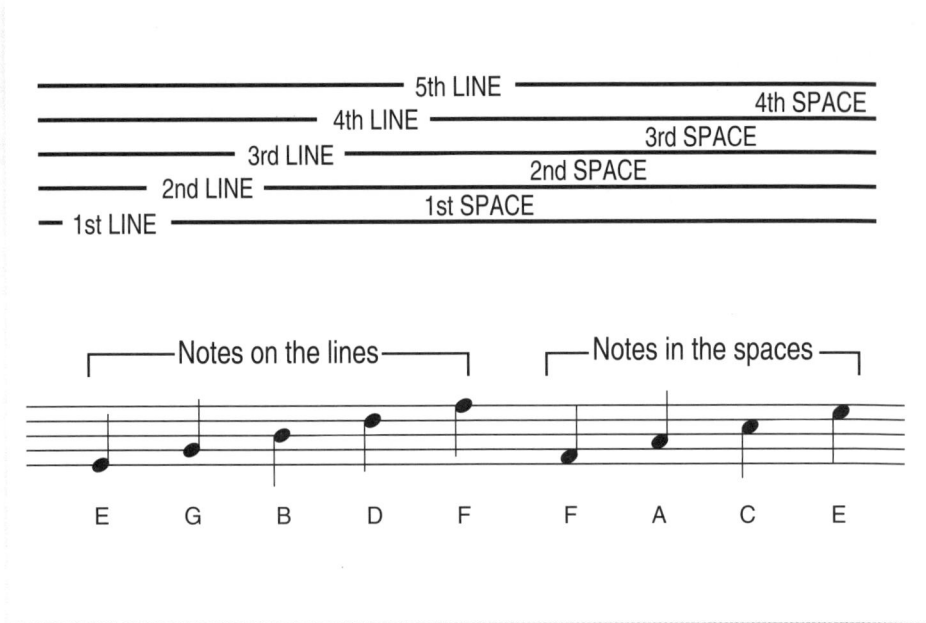

Measures and Bar Lines

Music is also divided into equal units of time, called MEASURES. One measure is divided from another by a BAR LINE.

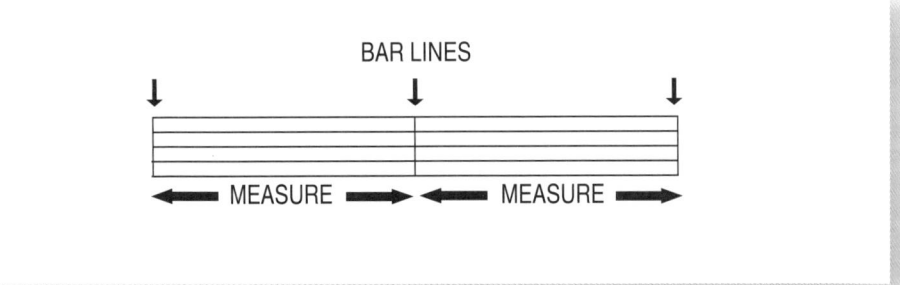

Clefs

During the evolution of music notation, the staff had from two to twenty lines, and symbols were invented to locate a reference line, or pitch, by which all other pitches were determined. These symbols were called CLEFS.

Music for the guitar is written in the G or treble clef. Originally the Gothic letter G was used on a four-line staff to establish the pitch of G. Notice how it wraps around the G line.

LED ZEPPELIN GUITAR METHOD

INSTRUCTIONAL MATERIAL BY RON MANUS & L. C. HARNSBERGER
WITH CONTRIBUTING EDITORS
BRAD TOLINSKI FROM GUITAR WORLD AND NATHANIEL GUNOD FROM NATIONAL GUITAR WORKSHOP

CONTENTS

Holding the Guitar	2
Getting Acquainted with Music	4
Getting Acquainted with Tablature	5
Chord Diagrams	5
Types of Guitars	6
Tuning Your Guitar	7
Notes on the First String E	8
Mixing It Up, More Mixing	9
Sound Off: How to Count Time	10
Time Signatures	10
Playing Different Kinds of Notes and Time Signatures	11
Notes on the Second String B	12
Two-String Rock	12
Stairway to Heaven (Melody)	13
Notes on the Third String G	14
Aura Lee	14
Ties	15
Boogie with Stu	15
Introducing Chords	16
Meet the Chords	16
The Three-String C Chord	17
Ode to Joy	17
Introducing the Quarter Rest	18
Rock 'n' Rhythm	18
The Three-String G7 Chord	19
The Lemon Song	19
Notes on the Fourth String D	20
Incomplete Measures	20
Chord Accompaniments	20
Your Time is Gonna Come	21
The Four-String G Chord	22
Whole Lotta Love	22
Going to California	23
Notes on the Fifth String A	24
Moby Dick	24
Introducing High A	26
Rockin' in Dorian Mode	26
Thank You	28
Notes on the Sixth String E	29
The Natural Scale	29
Tempo Signs	30
Three-Tempo Rock	30
How Many More Times (Bass Line)	30
The Four-String G7 Chord	31
The Lemon Song	31
The Four-String C Chord	32
Bron-Y-Aur Stomp	32
Eighth Notes	33
Eighth-Note Rock	33
Speed Drill	34
Communication Breakdown	35
Sharps, Flats, and Naturals	36
The Chromatic Scale	37
Chromatic Rock	37
Dazed and Confused	38
The Four-String F Chord	40
Communication Breakdown (Intro and Chorus)	40
Out on the Tiles (Solo, Duet, or Trio)	42
The Major Scale	44
Key Signatures	45
What Is and What Should Never Be (Verse)	46
Good Times Bad Times (Lick)	47
Introducing Dotted Notes	48
Heartbreaker (Riff)	49
How Many More Times (Solo, Duet, or Trio)	50
The Three Principal Chords	52
The Three Principal Chords in the Key of C Major	54
The Five-String C, Four-String F, and Six-String G7 Chords	54
Rhythm Patterns Using the Three Principal Chords in C Major	55
Introducing Triplets	56
You Shook Me	56
Key of A Minor	58
The Three Principal Chords in the Key of A Minor	58
The Four-String D7 Chord	59
Bring It On Home (Solo, Duet, or Trio)	60
New Chords: The Five-String A and Six-String Em Chords	62
When the Levee Breaks	62
The Six-String E Chord	64
Immigrant Song	64
Living Loving Maid (She's Just a Woman)	66
The Three Principal Chords in the Key of G Major	67
The Six-String G Chord, the Five-String C, and Four-String D7 Chords	67
Rock and Roll	68
The Dominant Major Chord	70
The Four-String D Major Chord	70
Thank You	70
Key of E Minor	72
The Three Principal Chords in the Key of E Minor	72
House of the Rising Sun	73
The Battle of Evermore	74
Power Chords	76
Misty Mountain Hop	76
Preparation for Bar (Barre) Chords	78
The Three Principal Chords in the Key of F Major	79
Important Open Chords	80
Most Commonly Used Barre Chords	81
Stairway to Heaven (Ending Section)	82
Sixteenth Notes	84
Dotted Eighth and Sixteenth Notes	85
Sixteenth-Note Triplets	85
Hammer-Ons and Pull-Offs	86
Over the Hills and Far Away	86
Fingerstyle	88
Bourée in E Minor	89
Babe I'm Gonna Leave You (Intro)	90
Important Small Barre Chords	91
Stairway to Heaven (Intro)	92
Chord Chart	94
Guitar Fingerboard Chart	96

Copyright © MMXII by Alfred Music Publishing Co., Inc.
All rights reserved. Printed in USA.

No part of this book shall be reproduced, arranged, adapted, recorded, publicly performed, stored in a retrieval system, or transmitted by any means without written permission from the publisher. In order to comply with copyright laws, please apply for such written permission and/or license by contacting the publisher at alfred.com/permissions.

ISBN-10: 0-7390-6354-5 (Book and CD)
ISBN-13: 978-0-7390-6354-5 (Book and CD)

Alfred Music Publishing Co., Inc.
P.O. Box 10003
Van Nuys, CA 91410-0003
alfred.com

Cover Photos
Large image of Jimmy Page back stage © Atlas Icons • Three small images of Led Zeppelin © Photofest

HOLDING THE GUITAR

Standing, with strap

Sitting

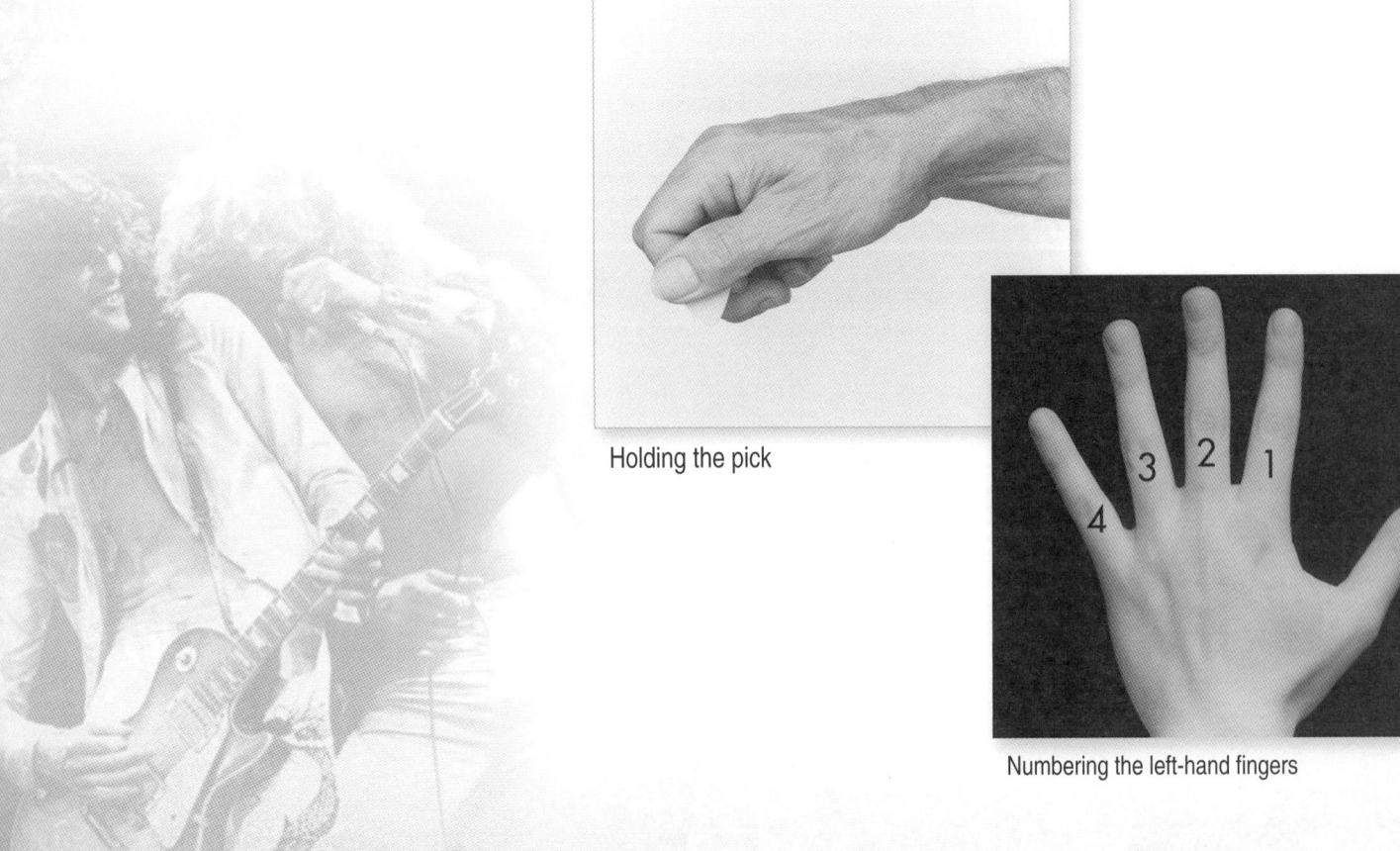

Holding the pick

Numbering the left-hand fingers

GETTING ACQUAINTED WITH TABLATURE

Tablature is a graphic method of showing how to play notes and chords on the guitar. It uses a six-line staff, with each line representing one string of the guitar.

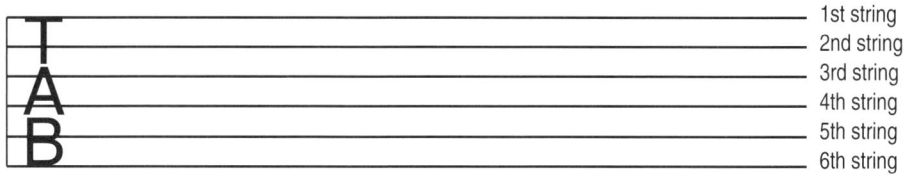

A number placed on a line means to finger that fret on the corresponding string. A 0 means the string is played open. Thus,

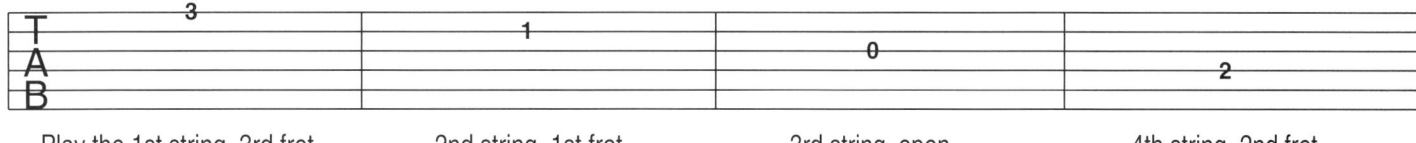

Play the 1st string, 3rd fret | 2nd string, 1st fret | 3rd string, open | 4th string, 2nd fret

Numbers placed one on top of the other are played simultaneously as chords.

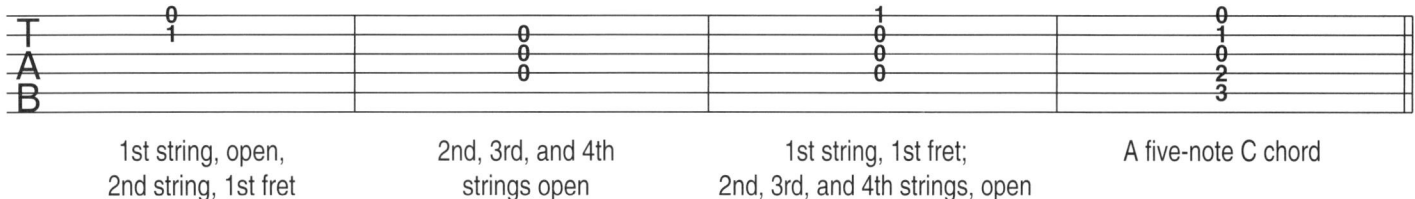

1st string, open, 2nd string, 1st fret | 2nd, 3rd, and 4th strings open | 1st string, 1st fret; 2nd, 3rd, and 4th strings, open | A five-note C chord

CHORD DIAGRAMS

Chord diagrams are used to indicate fingering for chords. The example to the right means to place your first finger on the 1st fret, 2nd string and second finger on the 2nd fret, 4th string. Then strum the first four strings only. The x's on the 5th and 6th strings indicate not to play those strings.

To make it as clear as possible, all the material in this book appears both in traditional music and in tablature. Chord diagrams are included where appropriate.

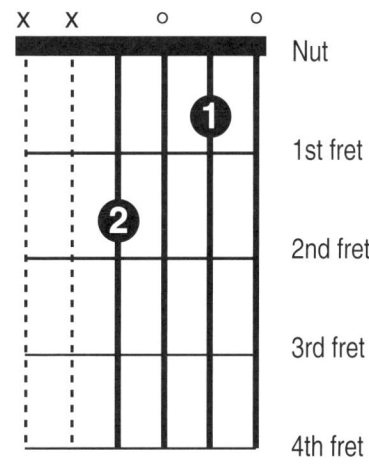

Strings: 6th 5th 4th 3rd 2nd 1st

TYPES OF GUITARS

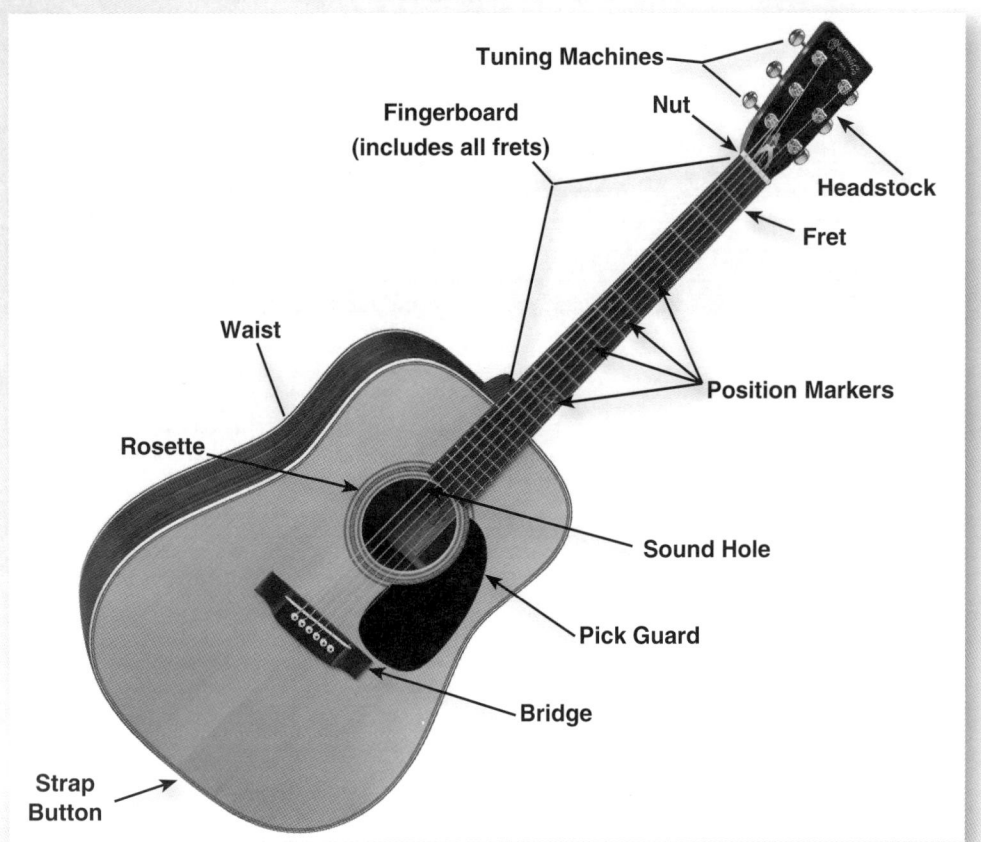

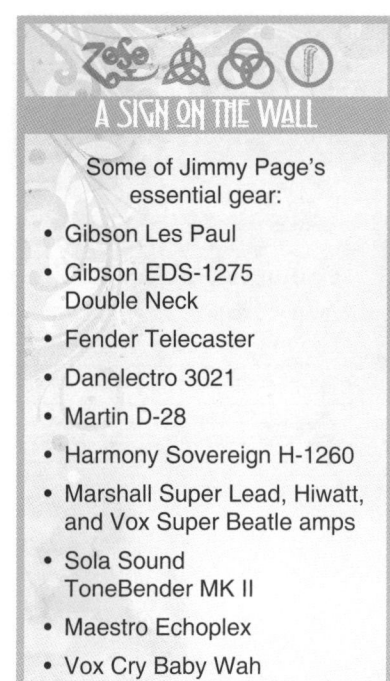

A SIGN ON THE WALL

Some of Jimmy Page's essential gear:
- Gibson Les Paul
- Gibson EDS-1275 Double Neck
- Fender Telecaster
- Danelectro 3021
- Martin D-28
- Harmony Sovereign H-1260
- Marshall Super Lead, Hiwatt, and Vox Super Beatle amps
- Sola Sound ToneBender MK II
- Maestro Echoplex
- Vox Cry Baby Wah

Acoustic Guitar

Acoustic guitars have narrow necks and steel strings. They are either strummed with a flat pick or played with one or more finger picks.

Strings: Steel
Gauge: Light or Medium

Solid Body Electric Guitar

Solid body electrics have narrow necks, light-gauge strings, and one or more electric pickups. The output of these pickups is fed through an amplifier and is sometimes modified further by using wah-wah pedals, distortion pedals, chorus effects, or other means of altering the tone.

Strings: Steel
Gauge: Light

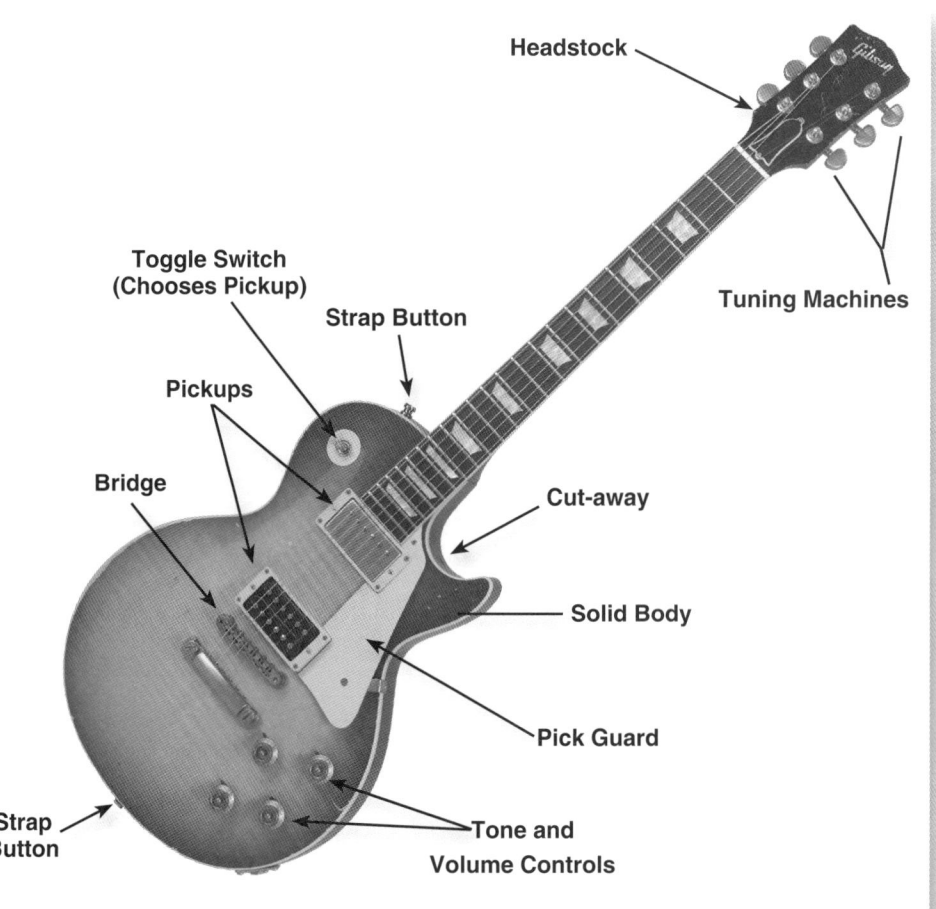

TUNING YOUR GUITAR

First, make sure the strings are wound properly around the tuning machines (sometimes called *pegs*). They should go from inside to outside. See below:

Turning the tuning peg counter-clockwise (always from the point of view of the player) raises the pitch. Turning the tuning peg clockwise lowers the pitch. Some guitars have the six tuning pegs on the same side of the head. Make sure all six strings are wound the same way, from inside out.

Once your strings are wound on the pegs properly, listen to the CD for this book, and follow the directions to get the guitar in perfect tune.

If you do not have the CD, follow the directions below (How to Tune Your Guitar Without Using the CD) to get the instrument in tune.

important:
Always remember that the thinnest, highest-sounding string—the one closest to the floor—is the 1st string. The thickest, lowest-sounding string—the one closest to the ceiling—is the 6th string. When guitarists say "the highest string," they mean the one highest in pitch, not the one highest in position.

How to Tune Your Guitar Without Using the CD

The six strings of your guitar have the same pitches as the six notes shown on the piano in the following illustration:

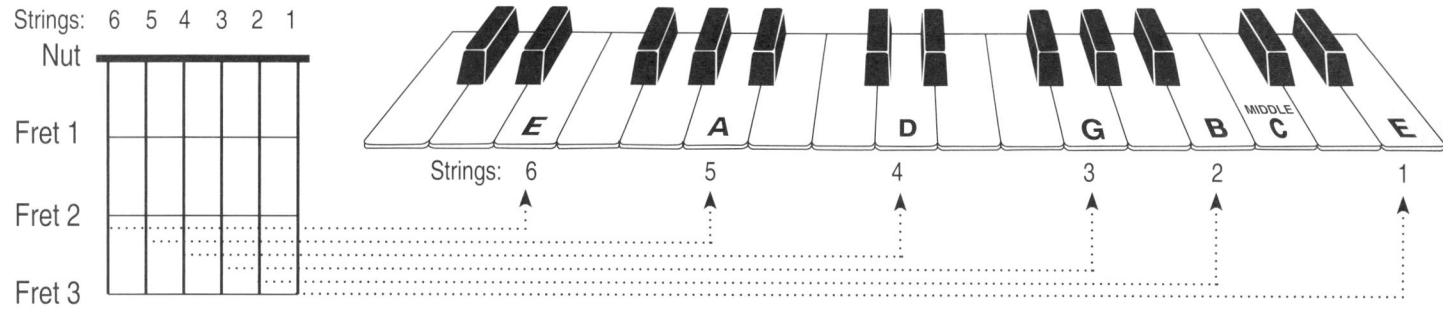

First, tune the 6th string to E on the piano. If no piano is available, we recommend you buy a tuning fork, tuning pipe, or electronic tuner. The first two are inexpensive and very handy, and all three are available from your music dealer. Tune the rest of the strings as follows:

Press 5th fret of 6th string to get pitch of 5th string (A).

Press 5th fret of 5th string to get pitch of 4th string (D).

Press 5th fret of 4th string to get pitch of 3rd string (G).

Press 4th fret of 3rd string to get pitch of 2nd string (B).

Press 5th fret of 2nd string to get pitch of 1st string (E).

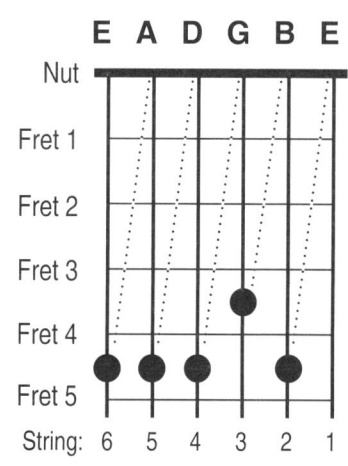

NOTES ON THE FIRST STRING E 🎵 Track 2

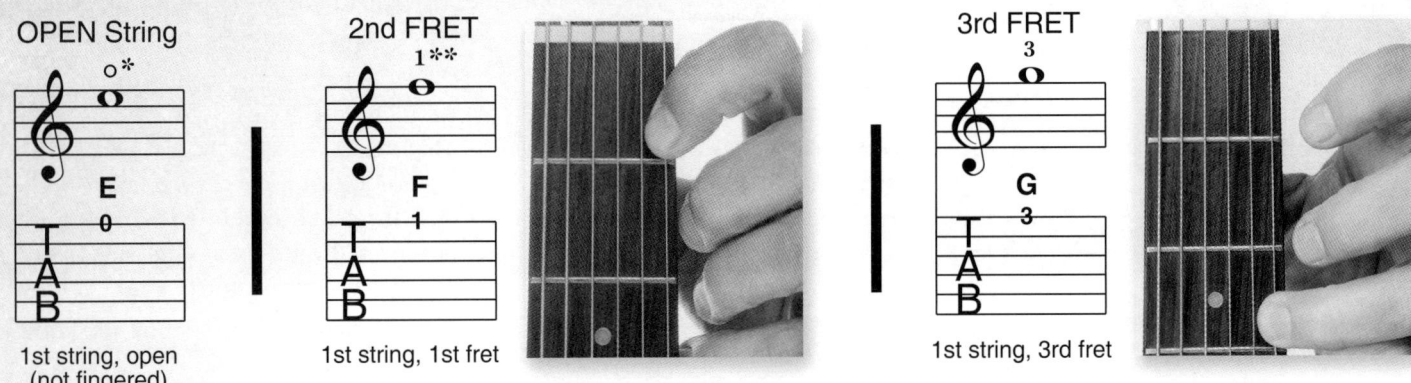

Playing the first string open (the note E):

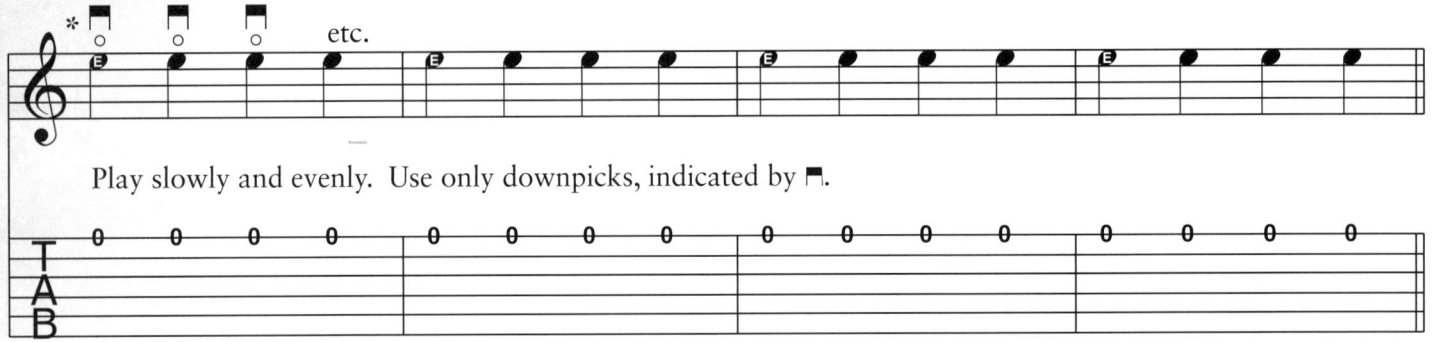

Play slowly and evenly. Use only downpicks, indicated by ⊓.

Combining the fingered notes F and G with the open string E:

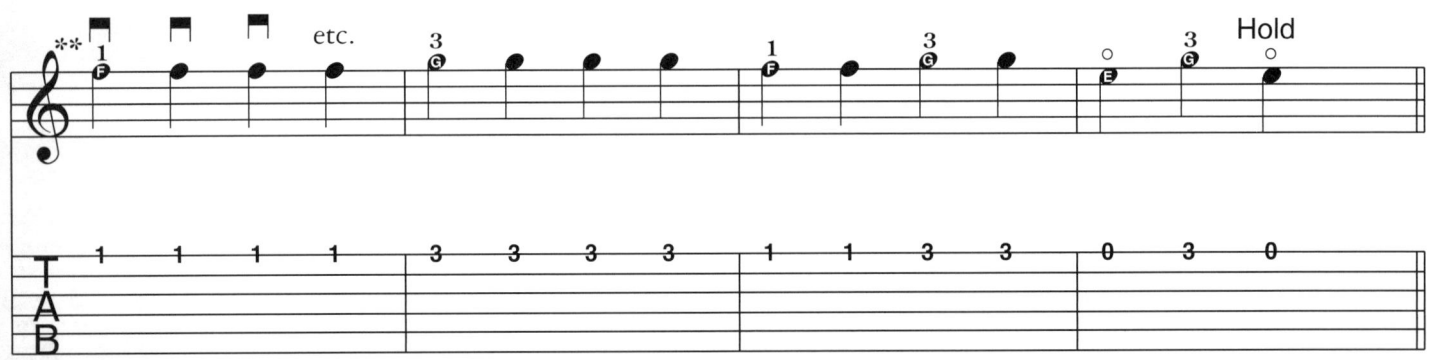

* o means OPEN STRING
** Numbers above the notes are fingerings and indicate which left-hand fingers are to be used.

Mixing It Up

Left-hand fingers: When playing from the 1st to the 3rd fret, keep the first finger down. Only the G will sound, but when you go back to the F, your finger will already be in place, making the transition sound smoother.

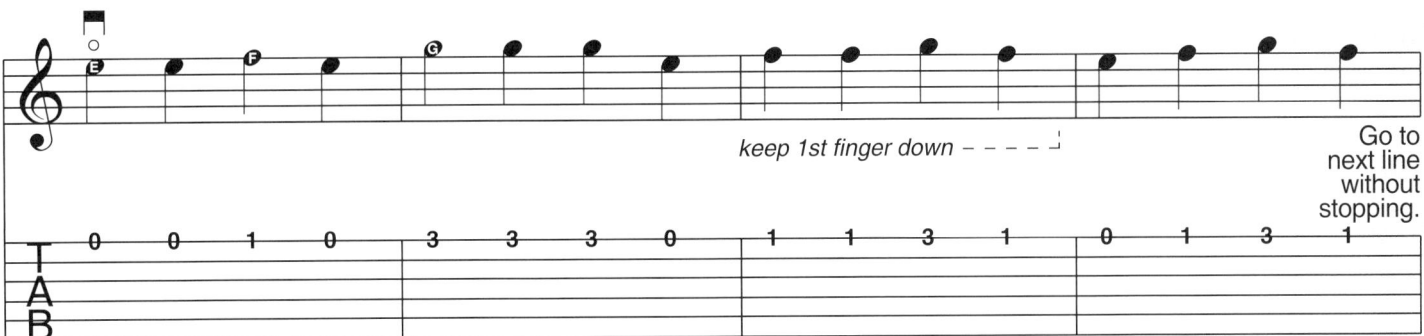

A double bar line marks the end of a piece.

More Mixing

Left-hand fingers: Place as close to the fret wires as possible without actually touching them.

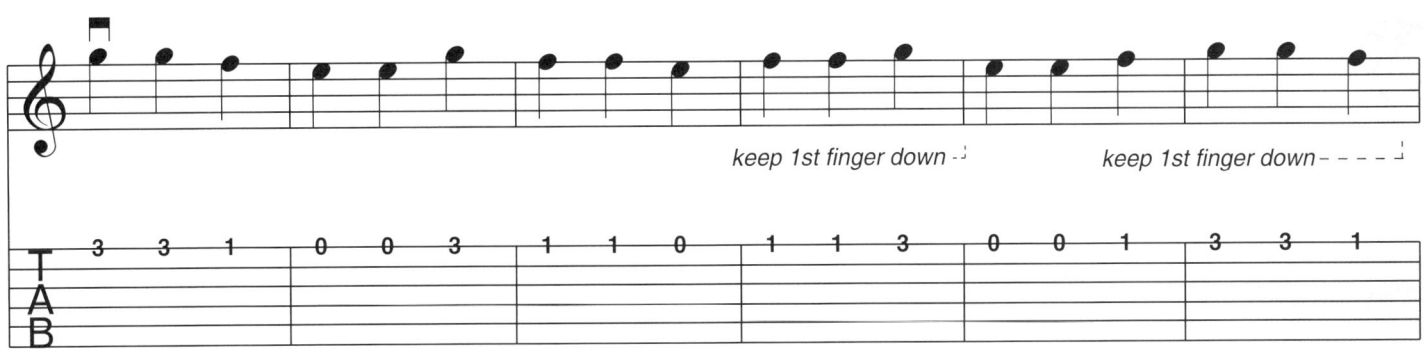

SOUND OFF: HOW TO COUNT TIME

Four Kinds of Notes

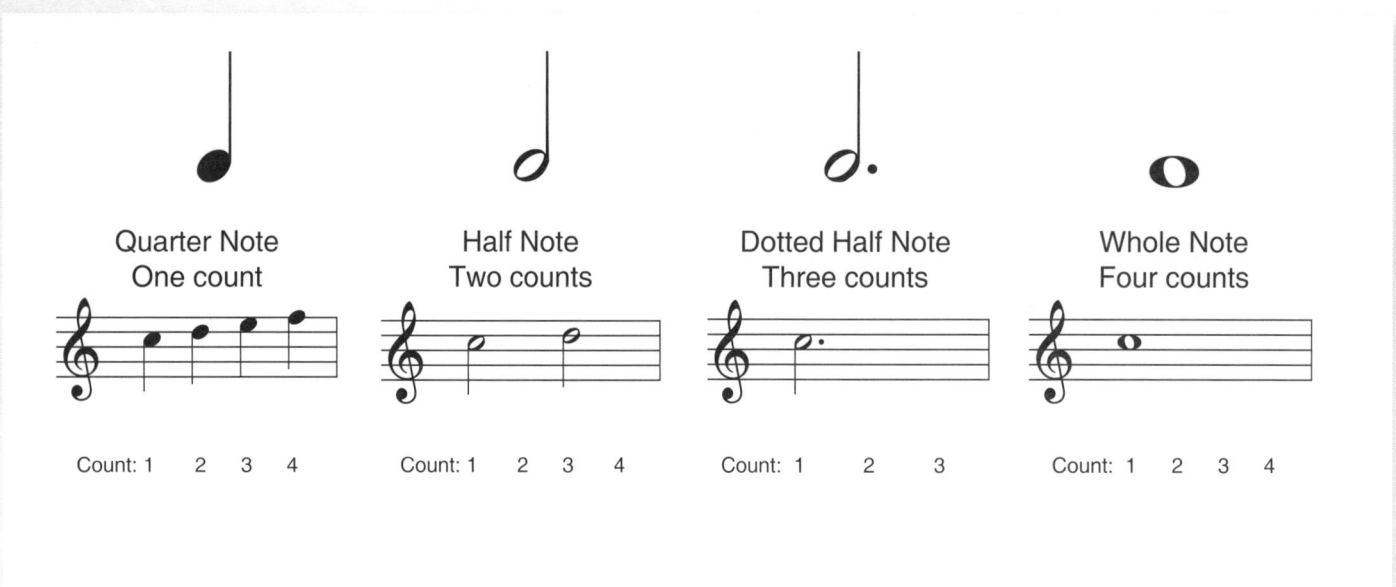

TIME SIGNATURES

Each piece of music has two numbers at its beginning called a TIME SIGNATURE. These numbers tell us how to count time for that particular piece.

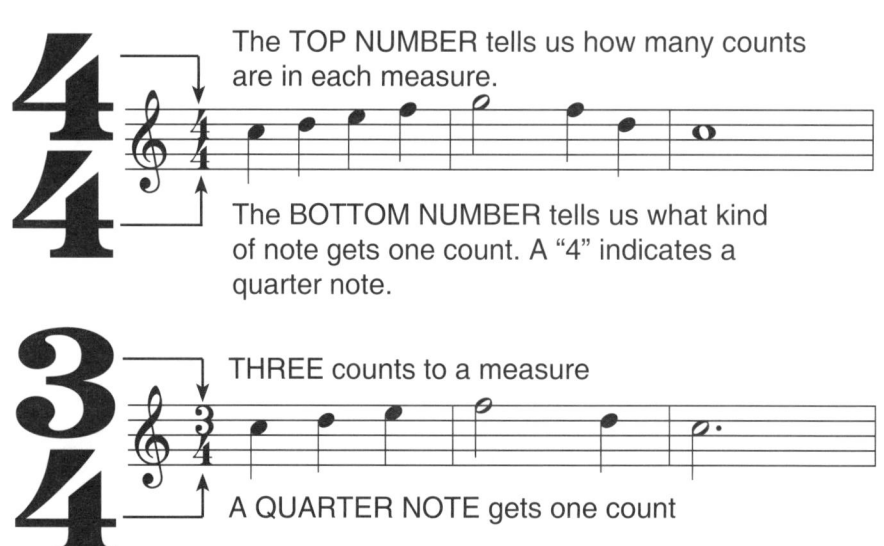

The TOP NUMBER tells us how many counts are in each measure.

The BOTTOM NUMBER tells us what kind of note gets one count. A "4" indicates a quarter note.

THREE counts to a measure

A QUARTER NOTE gets one count

important:

Fill in the missing time signatures of the songs already learned. Even though tablature players do not read standard music notation, it is still important to become familiar with the concept of time signatures.

PLAYING DIFFERENT KINDS OF NOTES AND TIME SIGNATURES

HALF NOTES (TWO COUNTS)

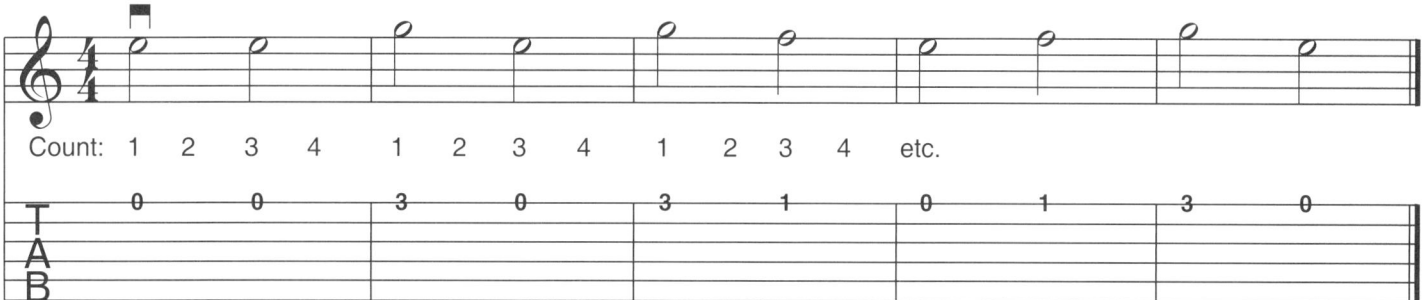

DOTTED HALF NOTES (THREE COUNTS)

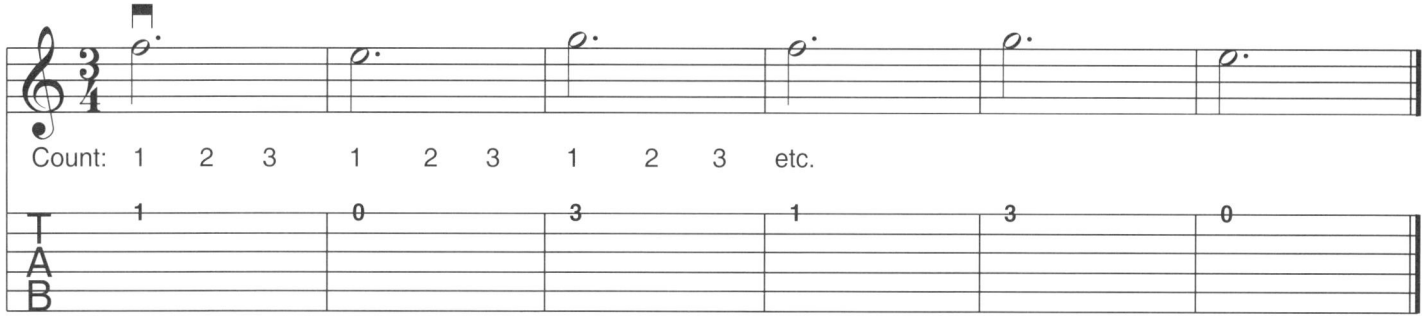

WHOLE NOTES (FOUR COUNTS)

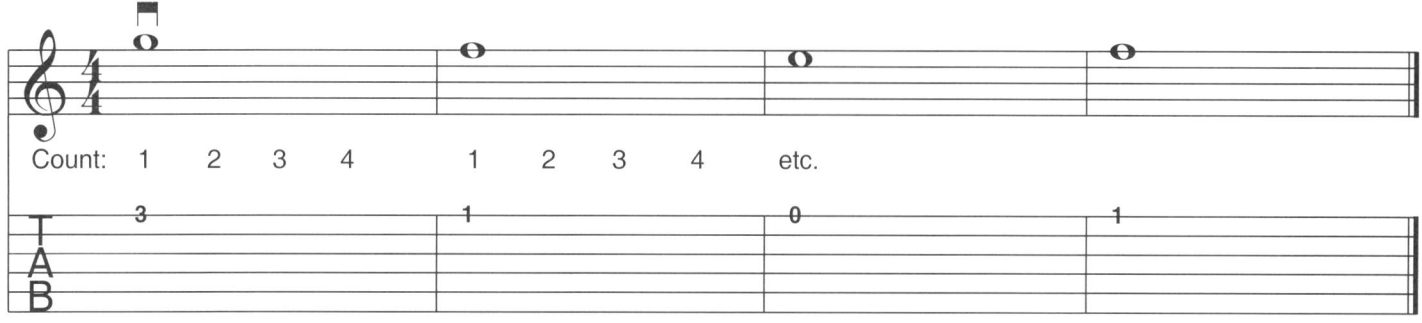

MIXED NOTES (REVIEW)

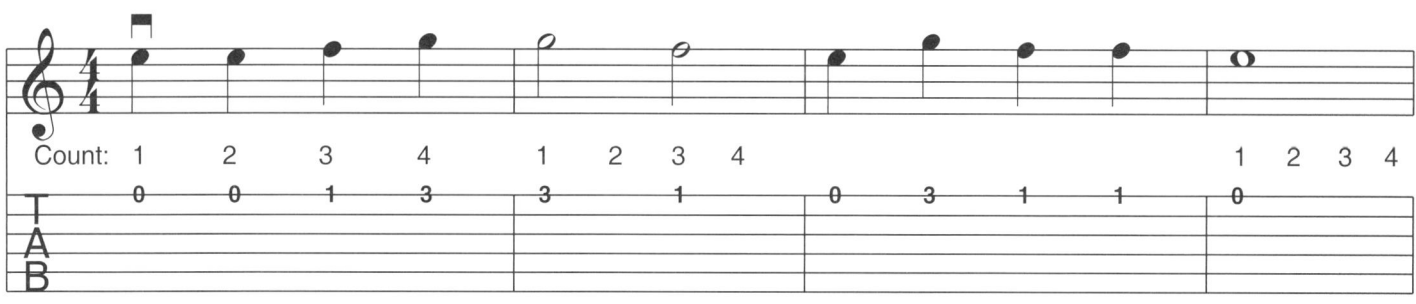

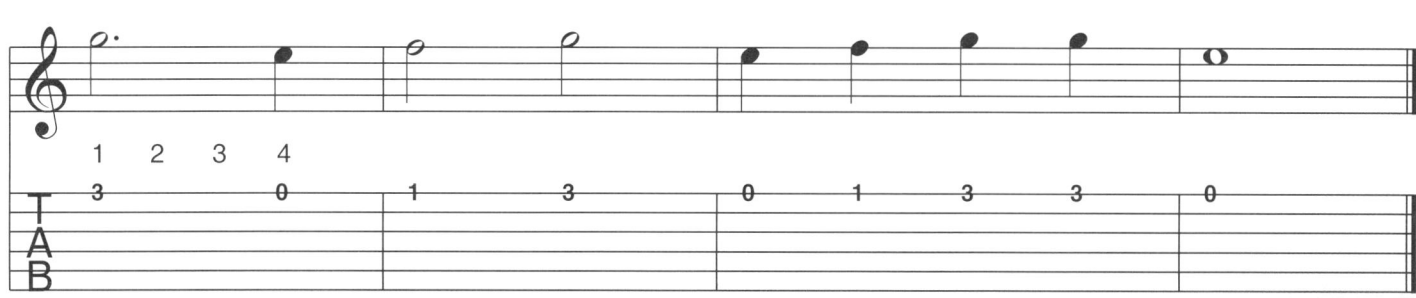

NOTES ON THE SECOND STRING B

Track 6

OPEN String

2nd string, open

1st FRET

2nd string, 1st fret

3rd FRET

2nd string, 3rd fret

Two-String Rock

Track 7

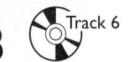

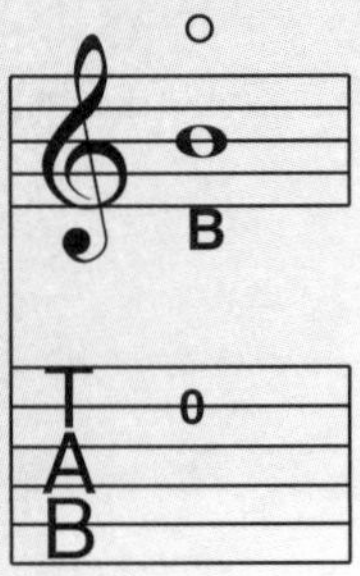

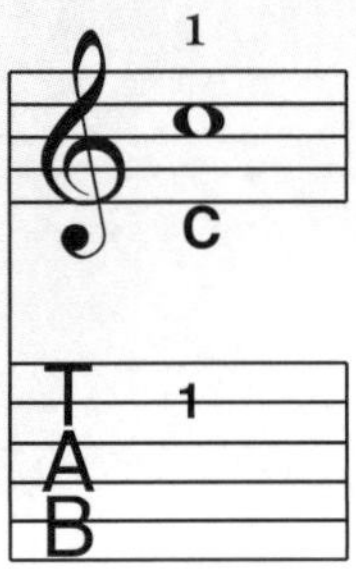

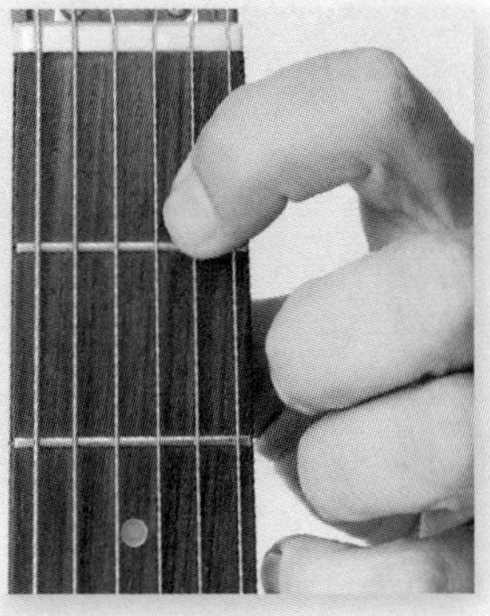

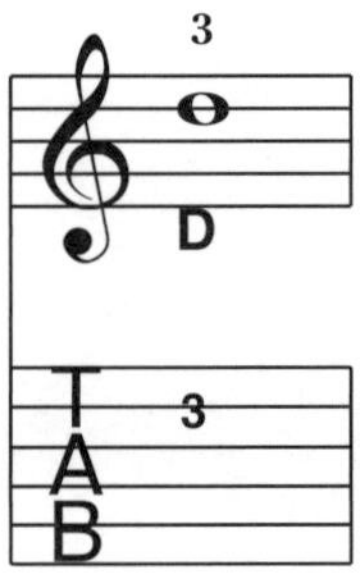

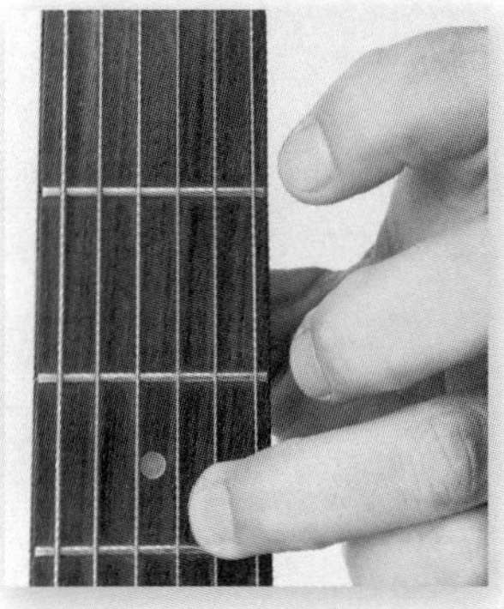

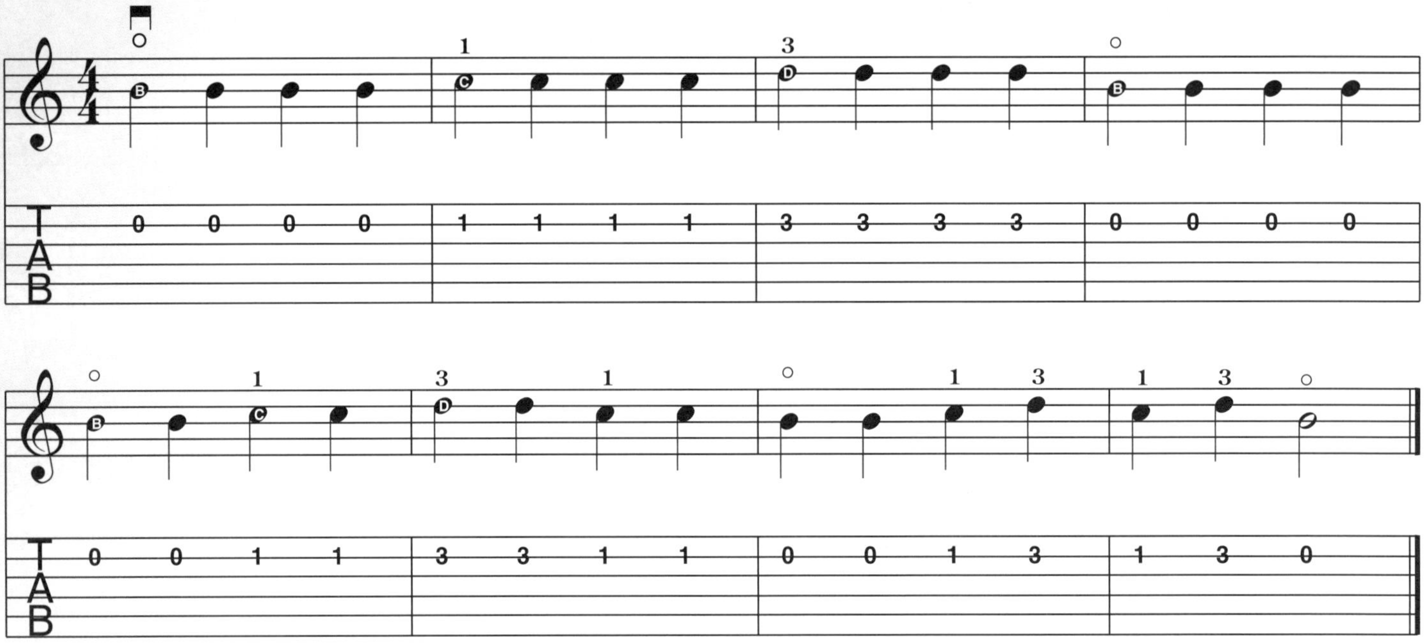

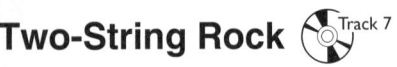

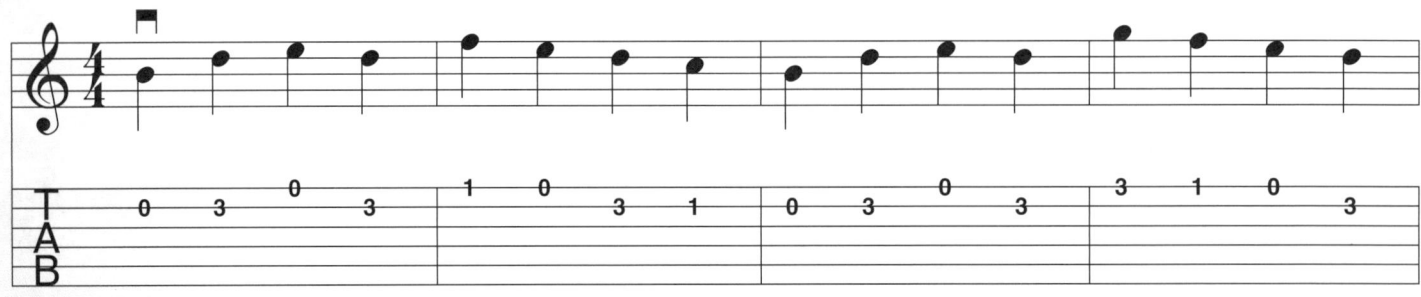

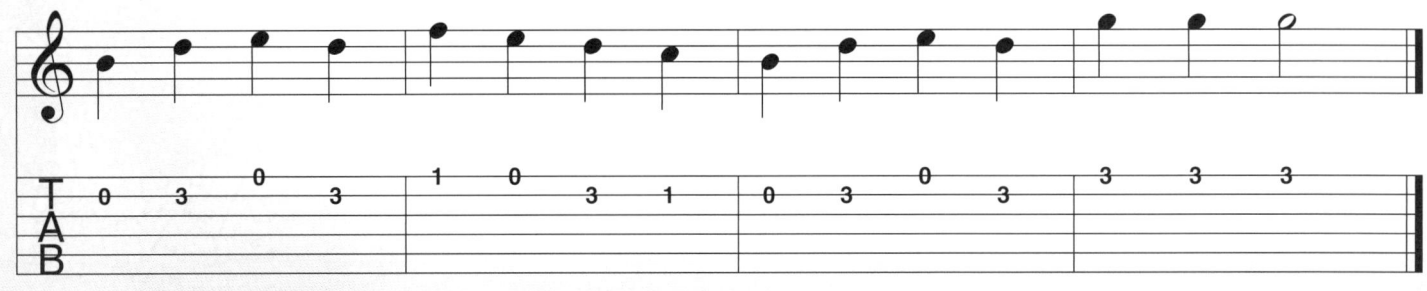

STAIRWAY TO HEAVEN (MELODY)

From the album 🎵

A number of the arrangements in this book will sound different from the original recordings. They have been simplified to help you learn the basics of playing guitar. You'll start with playing the vocal melodies first and then will be playing guitar parts later in the book.

Words and Music by
Jimmy Page and Robert Plant

Moderately Slow

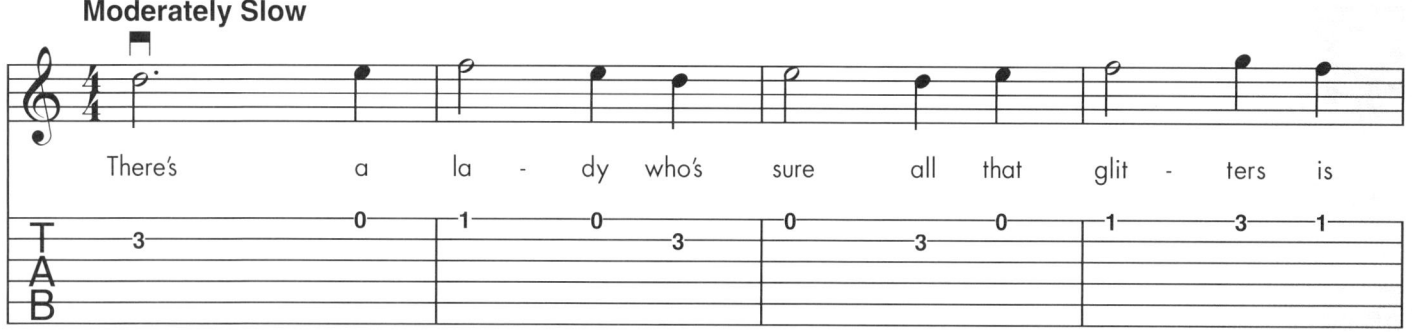

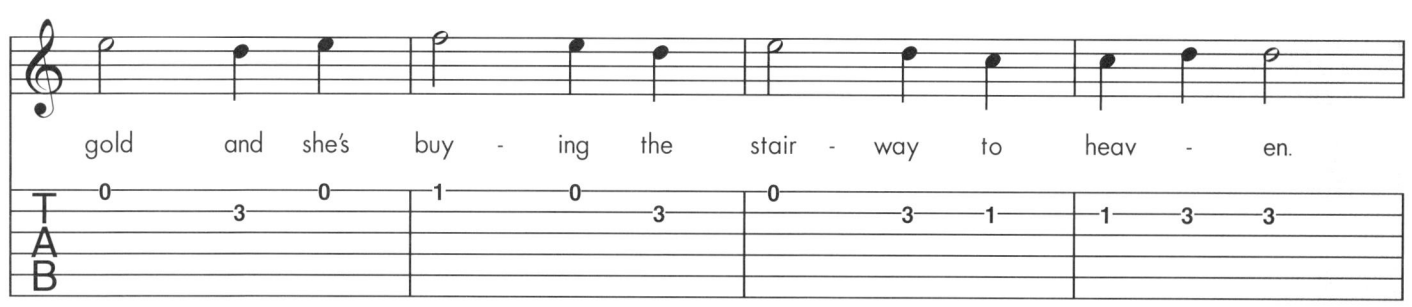

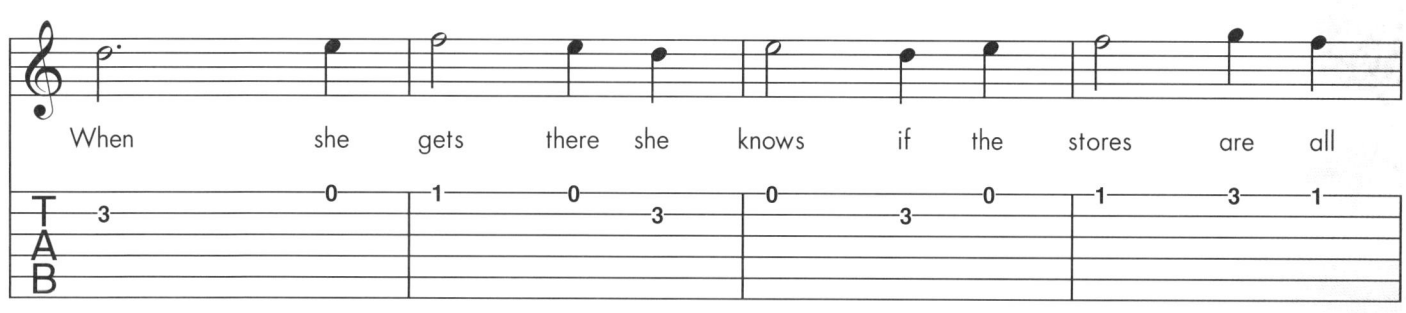

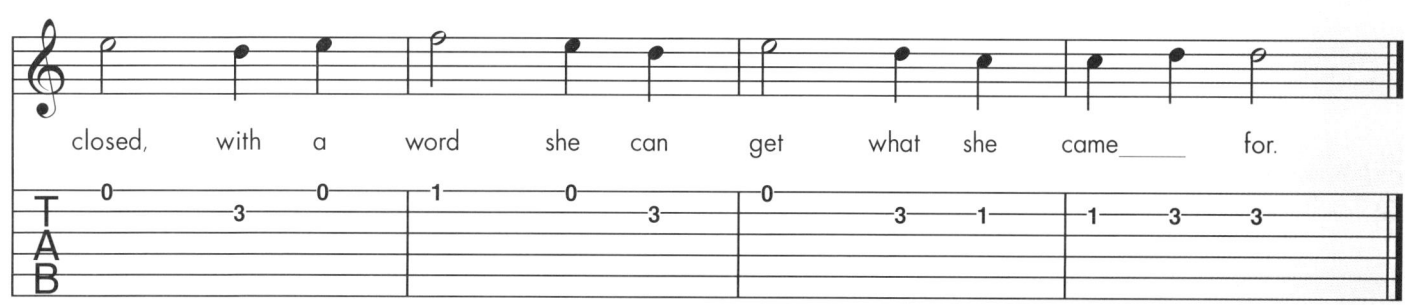

Copyright © 1972 (renewed) FLAMES OF ALBION MUSIC, INC.
All Rights Administered by WB MUSIC CORP.
Exclusive Print Rights for the World Excluding Europe Administered by ALFRED MUSIC PUBLISHING CO., INC.
All Rights Reserved

NOTES ON THE THIRD STRING G *Track 9*

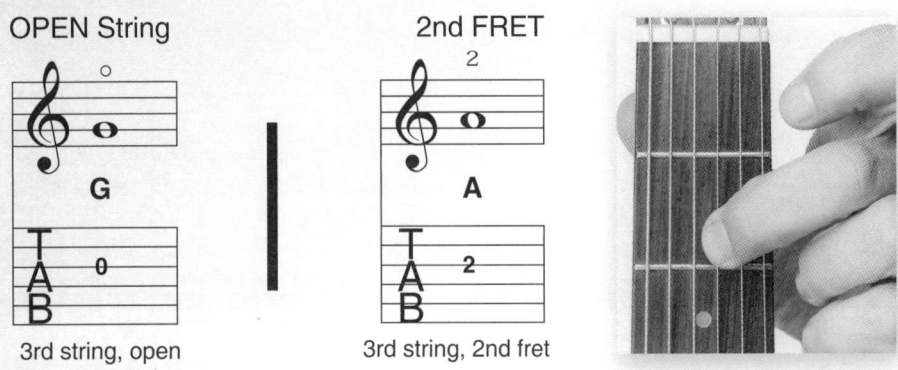

Aura Lee *Track 10*

A SIGN ON THE WALL

At the age of 13, Jimmy Page was inspired to play guitar when he heard Elvis Presley's recording of "Baby, Let's Play House," which featured guitarist Scotty Moore. In 1956, Elvis recorded the Civil War folk song "Aura Lee" with new lyrics and titled it "Love Me Tender."

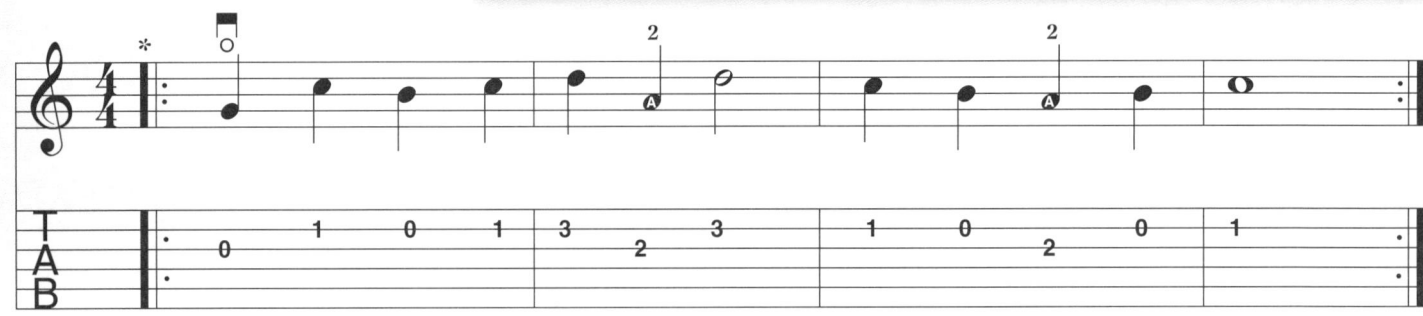

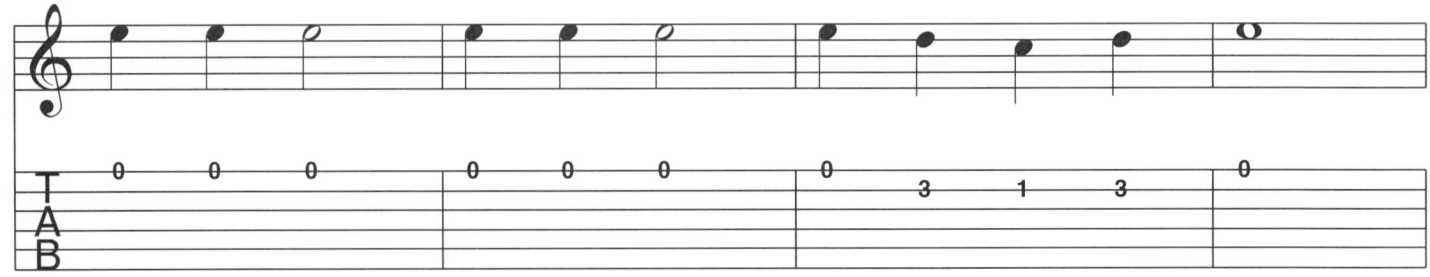

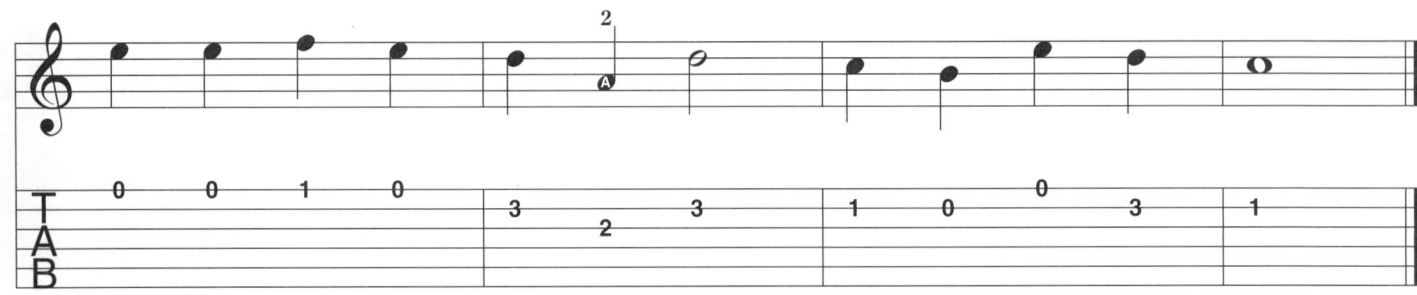

*The double dots on the inside of the double bars indicate that everything between the double bars must be REPEATED.

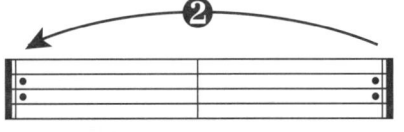
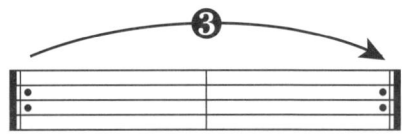

TIES

Ties are curved lines connecting two or more successive notes of the same pitch. When two notes are tied, the second one is not picked; its time value is added to the value of the first note. For example:

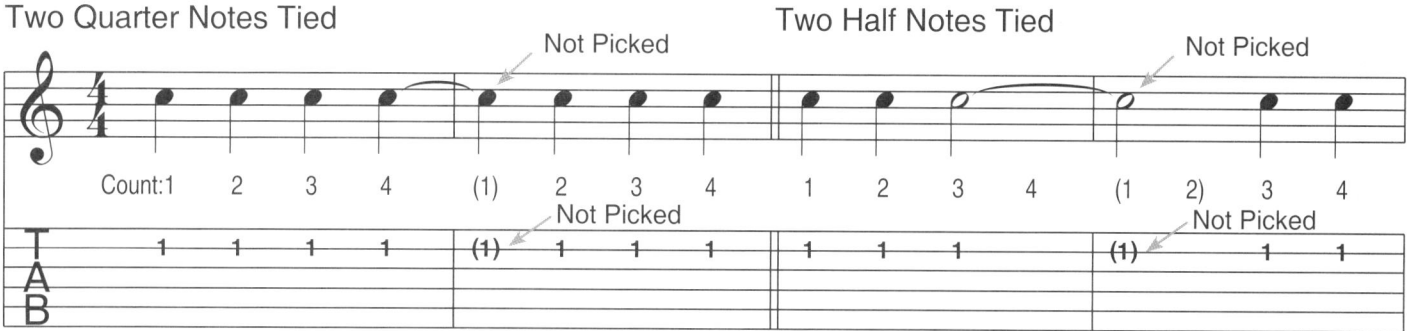

In TAB notation, the tie is indicated by a parenthesis **(1)** — do not pick that note again.

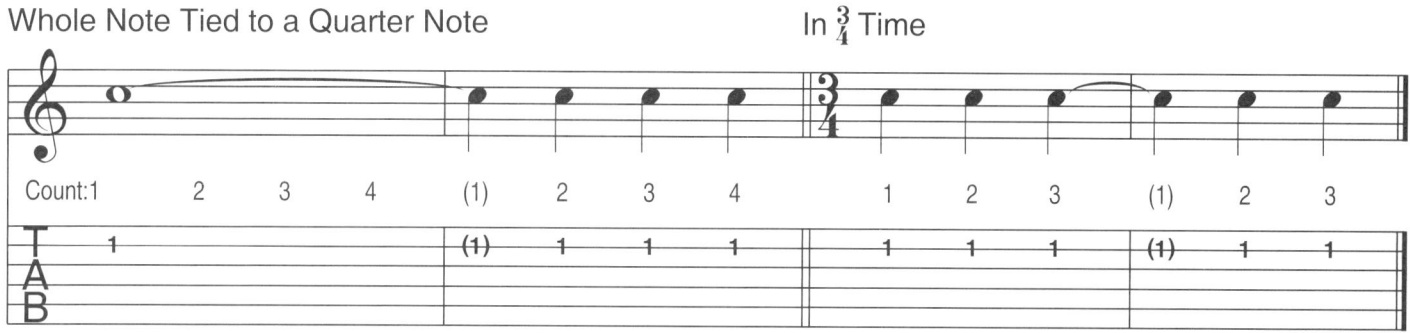

BOOGIE WITH STU

From the album PHYSICAL GRAFFITI

Moderate Boogie

Words And Music By Jimmy Page, Robert Plant, John Bonham, John Paul Jones, Ian Stewart, and Concepcion "Connie" Valenzuela

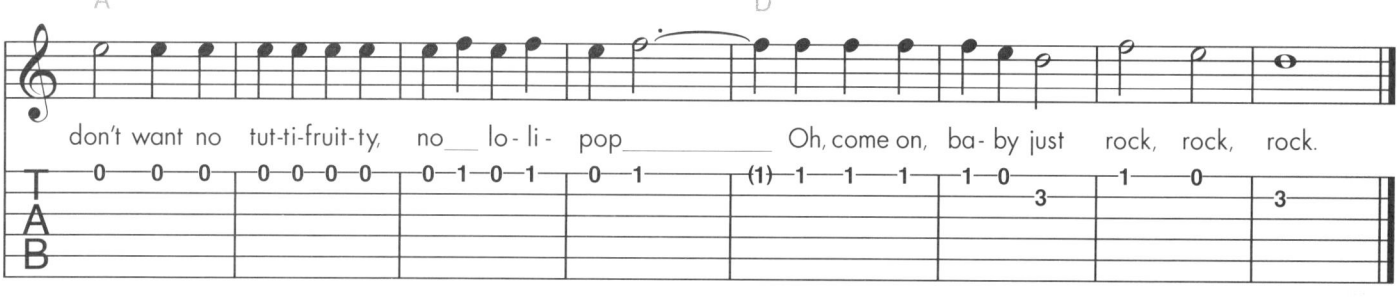

© 1975 (Renewed) FLAMES OF ALBION MUSIC, INC.
All Rights Administered by WB MUSIC CORP.
Exclusive Print Rights for the World Excluding Europe Administered by ALFRED MUSIC PUBLISHING CO., INC.
All Rights Reserved

INTRODUCING CHORDS

A CHORD is a combination of two or more harmonious notes. All note values except the whole note have a stem going up or down.

When notes are struck together as a CHORD, they are connected by the same stem.

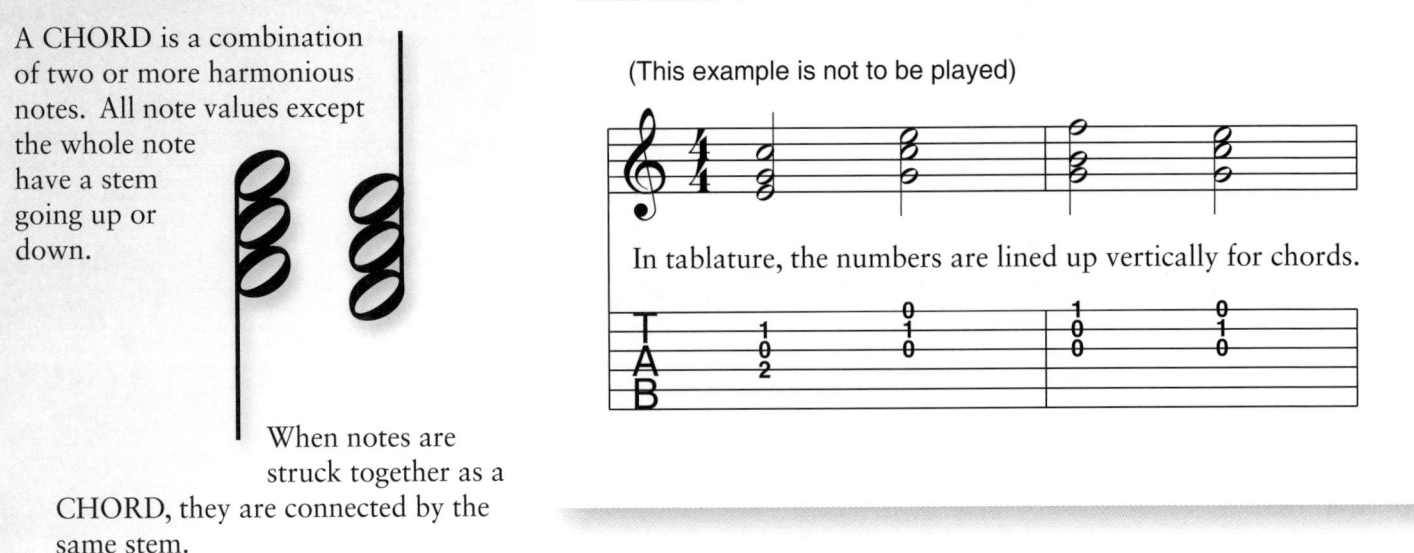

(This example is not to be played)

In tablature, the numbers are lined up vertically for chords.

Meet the Chords  Track 13

Two-note chords on the open B and E strings.

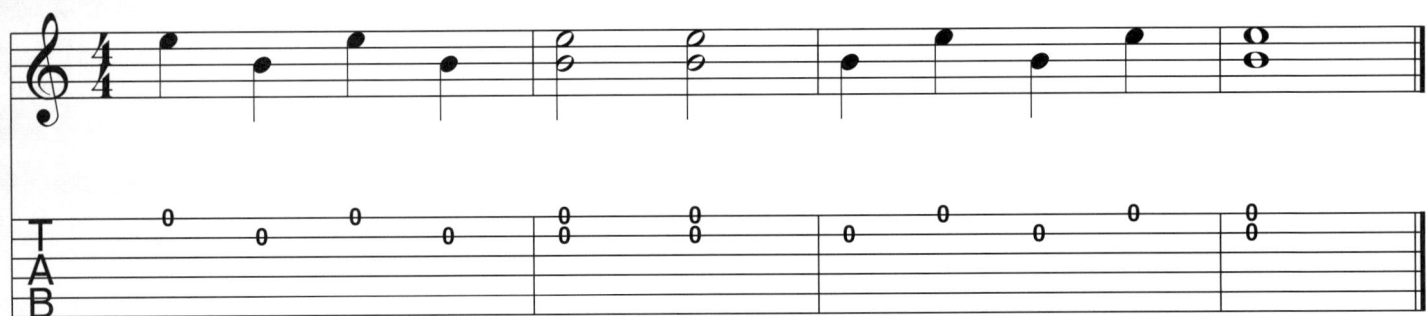

Two-note chords on the open G and B strings.

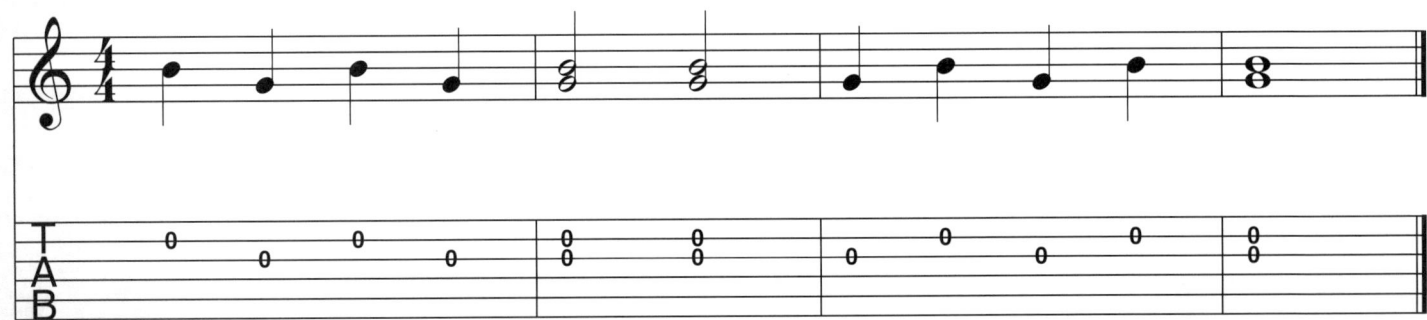

Three-note chords on the open G, B, and E strings.

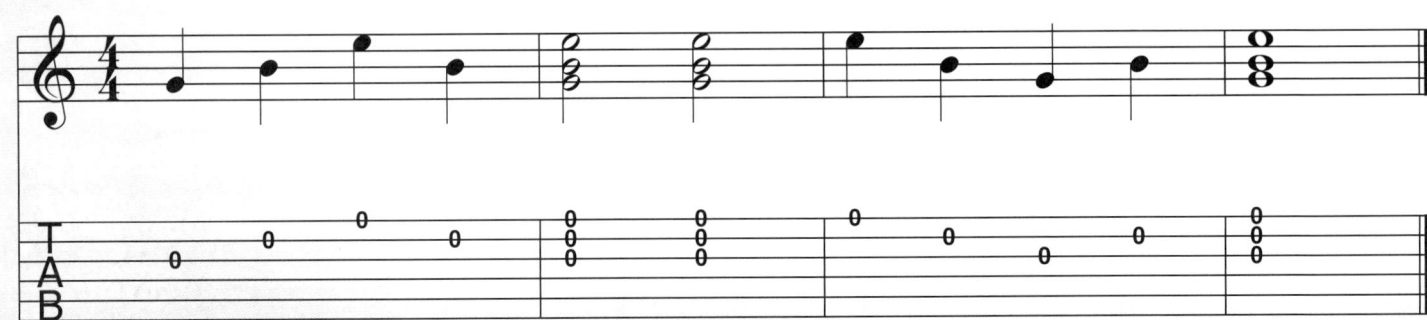

The Three-string C Chord

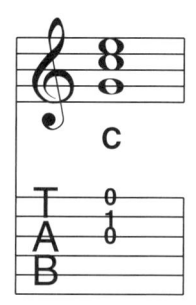 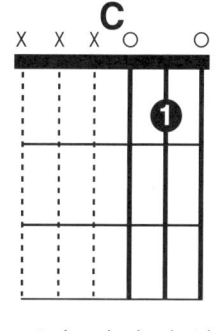 

Track 14

The chords you played on page 16 use only combinations of open strings. This next chord is called the C CHORD. It uses one finger plus the 1st and 3rd open strings.

Do not play dashed strings.

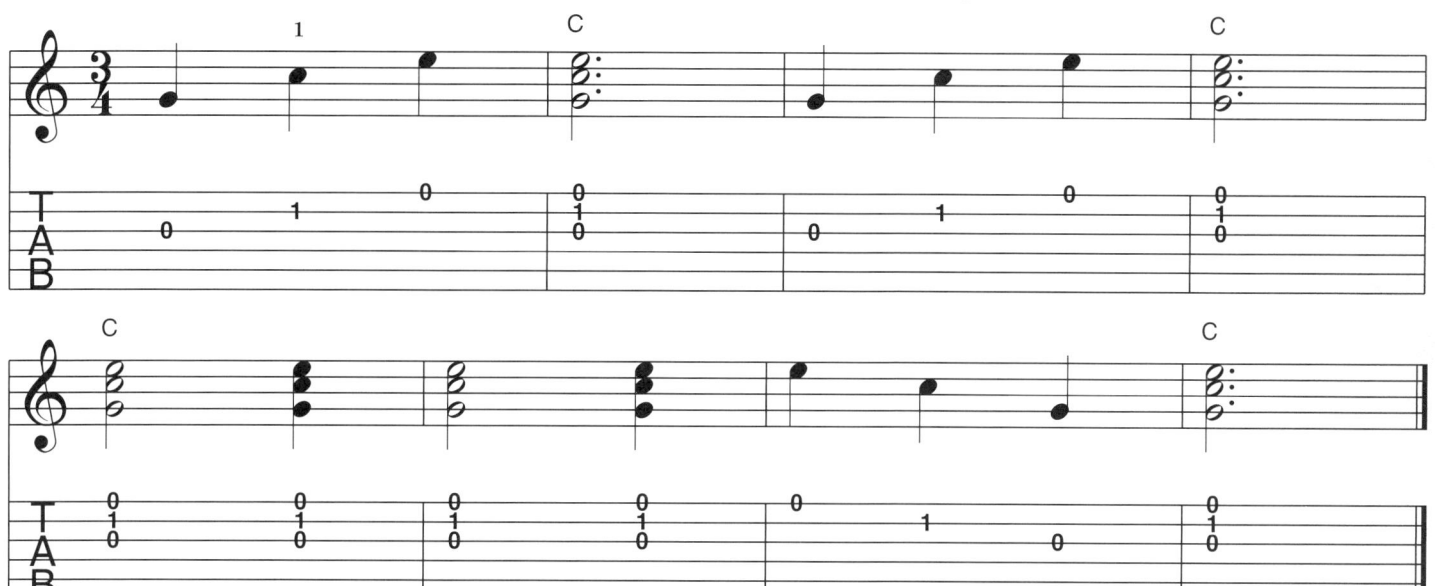

A Sign on the Wall

Before Led Zeppelin was formed, Jimmy Page worked as a session musician in recording studios that required him to read music. During that time, he took a few classical guitar lessons to improve his music reading skills. Classical music spans hundreds of years and thousands of composers, but two of the most famous composers are Beethoven and Bach. Beethoven's "Ode to Joy" is one of the most popular pieces of classical music, and Jimmy plays Bach's "Bouree in E Minor" during "Heartbreaker" on the live album *How the West Was Won* (see page 89).

Ode to Joy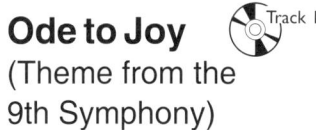
(Theme from the
9th Symphony)

Beethoven

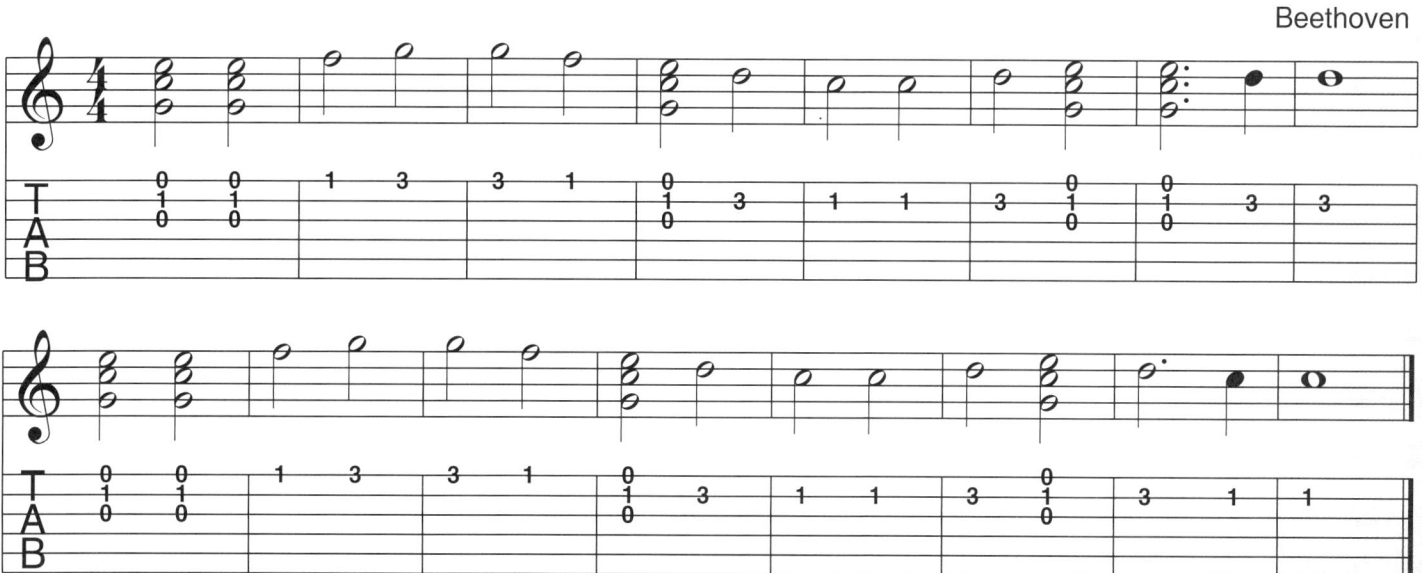

INTRODUCING THE QUARTER REST

Track 16

This symbol is a QUARTER REST, and it is used in music notation to mean one beat of silence. First, play the exercise, then try "Rock 'n' Rhythm."

For a cleaner effect when an open-string note is followed by a rest, you may stop the sound of the strings by touching them lightly with the "heel" of the right hand.

Rock 'n' Rhythm

Track 17

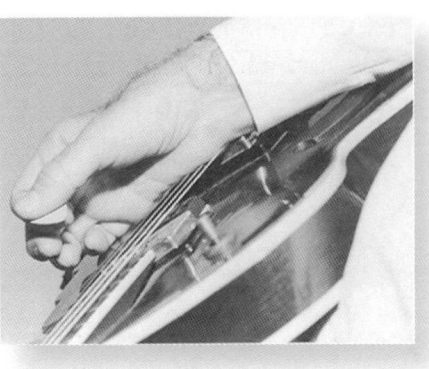

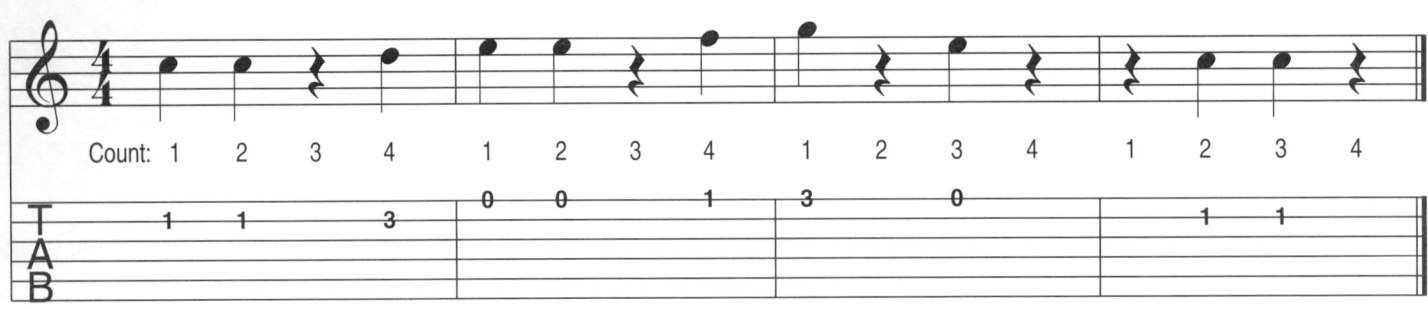

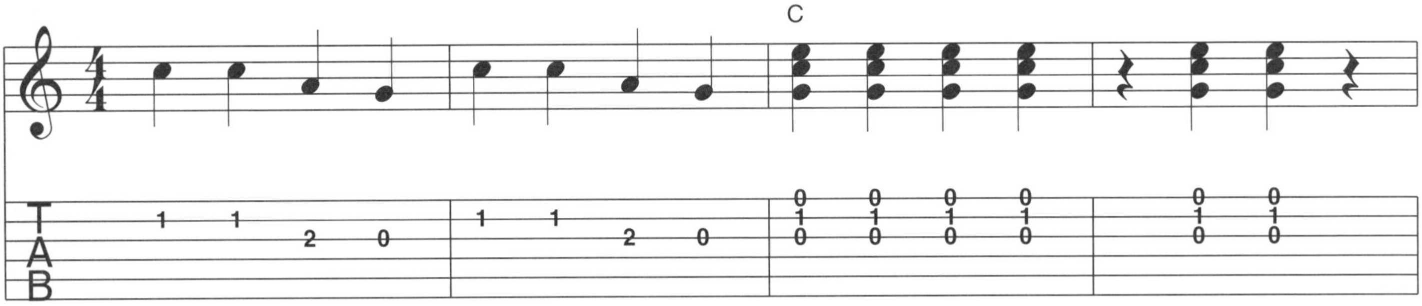

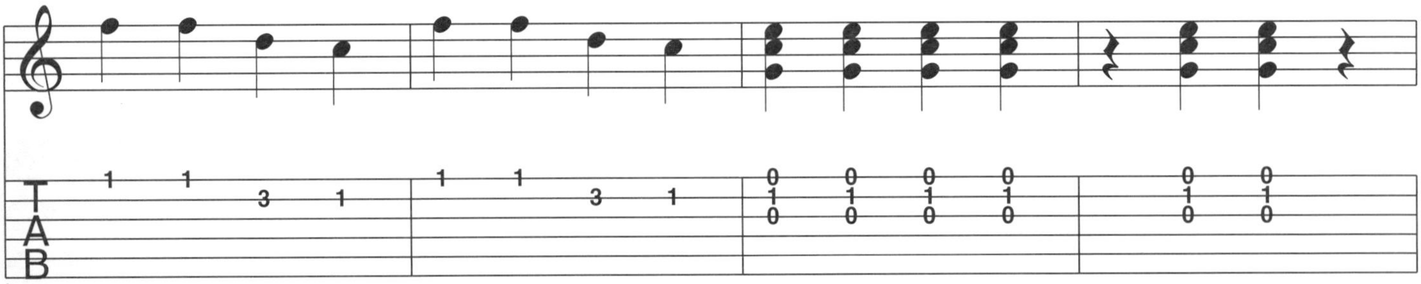

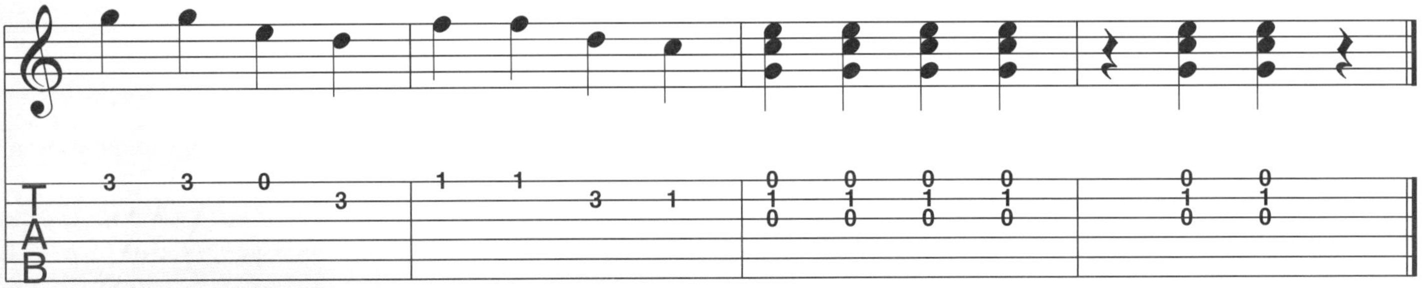

THE THREE-STRING G7 CHORD

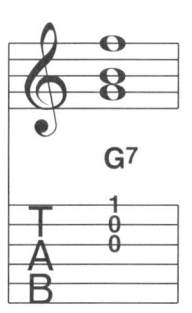
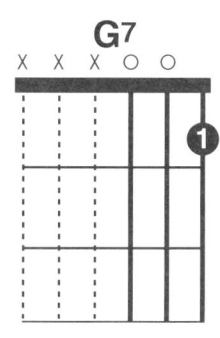
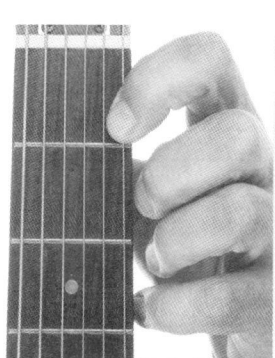

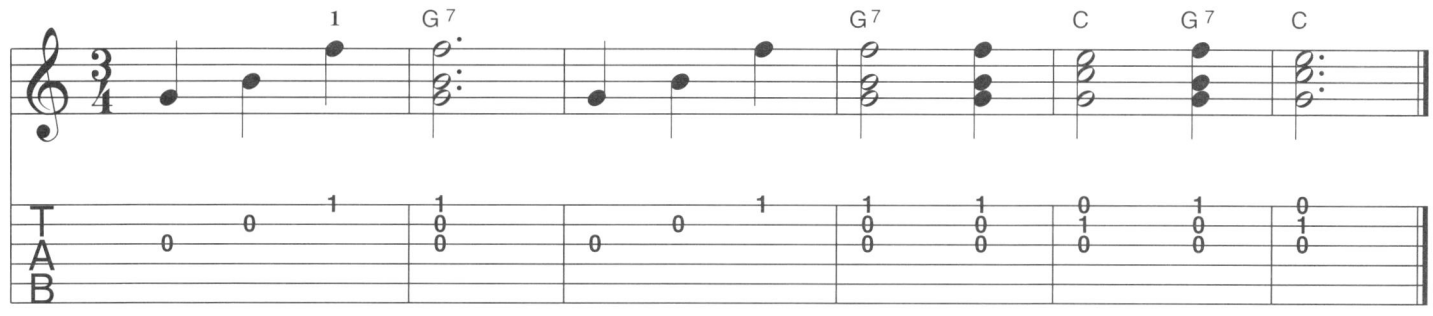

The Lemon Song

From the album LED ZEPPELIN II

Words and Music by
Jimmy Page, Robert Plant, John
Paul Jones, and John Bonham

© 1969 (Renewed) ARC MUSIC CORP.
All Rights Reserved   Used by Permission

NOTES ON THE FOURTH STRING D

Track 20

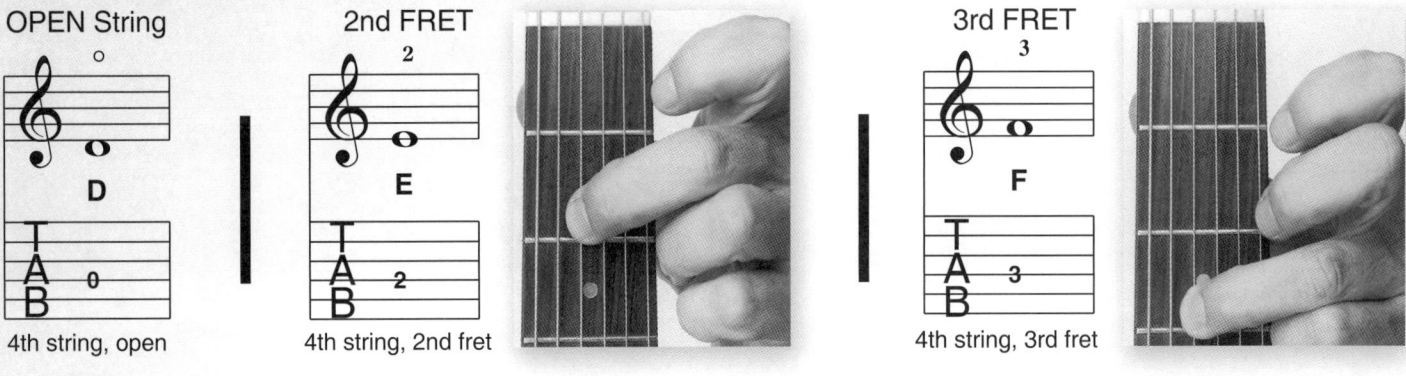

INCOMPLETE MEASURES

Not every piece of music begins on the first beat of a measure. Music sometimes begins with an incomplete measure, called the UPBEAT or PICKUP. If the pickup is one beat, the last measure will sometimes have only three beats in $\frac{4}{4}$, or two beats in $\frac{3}{4}$ to make up for the extra beat at the beginning.

"Your Time Is Gonna Come" (page 21) has a one-beat pickup. There are only three beats in the last measure to make up for the extra beat at the beginning.

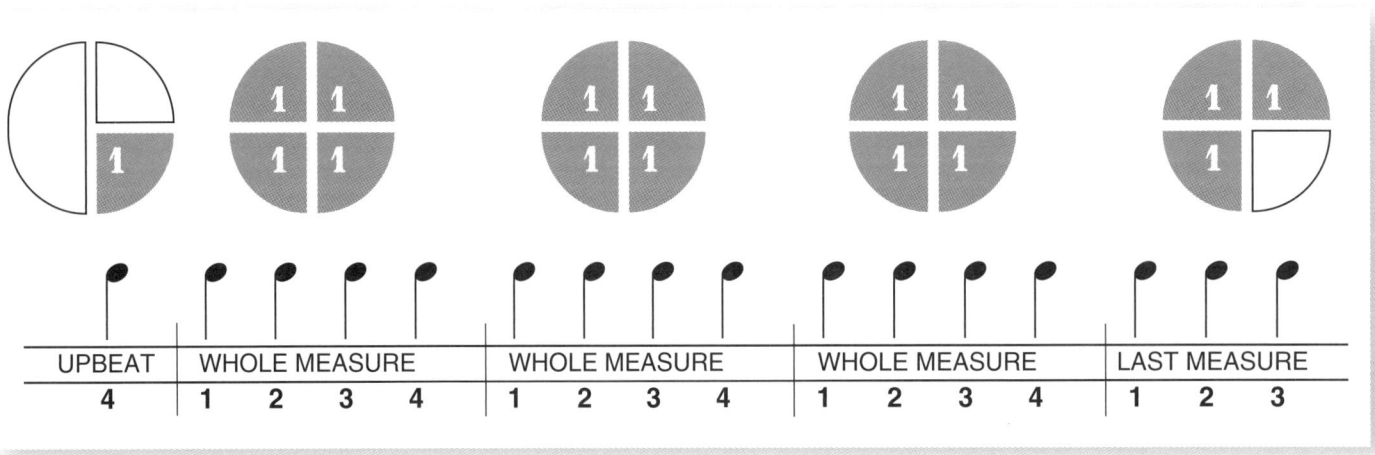

CHORD ACCOMPANIMENTS

Most of the songs throughout the rest of this book include grey letters above the music. These indicate chords that can be played by another guitarist, or pianist, to accompany you. Chord frames showing how to play all of these chords on the guitar are included on pages 94 and 95.

LED ZEPPELIN GUITAR METHOD 21

YOUR TIME IS GONNA COME
From the album Led Zeppelin

Track 21

Words and Music by
Jimmy Page and John Paul Jones

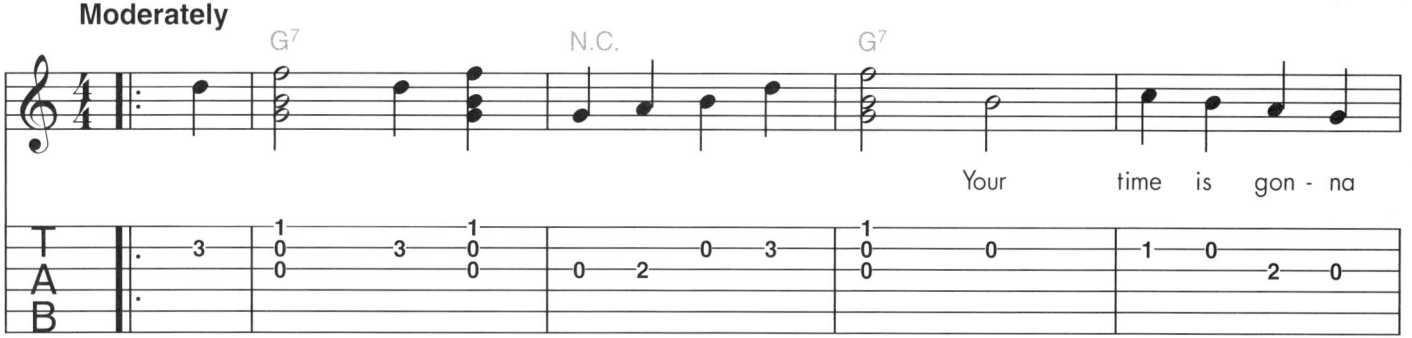
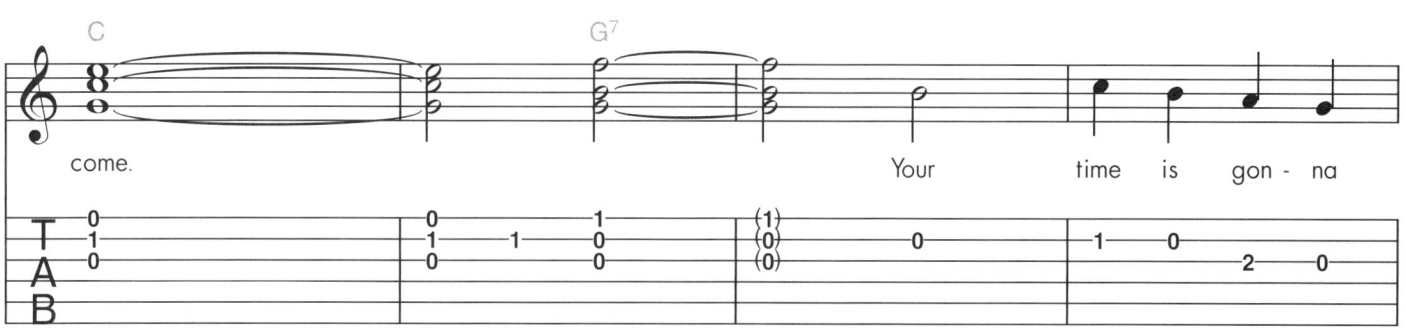

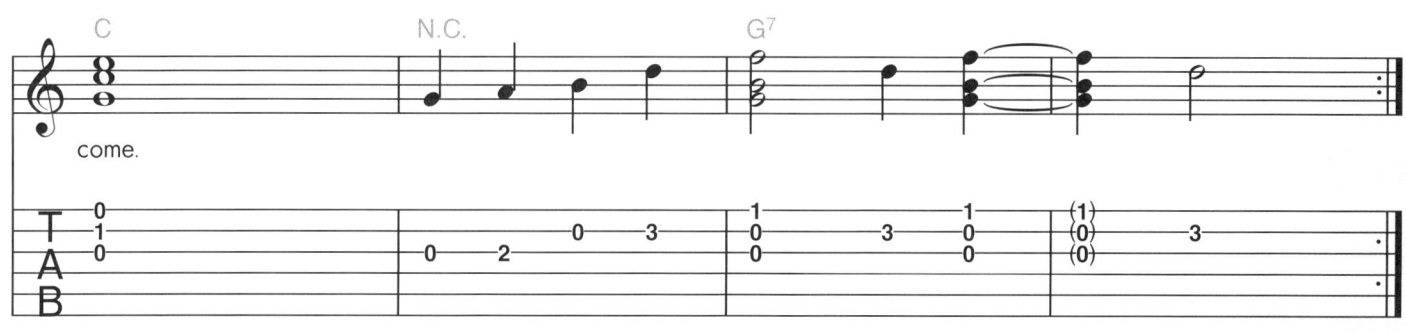

© 1969 (Renewed) FLAMES OF ALBION MUSIC, INC.
All Rights Administered by WB MUSIC CORP.
Exclusive Print Rights for the World Excluding Europe Administered by ALFRED MUSIC PUBLISHING CO., INC.
All Rights Reserved

THE FOUR-STRING G CHORD

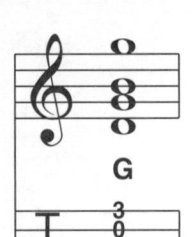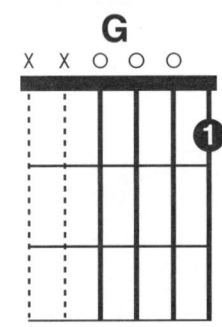

WHOLE LOTTA LOVE

From the album LED ZEPPELIN II

Words and Music by Jimmy Page, Robert Plant, John Paul Jones, John Bonham, and Willie Dixon

Slow Blues

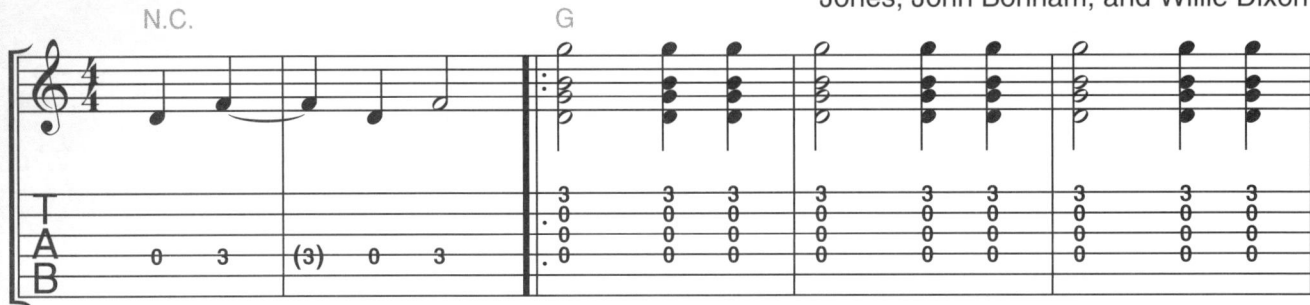
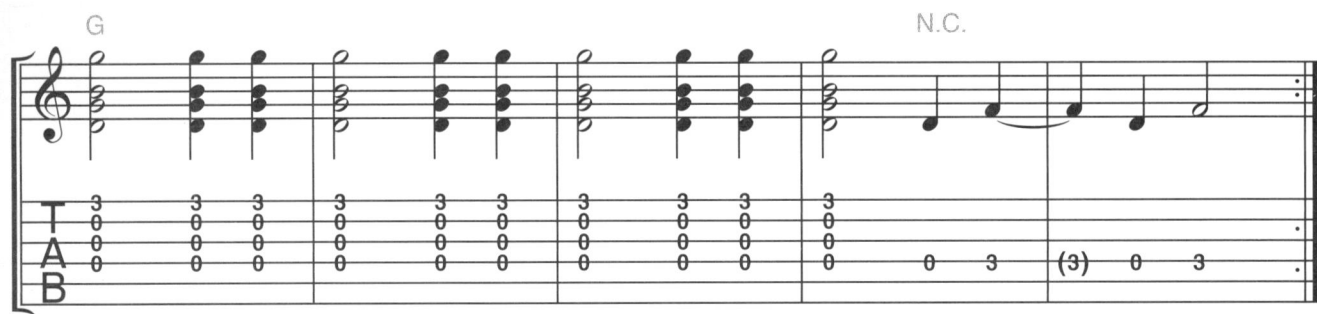
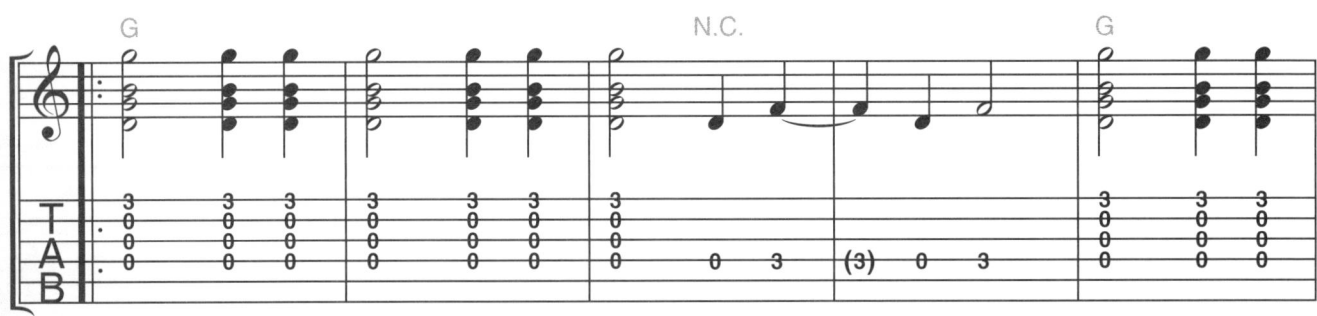

© 1969 (Renewed) FLAMES OF ALBION MUSIC, INC.
All Rights Administered by WB MUSIC CORP.
Exclusive Print Rights for the World Excluding Europe Administered by ALFRED MUSIC PUBLISHING CO., INC.
All Rights Reserved

Going to California

From the album

Moderately

Words and Music by
Jimmy Page and Robert Plant

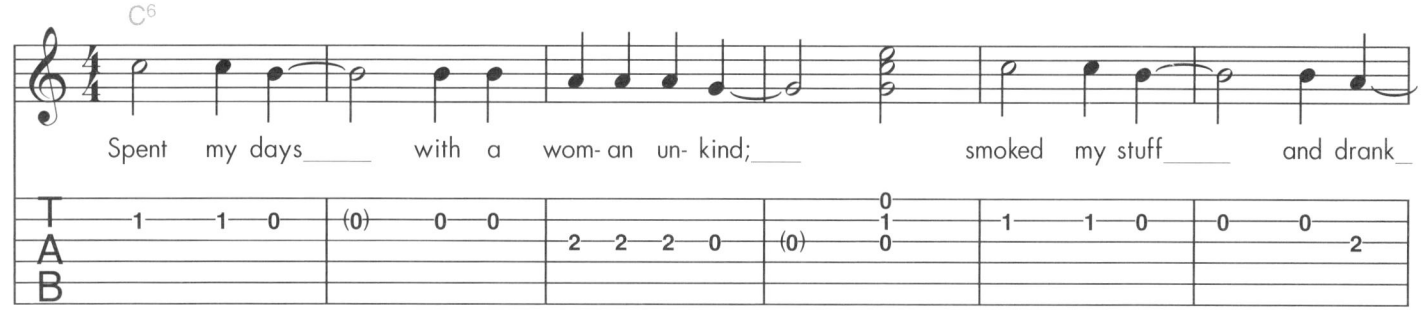
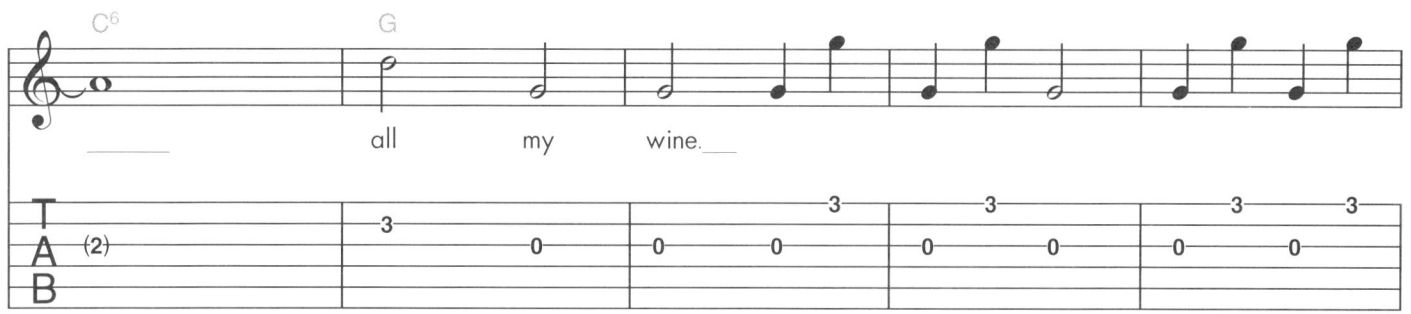

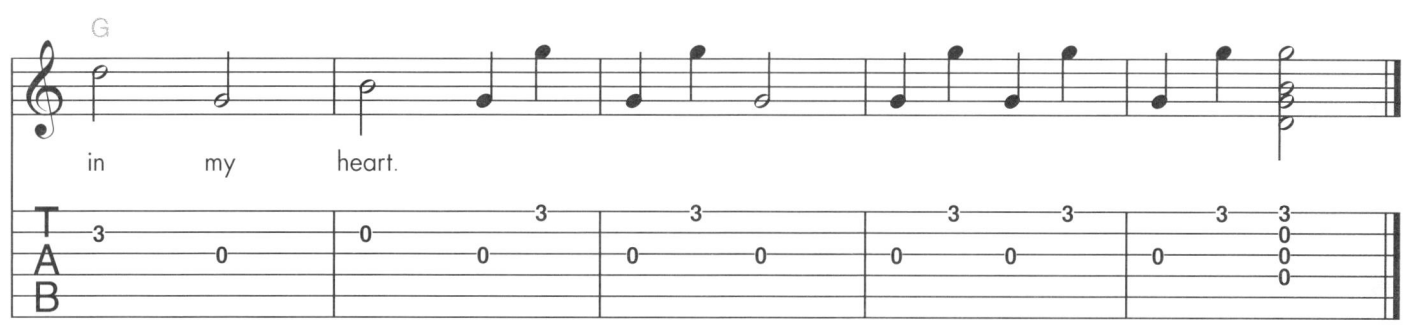

© 1972 (Renewed) FLAMES OF ALBION MUSIC, INC.
All Rights Administered by WB MUSIC CORP.
Exclusive Print Rights for the World Excluding Europe Administered by ALFRED MUSIC PUBLISHING
All Rights Reserved

NOTES ON THE FIFTH STRING A — Track 25

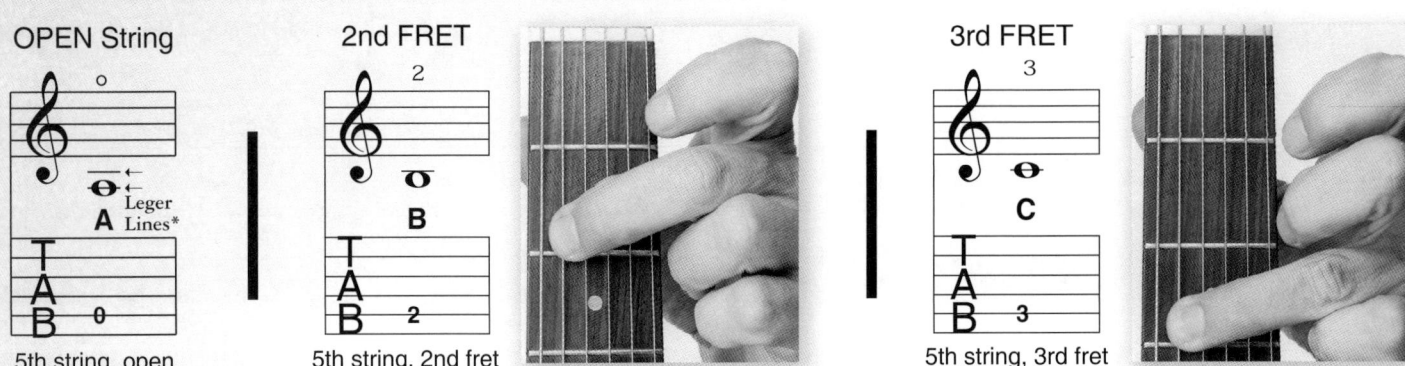

* The short line that extends the staff downwards is called a *leger* (pronounced ledger) line.

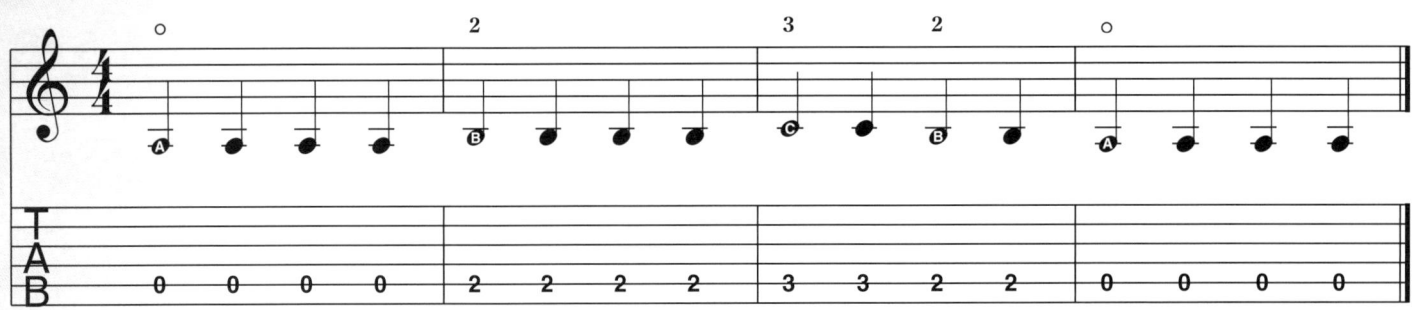

MOBY DICK — Track 26
From the album LED ZEPPELIN II

Music by John Bonham, John Paul Jones, and Jimmy Page

Moderately Fast

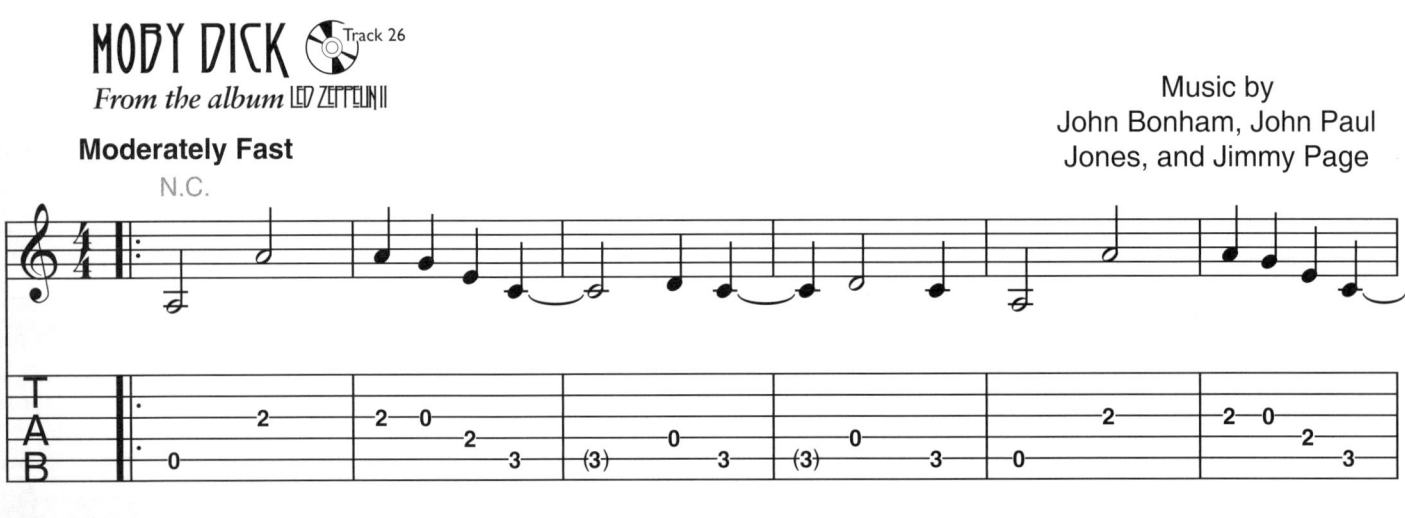

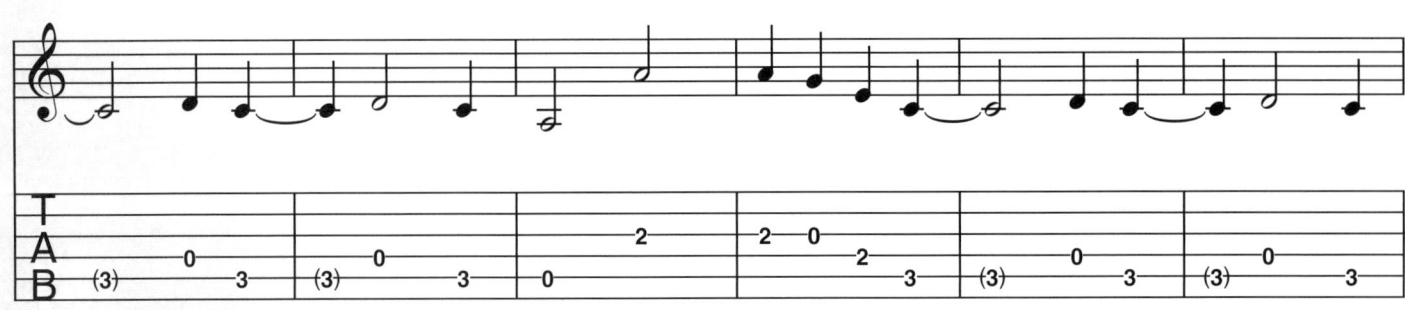

© 1969 (Renewed) FLAMES OF ALBION MUSIC, INC.
All Rights Administered by WB MUSIC CORP.
Exclusive Print Rights for the World Excluding Europe Administered by ALFRED MUSIC PUBLISHING CO., INC.
All Rights Reserved

INTRODUCING HIGH A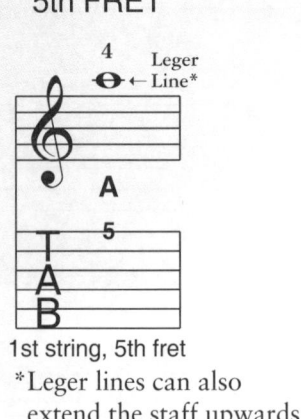

Track 27

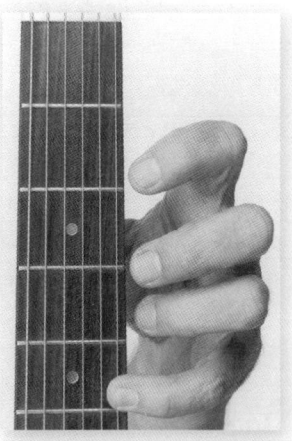

Notice that high A is played on the 5th fret, but the fourth finger is used. Slide your hand up the fretboard so that the fourth finger can reach the 5th fret.

*Leger lines can also extend the staff upwards.

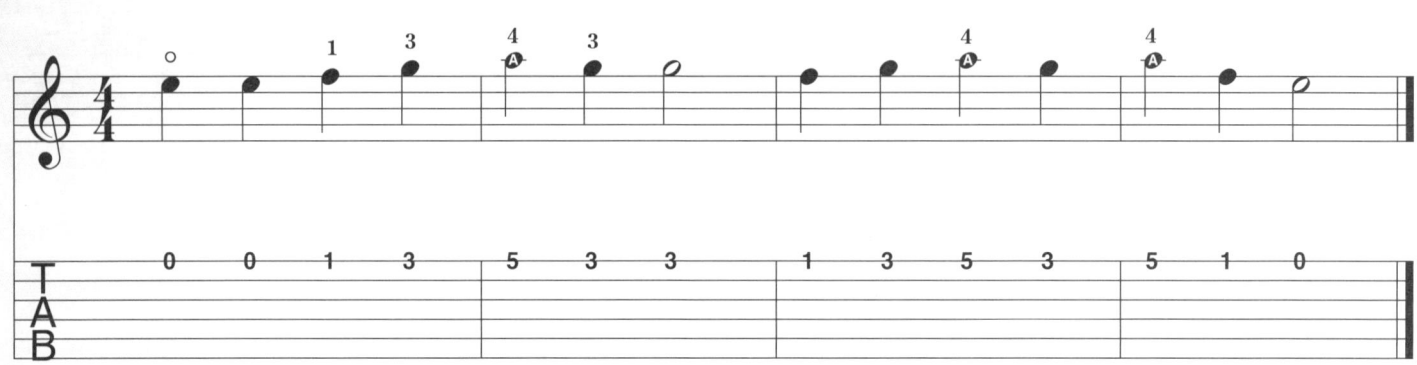

Rockin' in Dorian Mode Track 28

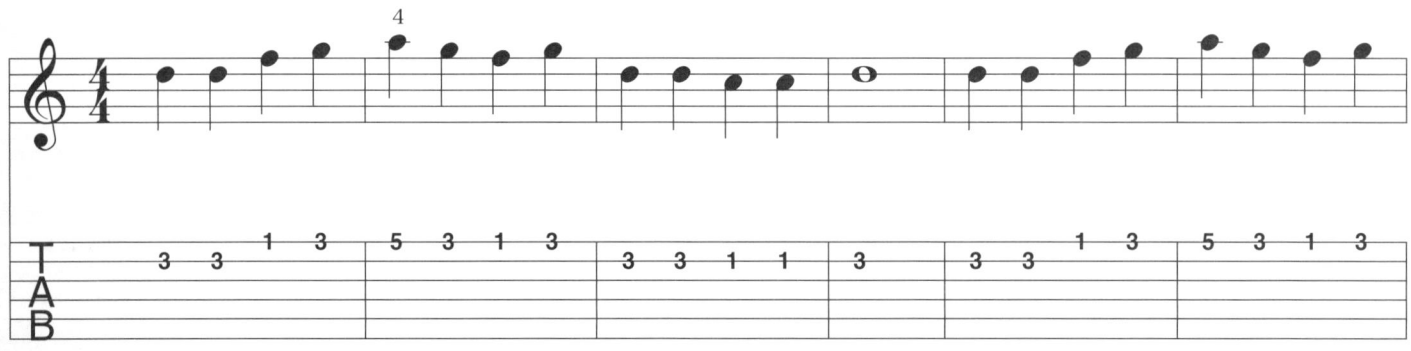

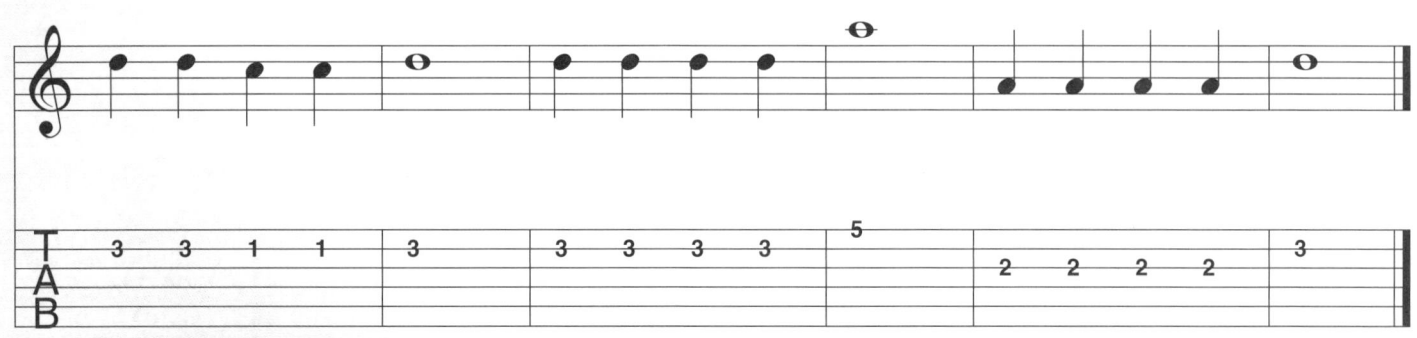

A SIGN ON THE WALL

Led Zeppelin was formed in 1968 by Jimmy Page (guitar), and featured Robert Plant (vocals, harmonica), John Paul Jones (bass guitar, keyboards, mandolin), and John Bonham (drums).   Their epic concerts helped them to become the highest-grossing band of the 1970s. During their 12 years together, they were arguably the biggest rock band in the world, and they continue to be one of the most influential and innovative groups of all time.

© ROBERT KNIGHT • WWW.ROBERTMKNIGHT.COM

A SIGN ON THE WALL

Led Zeppelin continues to inspire generations with their groundbreaking blues-infused, guitar-driven rock 'n' roll. To date, they have sold over 200 million albums worldwide, and their catalog of songs has proven to be one of the most enduring collections written in the 20th century. In 1995 they were inducted into the Rock & Roll Hall of Fame, and they were added to the UK Music Hall of Fame in 2004. They received the Grammy Lifetime Achievement Award in 2005, and were then ranked number one on VH1's *100 Greatest Artists of Hard Rock*.

THANK YOU

From the album LED ZEPPELIN II

Words and Music by
Jimmy Page and Robert Plant

Moderately Slow

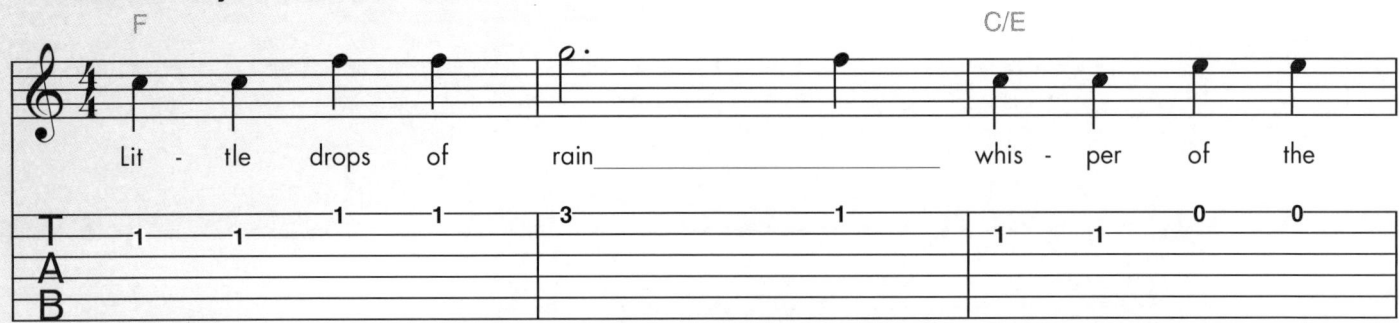

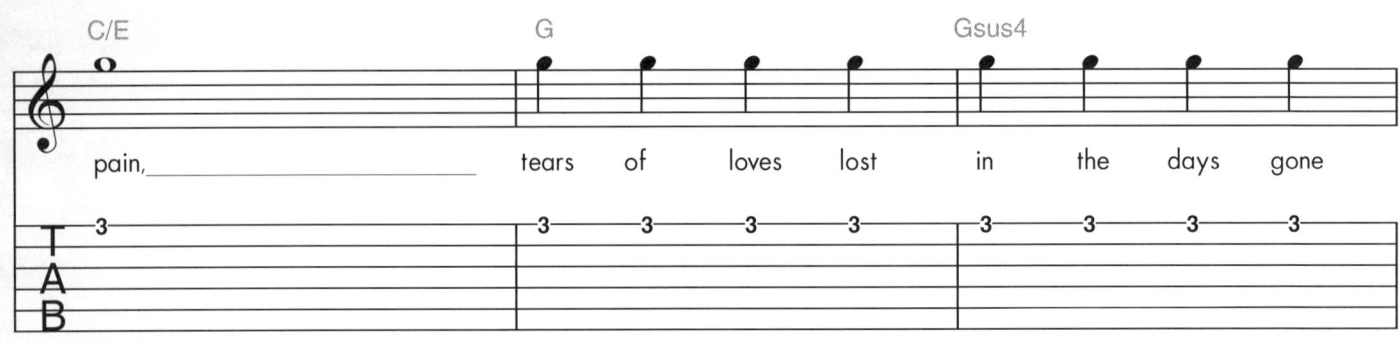

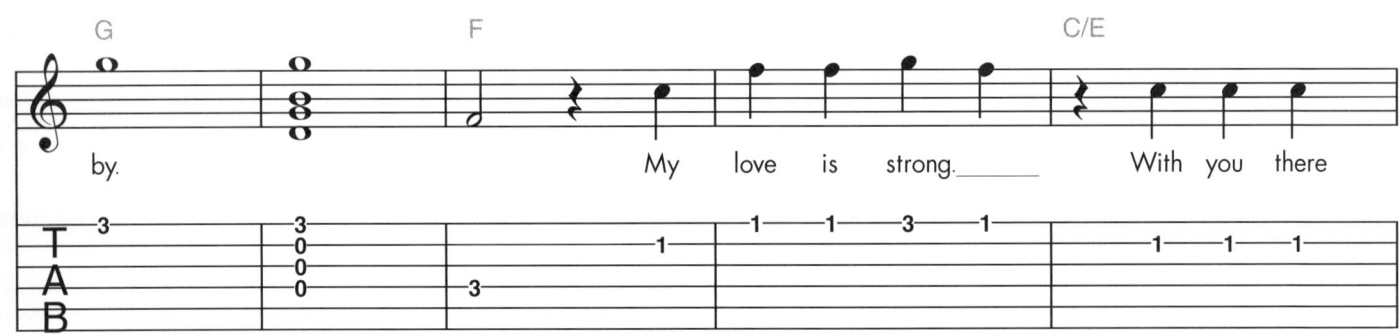

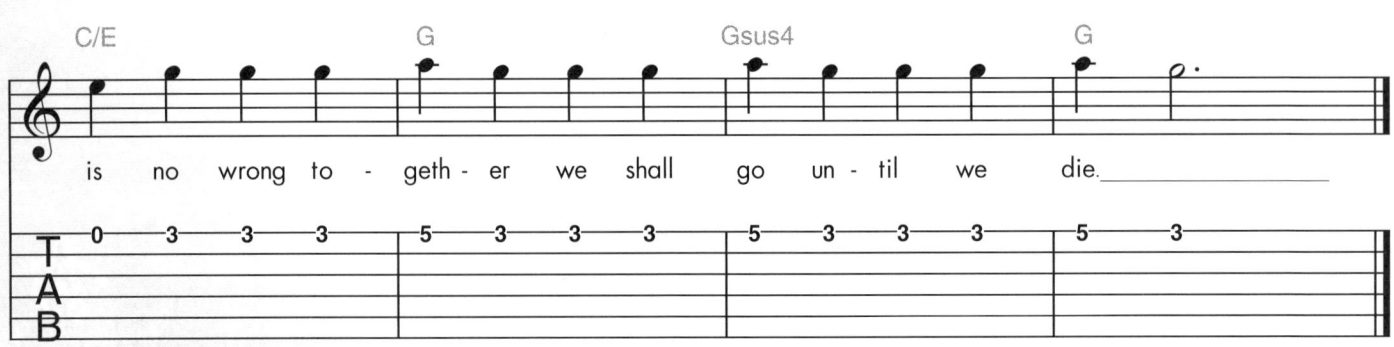

© 1969 (Renewed) FLAMES OF ALBION MUSIC, INC.
All Rights Administered by WB MUSIC CORP.
Exclusive Print Rights for the World Excluding Europe Administered by ALFRED MUSIC PUBLISHING CO., INC.
All Rights Reserved

NOTES ON THE SIXTH STRING E *Track 30*

OPEN String — 6th string, open — E

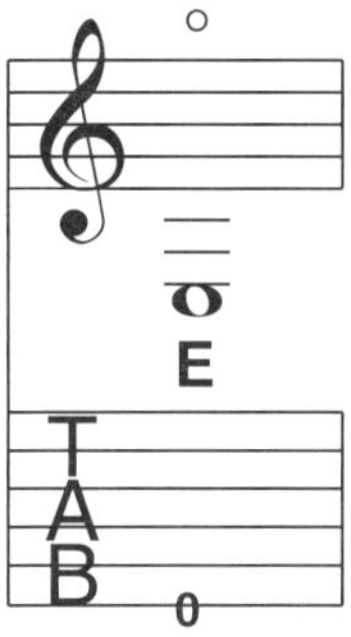

1st FRET — 6th string, 1st fret — F

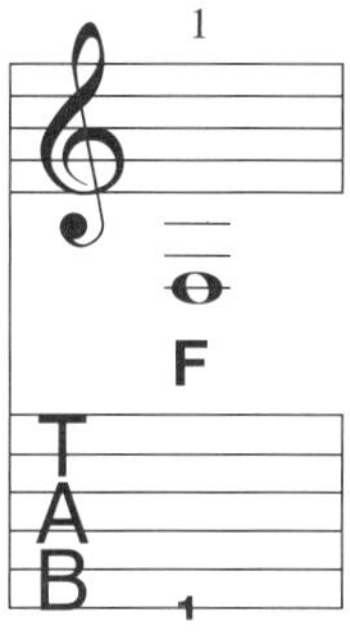

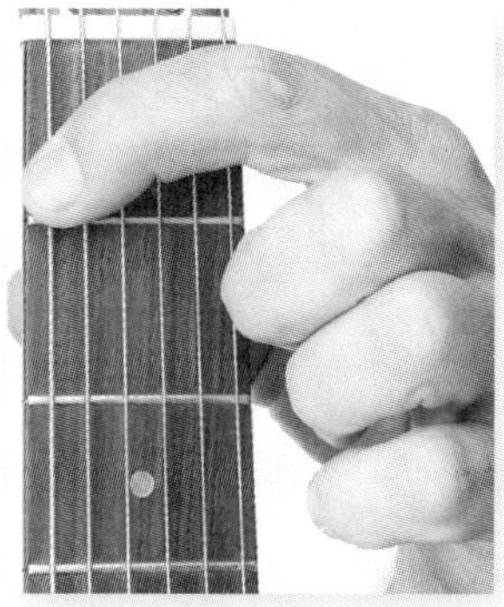

3rd FRET — 6th string, 3rd fret — G

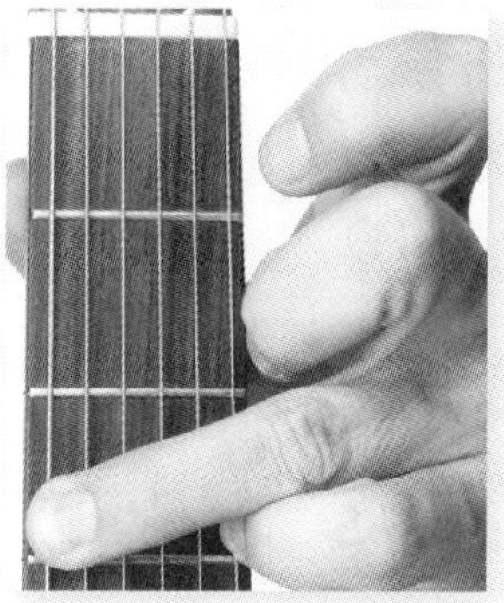

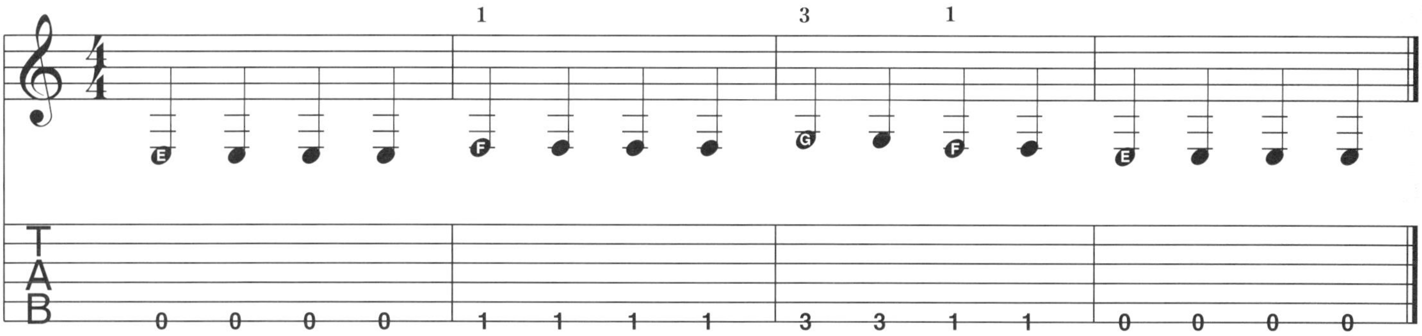

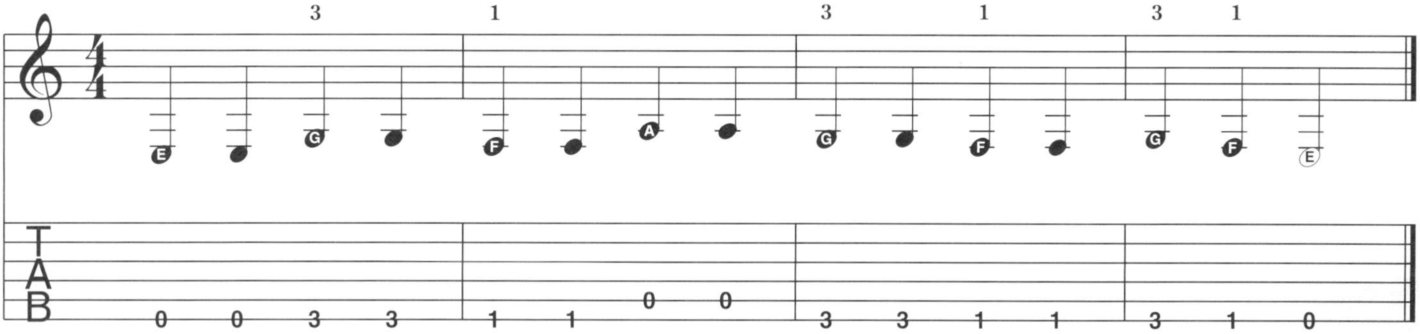

THE NATURAL SCALE

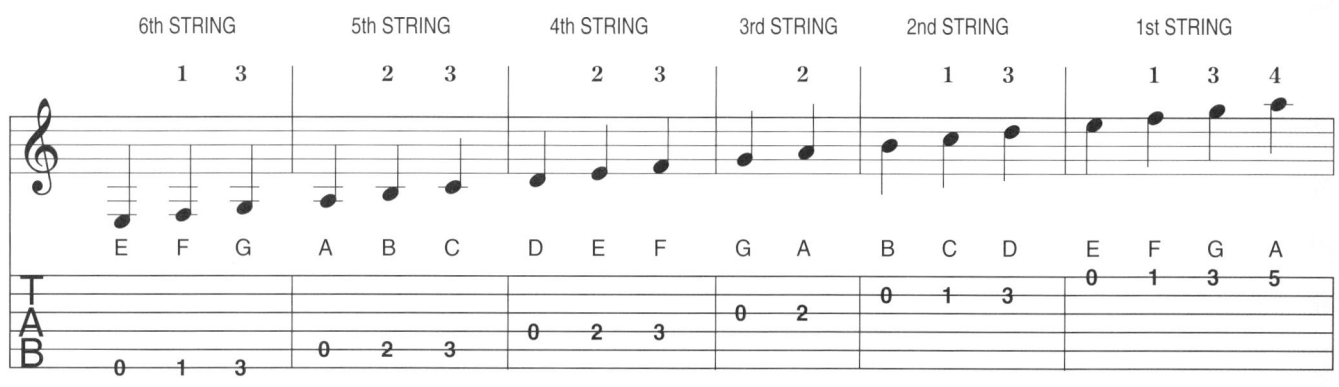

TEMPO SIGNS

Tempo signs tell how fast or slow to play.
The three most common TEMPO SIGNS are: *Andante* (slow)   *Moderato* (moderately)   *Allegro* (fast)
                                               say: on-*don*-tay   mah-duh-*rah*-toe   al-*lay*-grow

Three-Tempo Rock   Play three times: 1st time *Andante*, 2nd time *Moderato*, 3rd time *Allegro*.

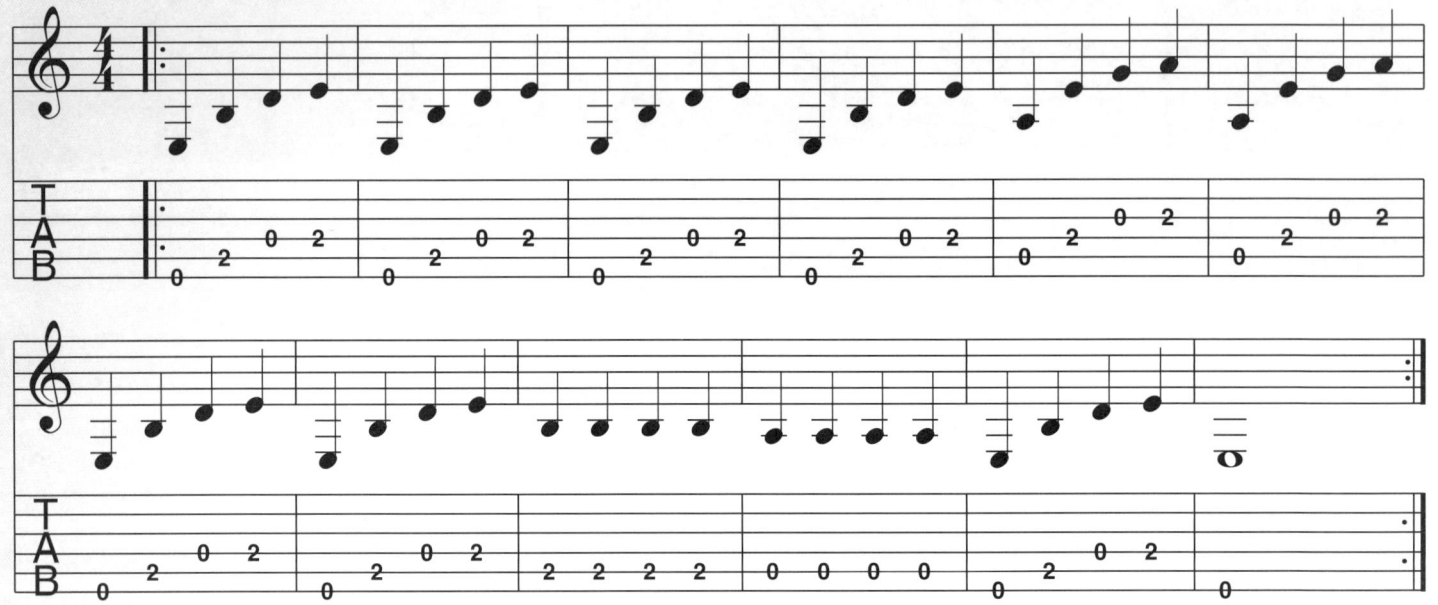

HOW MANY MORE TIMES (BASS LINE) Track 31

From the album LED ZEPPELIN

This song is a fast blues. When playing the blues, rhythms are usually played differently than they are written. First practice this song as written and then listen to the recording and play the blues feel you hear.

Words and Music by
Jimmy Page, John Paul
Jones, and John Bonham

Allegro

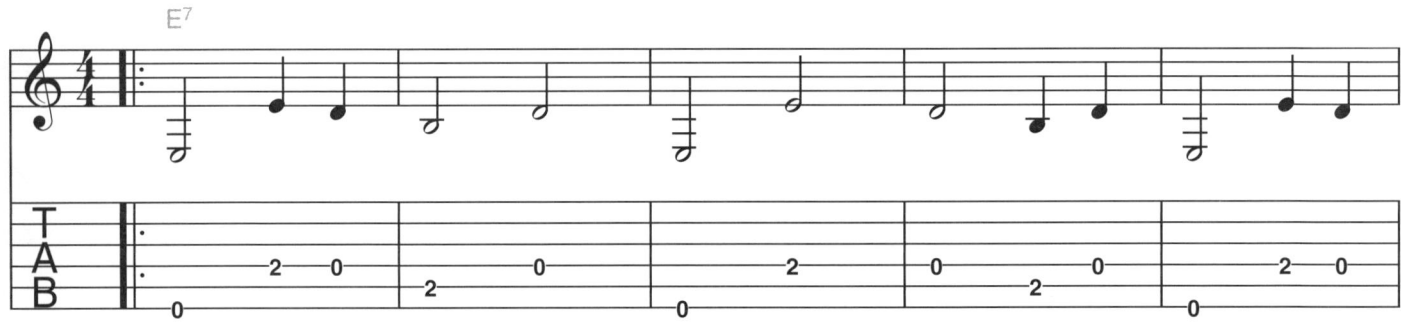

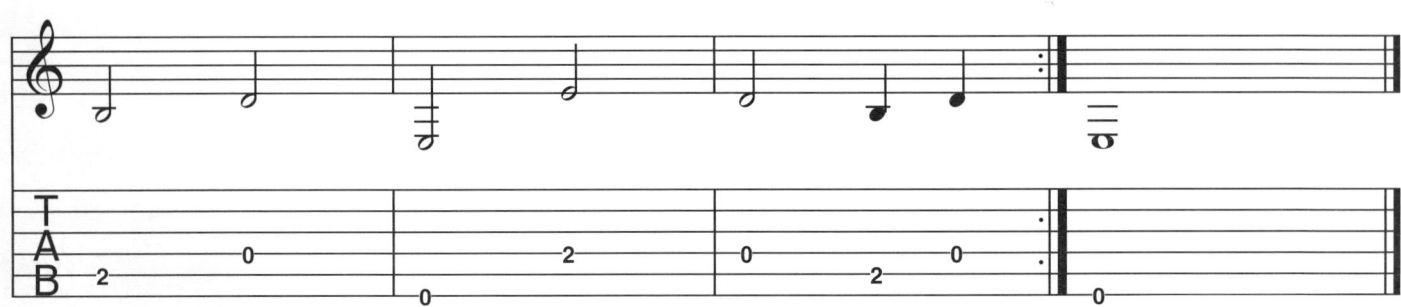

© 1969 (Renewed) FLAMES OF ALBION MUSIC, INC.
All Rights Administered by WB MUSIC CORP.
Exclusive Print Rights for the World Excluding Europe Administered by ALFRED MUSIC PUBLISHING CO., INC.
All Rights Reserved

THE FOUR-STRING G7 CHORD *Track 32*

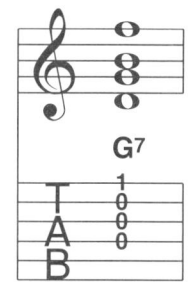 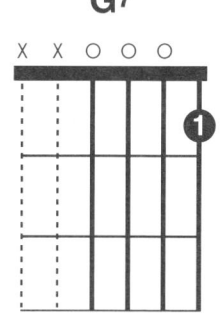 

The three-note G7 chord you learned earlier can be expanded to a fuller and richer sounding four-note chord by simply adding the open 4th string.

THE LEMON SONG *Track 33*
From the album LED ZEPPELIN II

This version of "The Lemon Song" uses notes on the 6th string and the four-string G7 chord.

Words and Music by Jimmy Page, Robert Plant, John Paul Jones, and John Bonham

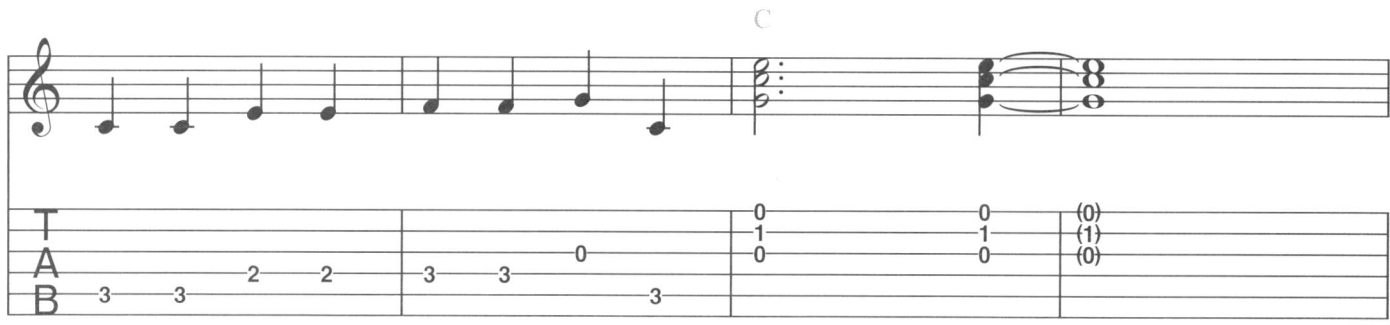
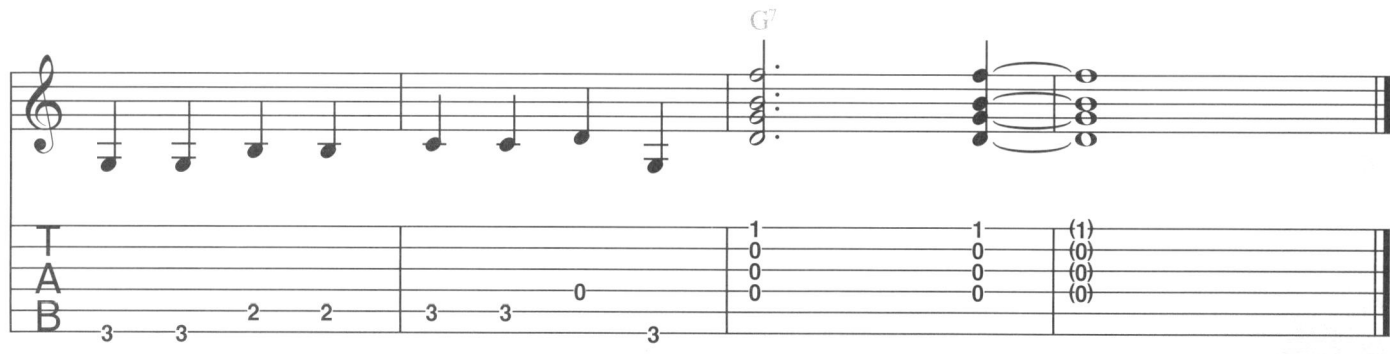

© 1969 (Renewed) ARC MUSIC CORP.
All Rights Reserved   Used by Permission

THE FOUR-STRING C CHORD 🎵 Track 34

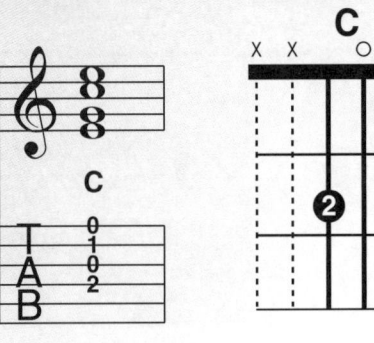
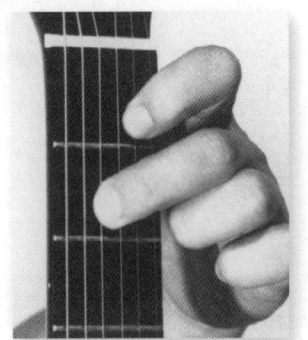

Bron-Y-Aur Stomp 🎵 Track 35
From the album Led Zeppelin III

Words and Music by
Jimmy Page, Robert Plant,
and John Paul Jones

Play accented notes (those marked with a >) louder than the unaccented ones.

Allegro

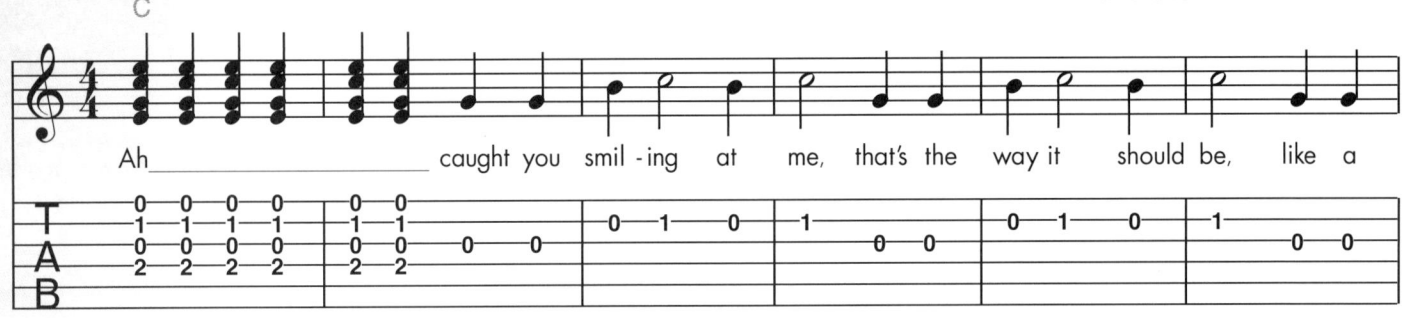
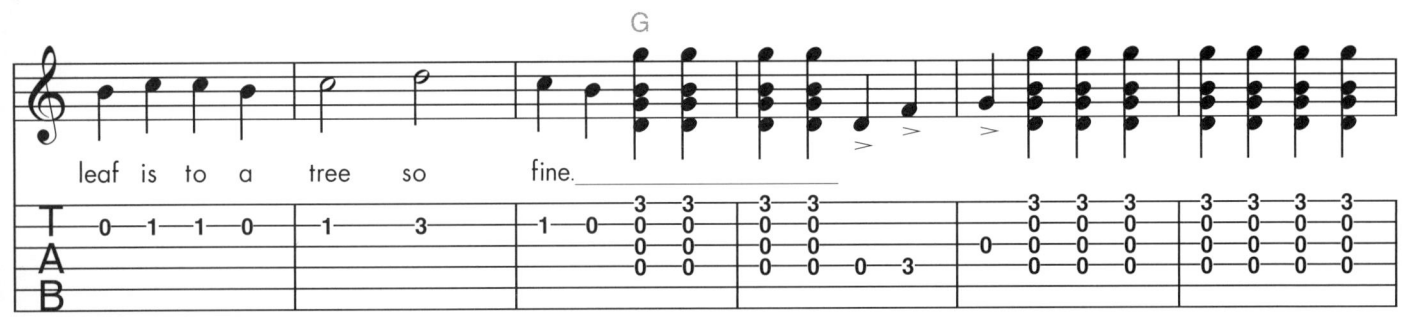

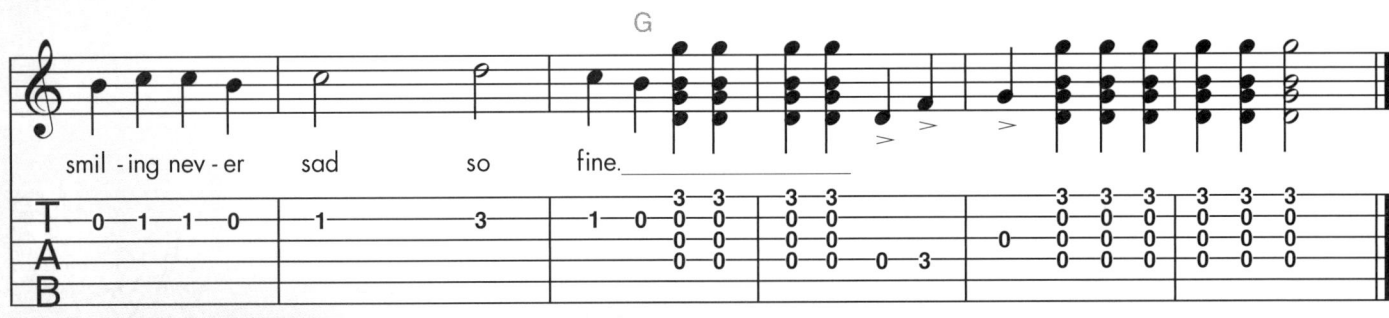

© 1970 (Renewed) FLAMES OF ALBION MUSIC, INC.
All Rights Administered by WB MUSIC CORP.
Exclusive Print Rights for the World Excluding Europe Administered by ALFRED MUSIC PUBLISHING CO., INC.
All Rights Reserved

EIGHTH NOTES Track 36

Eighth notes are black notes with a flag added to the stem, ♪ or ♪.

Two or more eighth notes are written with connecting beams, ♫ or ♫. The eighth rest is 𝄾.

Two eighth notes are played in the same time as one quarter note.

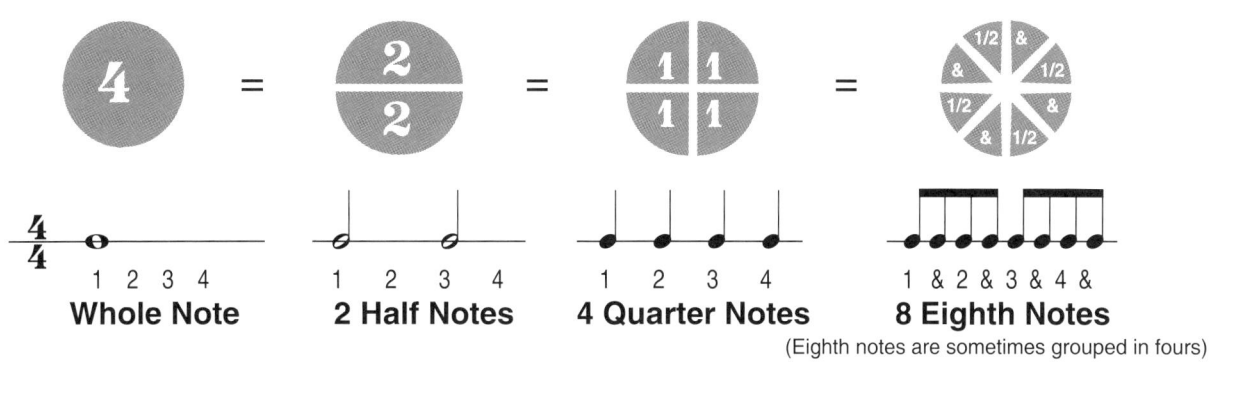

Until now, you have been playing using downstrokes only.
To be able to play more quickly, you will now also use upstrokes.

Use alternating downstrokes ⊓
and upstrokes ∨ on eighth notes:

Eighth-Note Rock Track 37

Allegro moderato (moderately fast)

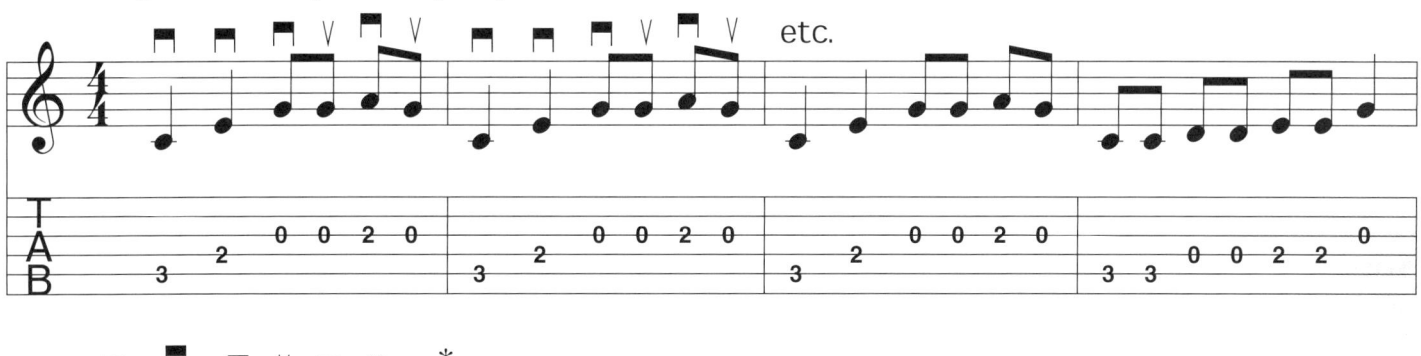

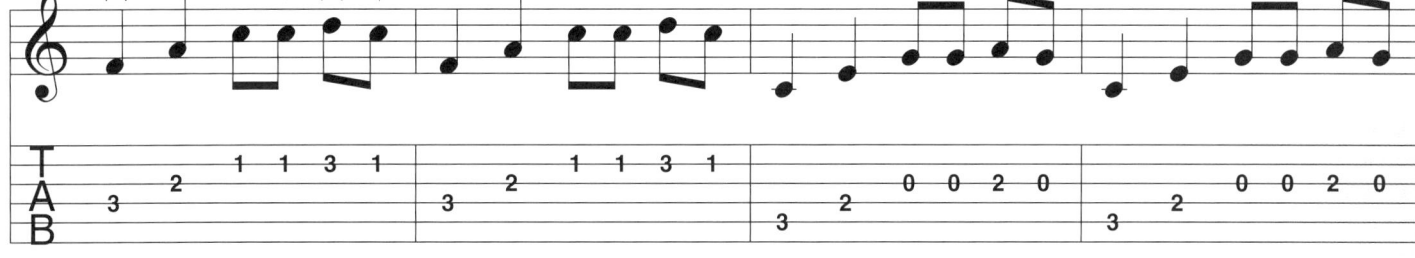

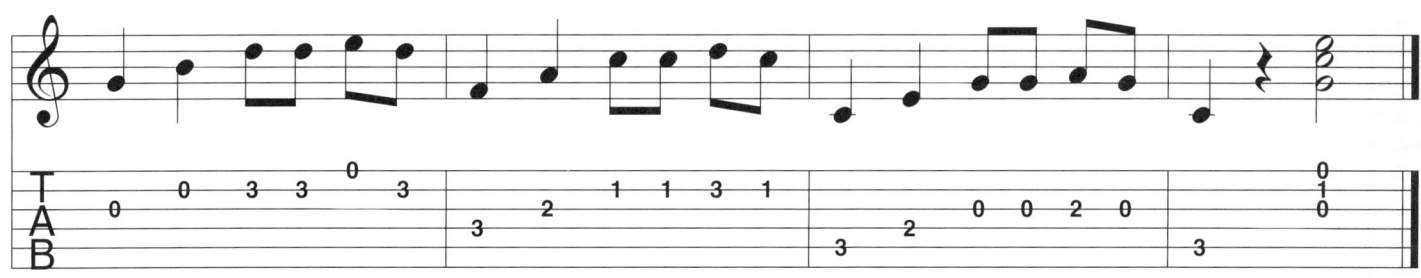

* Fill in the rest of the page with downstrokes and upstrokes.

Speed Drill

Speed drills are for the development of technique and should be practiced daily. Start all speed drills slowly, and be sure that each note is clear and distinct. On each repetition, increase the tempo a little. We recommend you practice with a metronome to maintain an even tempo.

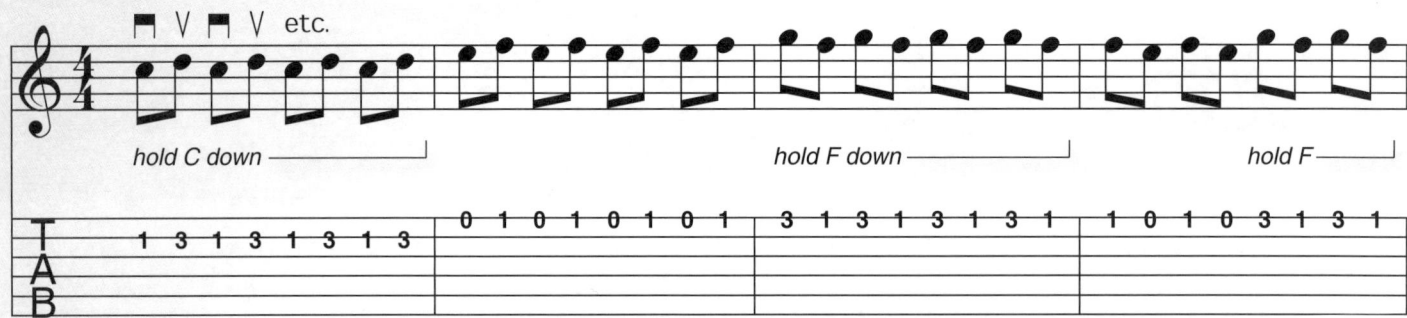

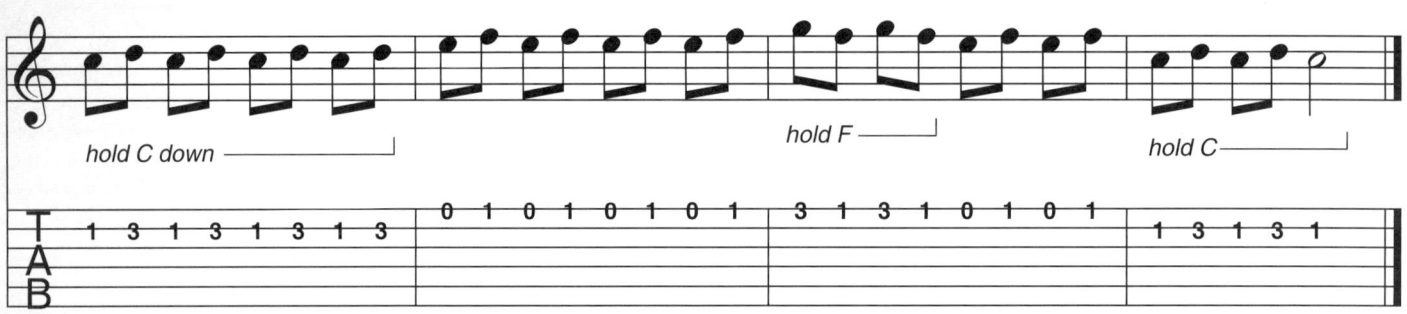

PHOTO BY ROBERT KNIGHT

A SIGN ON THE WALL

Jimmy Page is the guitarist, co-songwriter, and producer for Led Zeppelin. His heavy riffs, wild solos, and intense stage presence helped define what it means to be a rock guitarist. His guitar solo on "Stairway to Heaven" was voted the "greatest guitar solo of all time" by *Guitar World* magazine. He combined his roots in the blues with other influences, such as folk, funk, and Middle Eastern music, to create his own distinct hard-rock style.

LED ZEPPELIN GUITAR METHOD 35

COMMUNICATION BREAKDOWN (INTRO)

From the album LED ZEPPELIN

 Track 39

Words and Music by
Jimmy Page, John Paul Jones, and
John Bonham

Moderately Rock

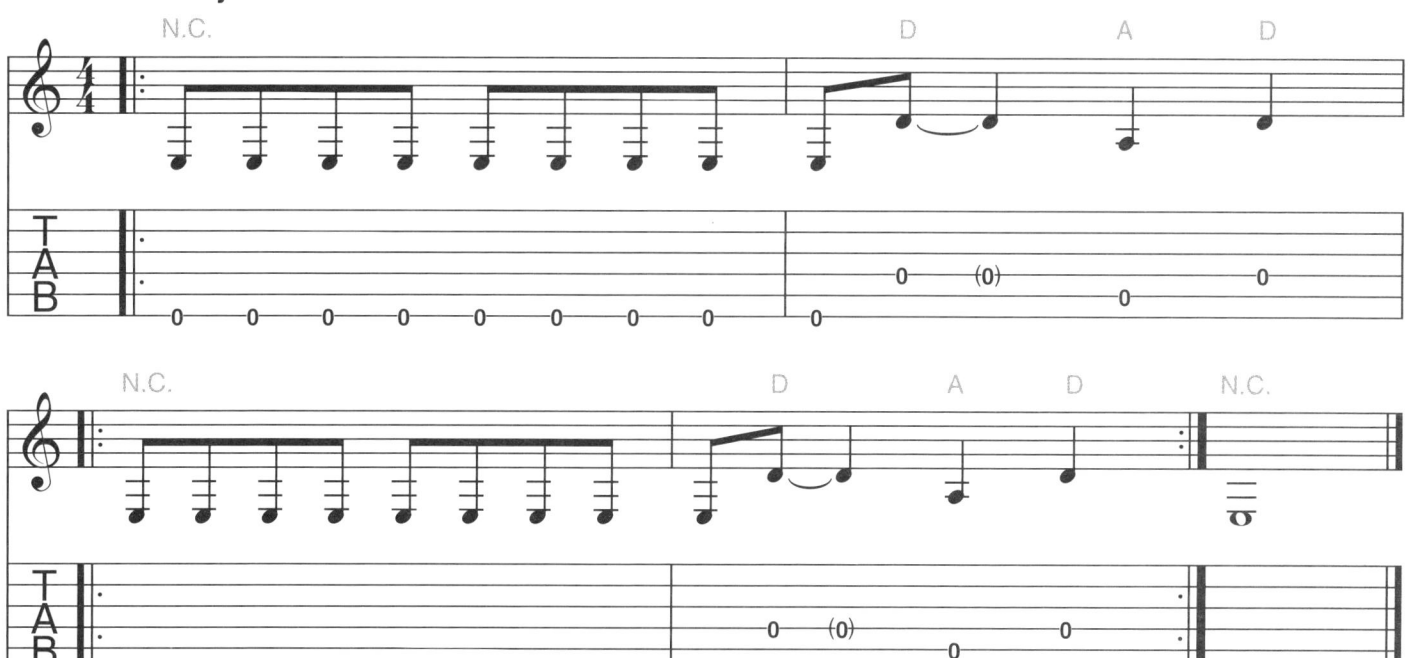

© 1969 (Renewed) FLAMES OF ALBION MUSIC, INC.
All Rights Administered by WB MUSIC CORP.
Exclusive Print Rights for the World Excluding Europe Administered by ALFRED MUSIC PUBLISHING CO., INC.
All Rights Reserved

PHOTO BY ROBERT KNIGHT

A SIGN ON THE WALL

If one person can hold the title as the greatest, most influential, and most emulated rock drummer in history, it would be John Bonham. Bonham was a rock-solid powerhouse, laying down the most enormous-sounding and authoritative drum beats in the history of rock 'n' roll. Bonham played with Led Zeppelin right up until his unfortunate and premature death on September 25th, 1980. John will forever be remembered with a deep fondness, not just by the drummers he influenced, but also by the millions of listeners he touched even long after his passing.

SHARPS ♯, FLATS ♭, AND NATURALS ♮

The distance from one fret to the next fret, up or down, is a HALF STEP.

TWO half steps make a WHOLE STEP.

SHARPS RAISE the note a half step. Play the next fret higher.

FLATS LOWER the note a half step. If the note is fingered, play the next fret lower. If the note is open, play the 4th fret of the next lower string except if that string is G (3rd string), then play the 3rd fret.

NATURALS CANCEL a previous sharp or flat.

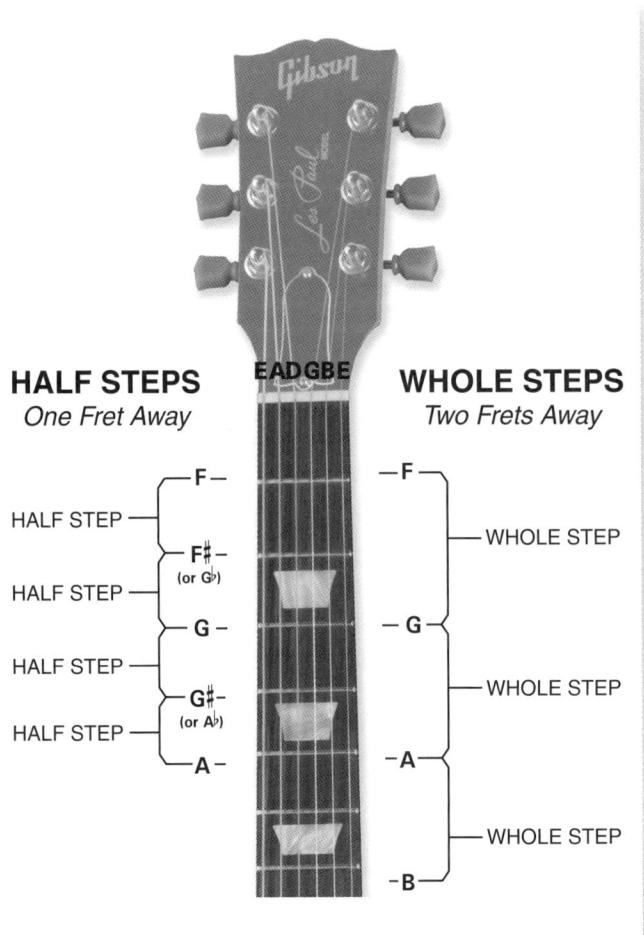

THE CHROMATIC SCALE 🔘 Track 40

The CHROMATIC SCALE is formed exclusively of HALF STEPS.
Ascending, the CHROMATIC SCALE uses SHARPS (♯), but descending, uses FLATS (♭).

ASCENDING CHROMATIC SCALE

C means common time (same as 4/4)

DESCENDING CHROMATIC SCALE

Chromatic Rock

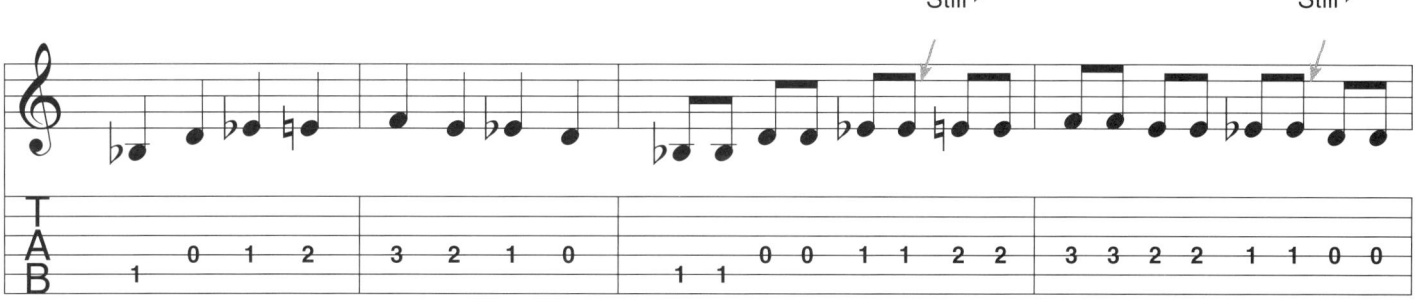

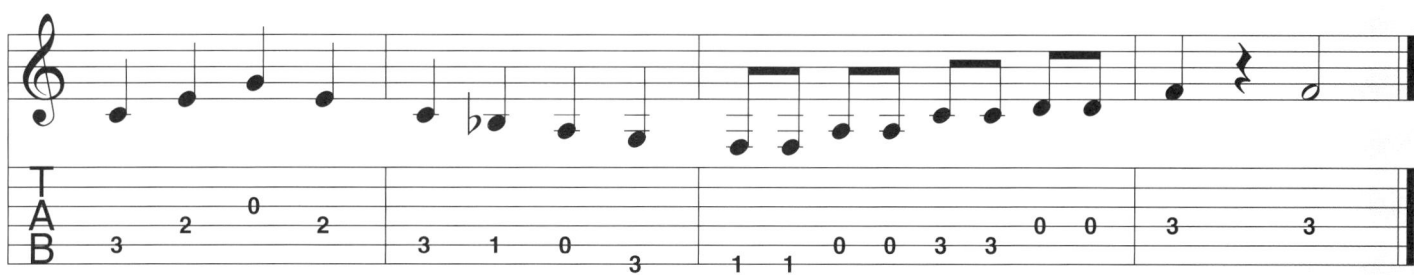

* When a sharp or flat note appears more than once in the same measure, it is still played as a sharp or flat unless cancelled by a natural sign (♮). It's also important to know that these signs, called ACCIDENTALS, only apply to the measure in which they appear.

Dazed and Confused

From the album Led Zeppelin

Track 42

Words and Music by Jimmy Page

Slow Blues

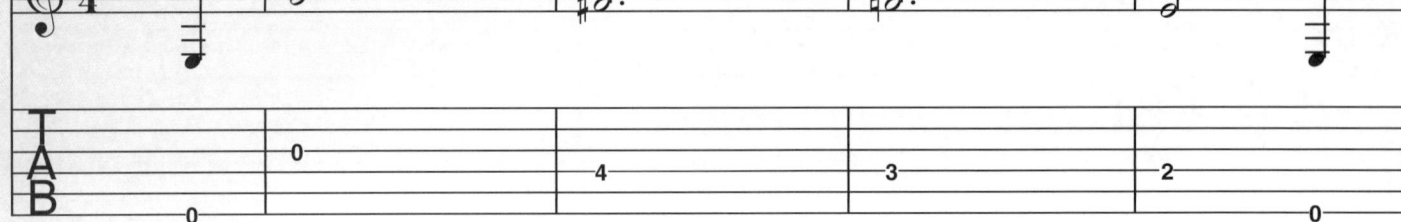
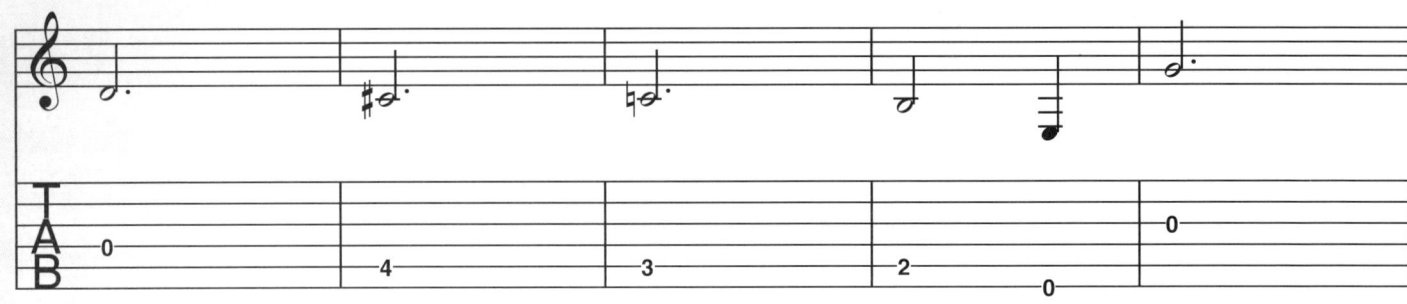
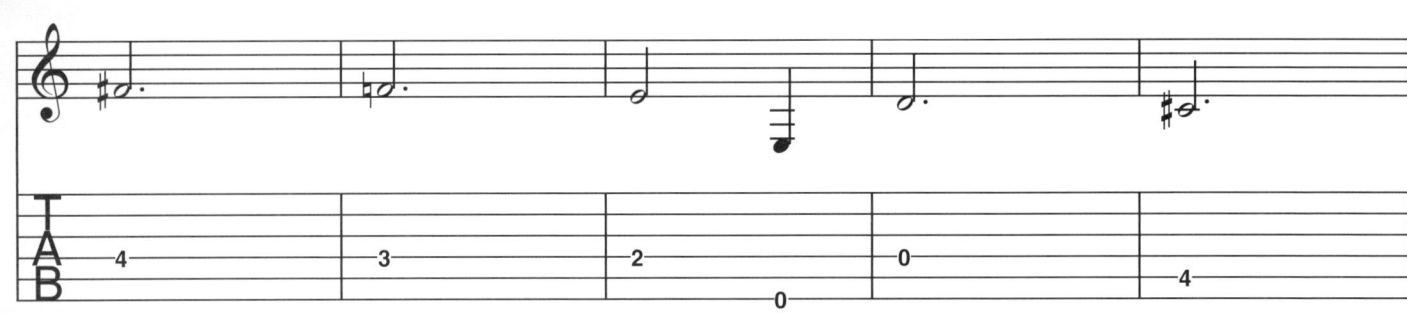
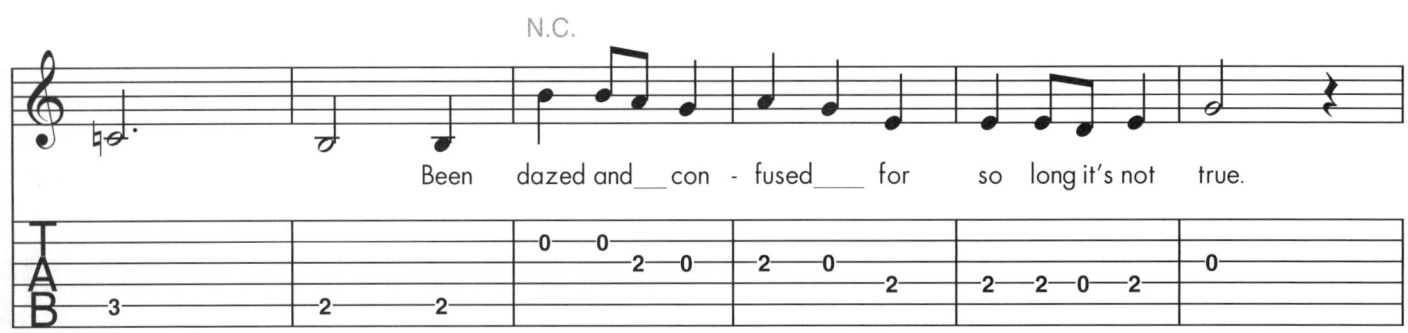
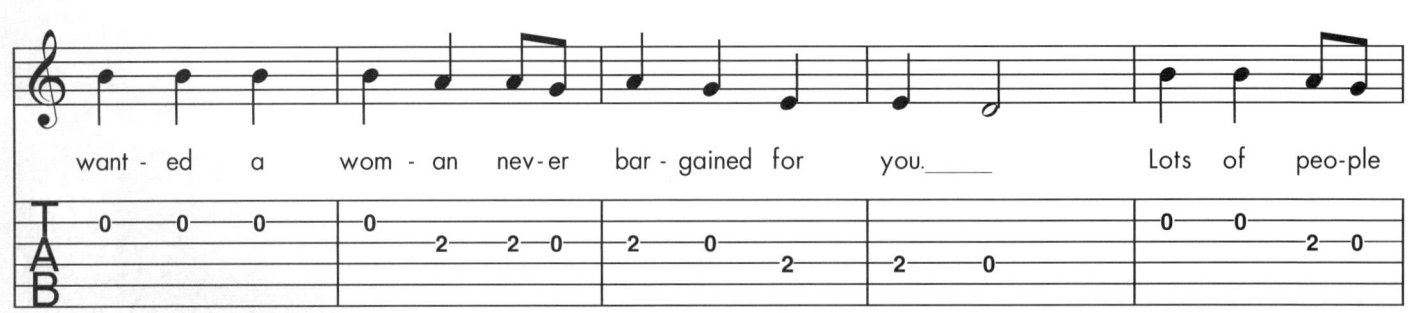

© 1969 (Renewed) FLAMES OF ALBION MUSIC, INC.
All Rights Administered by WB MUSIC CORP.
Exclusive Print Rights for the World Excluding Europe Administered by ALFRED MUSIC PUBLISHING CO., INC.
All Rights Reserved

LED ZEPPELIN GUITAR METHOD 39

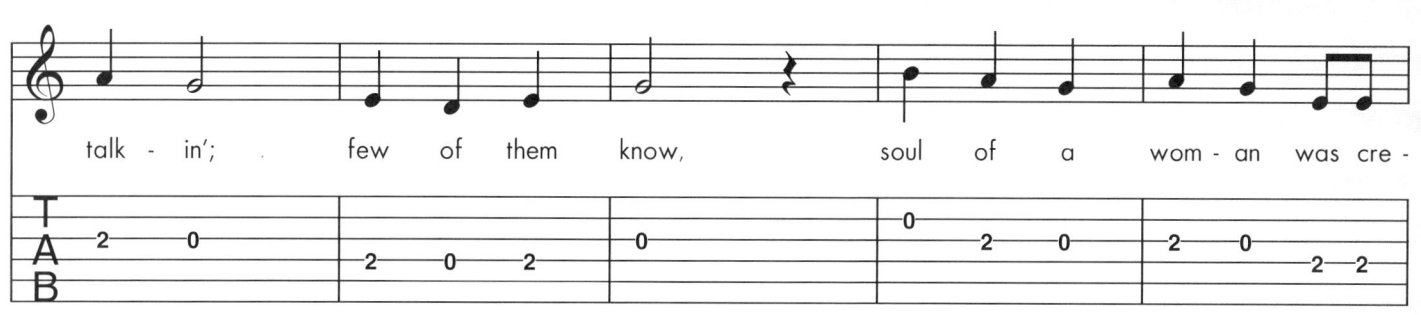
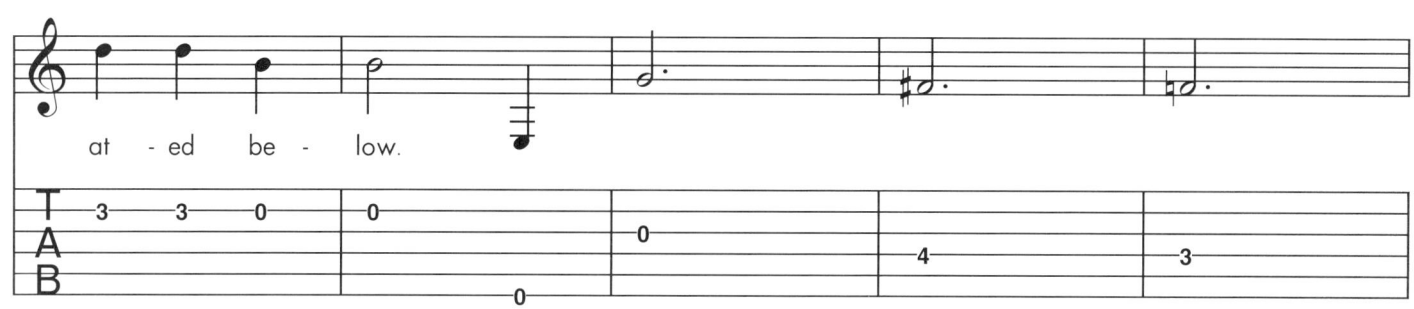
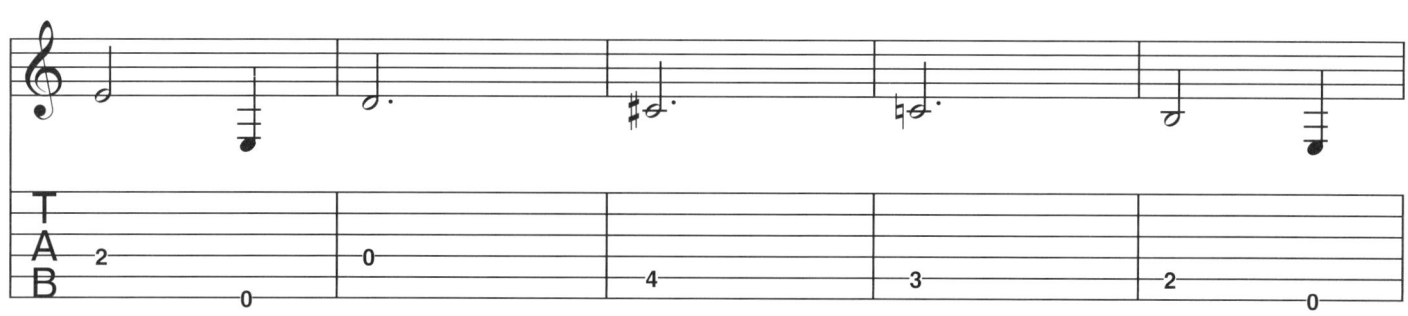
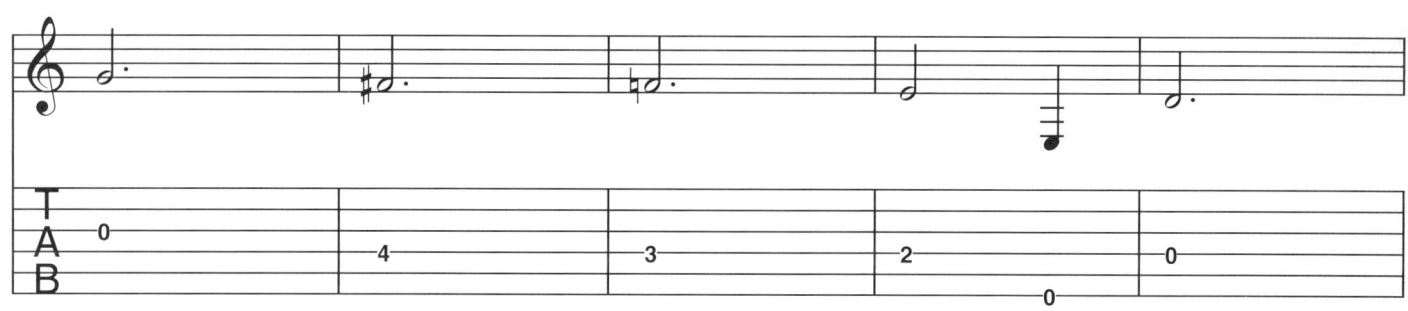
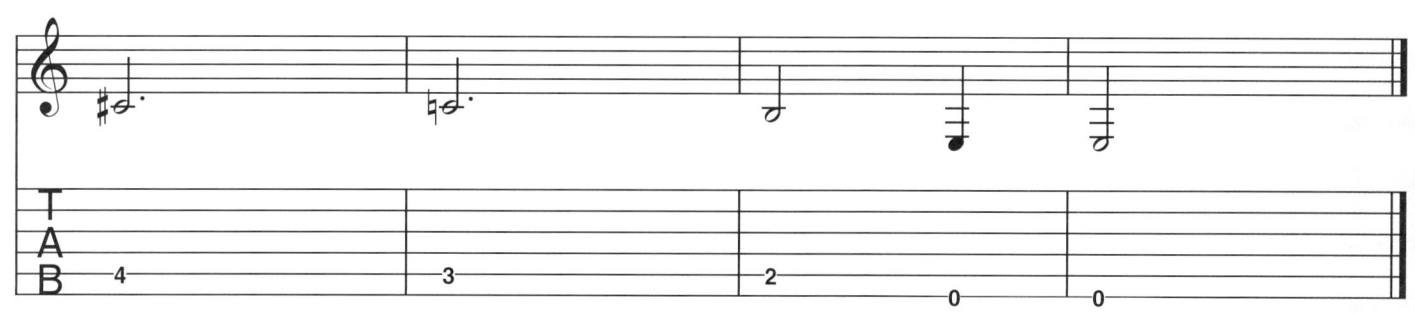

THE FOUR-STRING F CHORD  Track 43

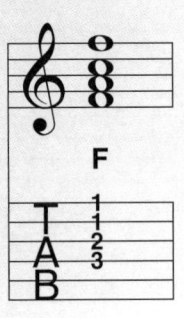
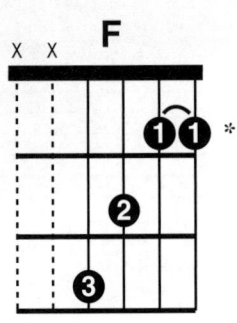
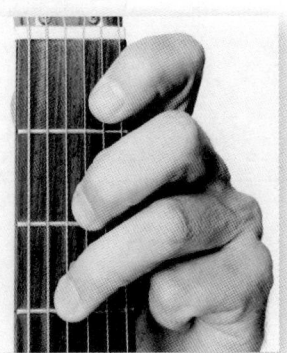

*Depress both the 1st and 2nd strings at the 1st fret with your first finger.

hold fingers down

COMMUNICATION BREAKDOWN Track 44
(INTRO AND CHORUS)
From the album LED ZEPPELIN

Words and Music by
Jimmy Page, John Paul Jones, and John Bonham

Moderately Rock

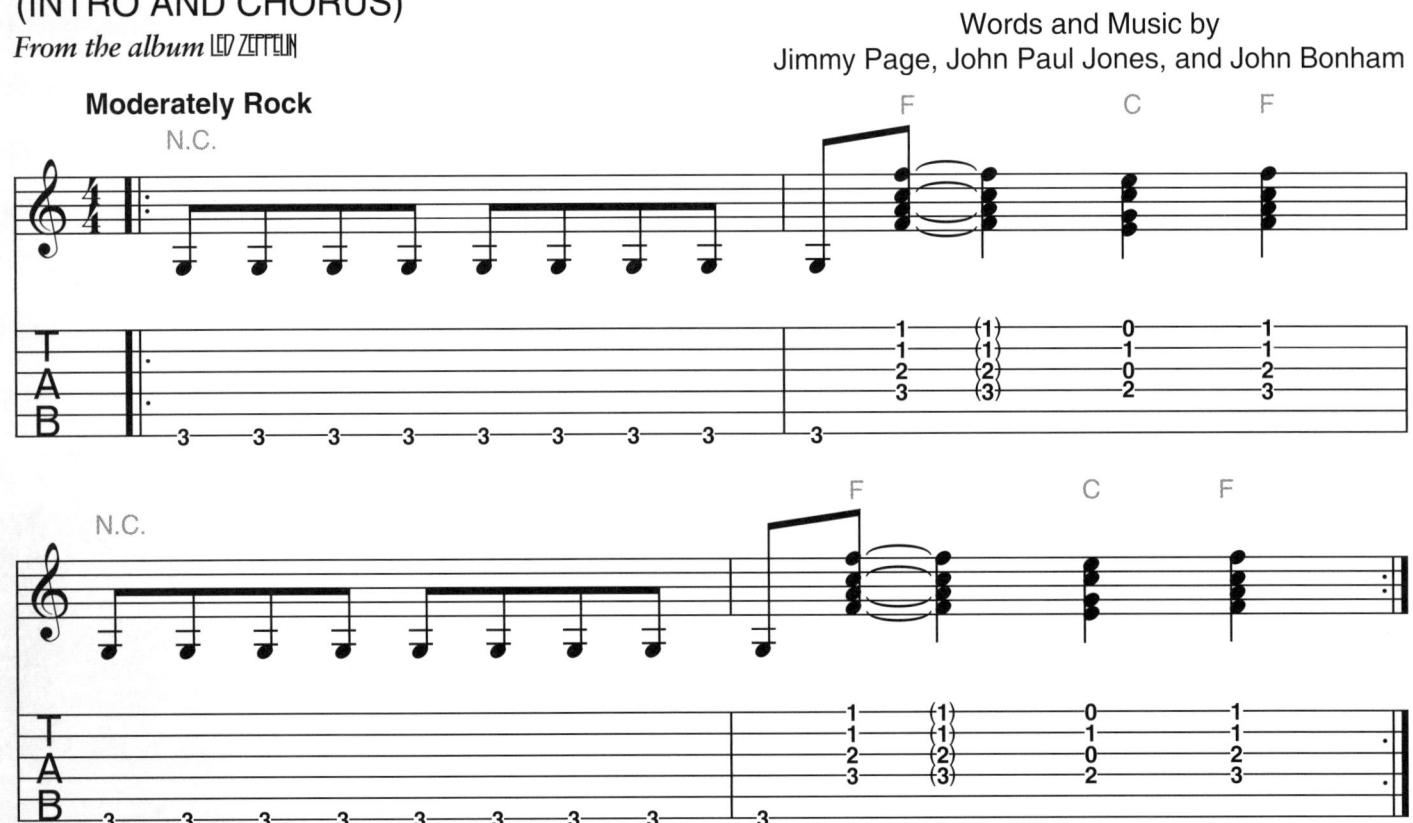

Copyright © 1969 (renewed) FLAMES OF ALBION MUSIC, INC.
All Rights Administered by WB MUSIC CORP.
Exclusive Print Rights for the World Excluding Europe Administered by ALFRED MUSIC PUBLISHING CO., INC.
All Rights Reserved

OUT ON THE TILES
(SOLO, DUET, OR TRIO)

From the album Led Zeppelin III

Words and Music by Jimmy Page, Robert Plant, and John Bonham

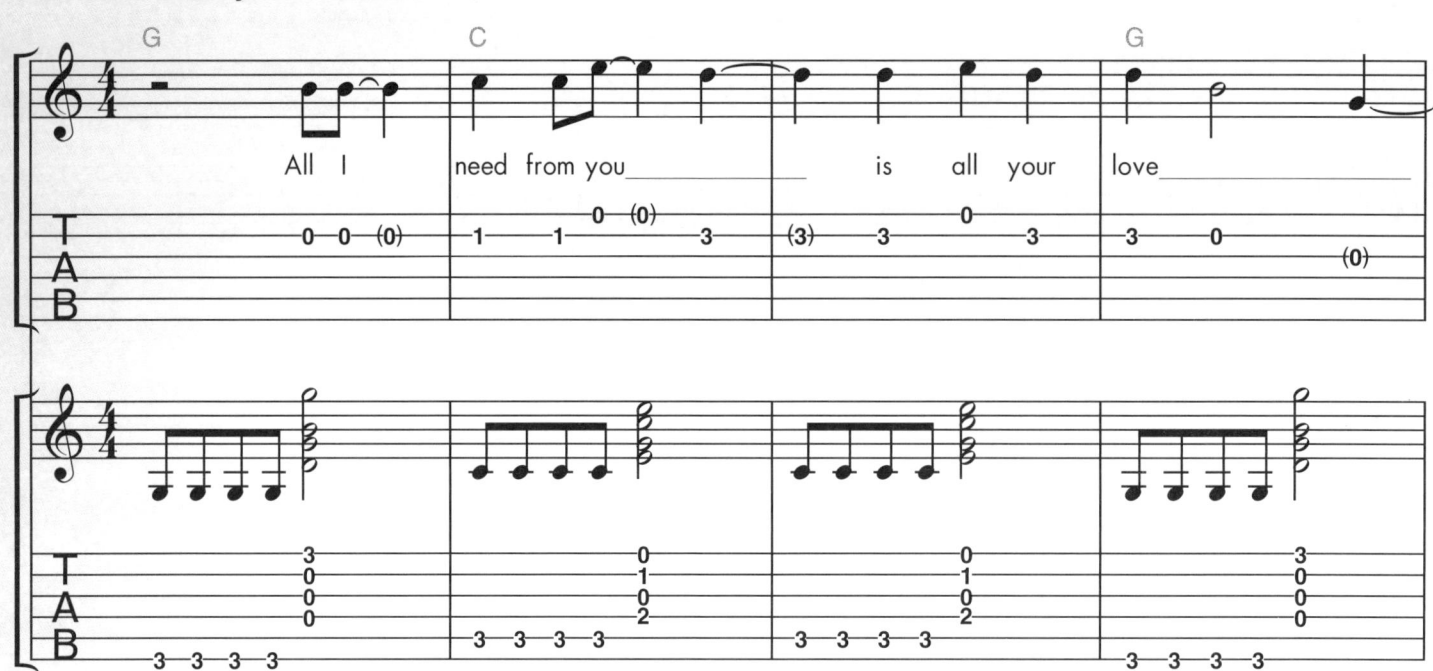

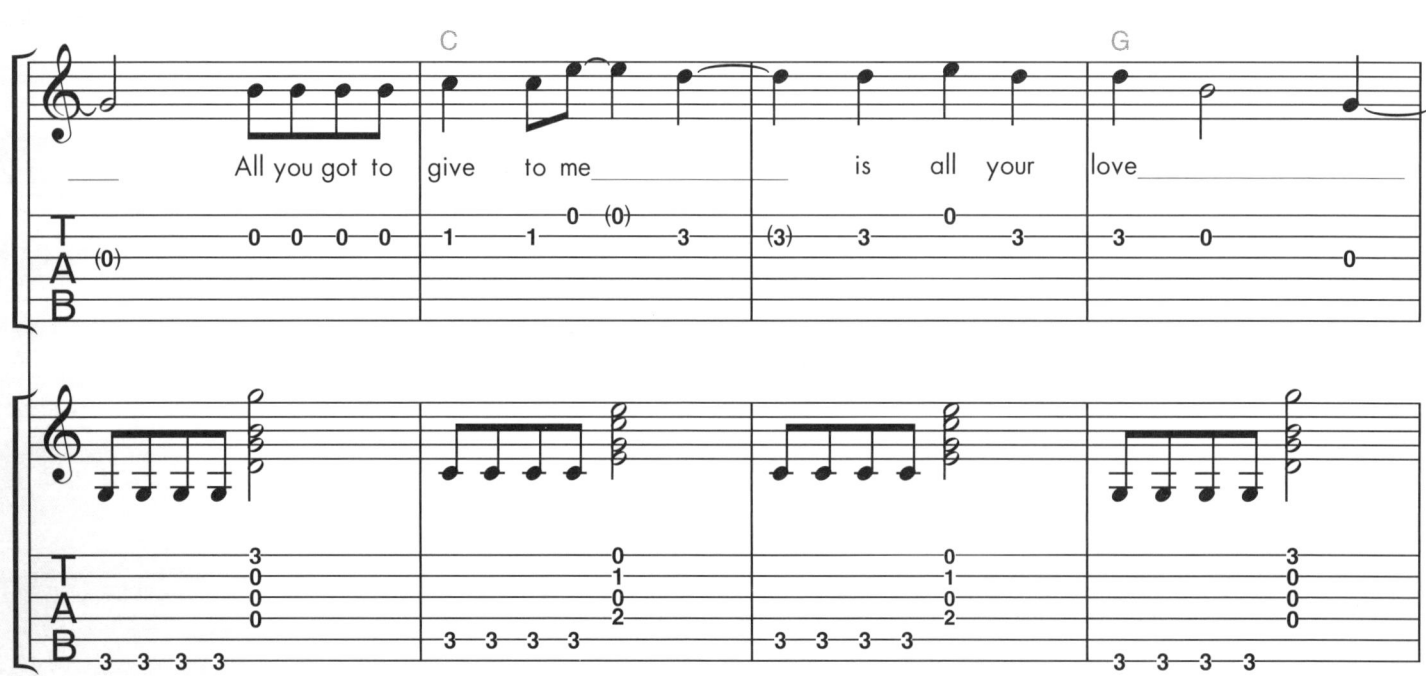

© 1970 (Renewed) FLAMES OF ALBION MUSIC, INC.
All Rights Administered by WB MUSIC CORP.
Exclusive Print Rights for the World Excluding Europe Administered by ALFRED MUSIC PUBLISHING CO., INC.
All Rights Reserved

* A whole rest ▬ means to be silent for a complete measure.

THE MAJOR SCALE

A scale is a series or succession of tones. All MAJOR SCALES are made of eight tones, which ascend in alphabetical order. The major scale always follows this pattern of alternating whole and half steps:

The Octave Note
This scale has eight notes. The highest note, having the same name as the first note, is called the OCTAVE note.

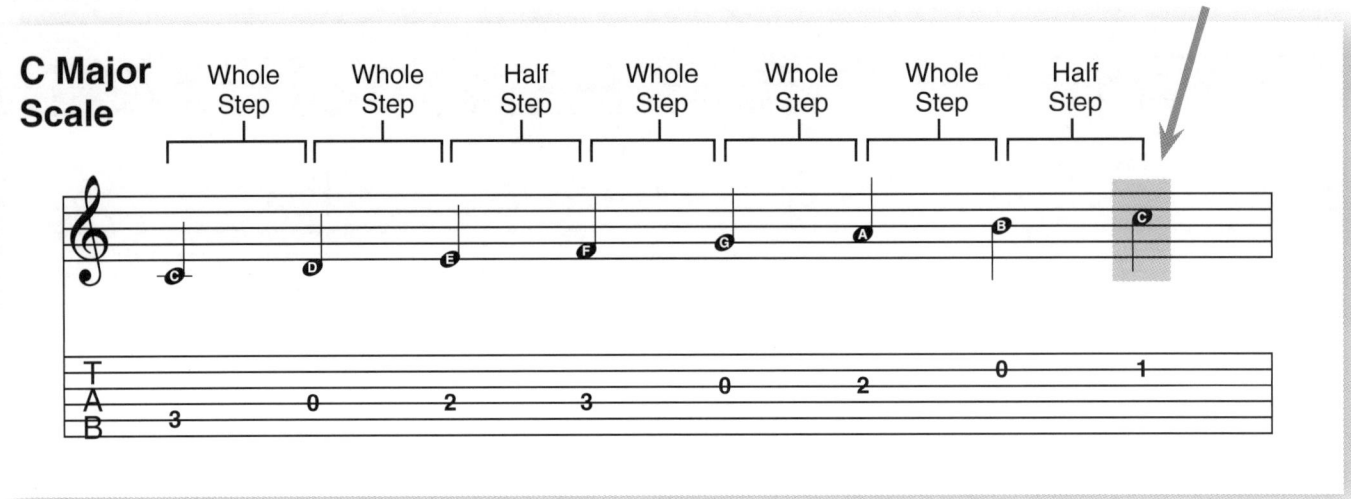

It is easier to visualize whole steps and half steps on a piano keyboard. Notice that there are whole steps between every white key except E–F and B–C.

Whole Steps—One Key Between
Half Steps—No Key Between

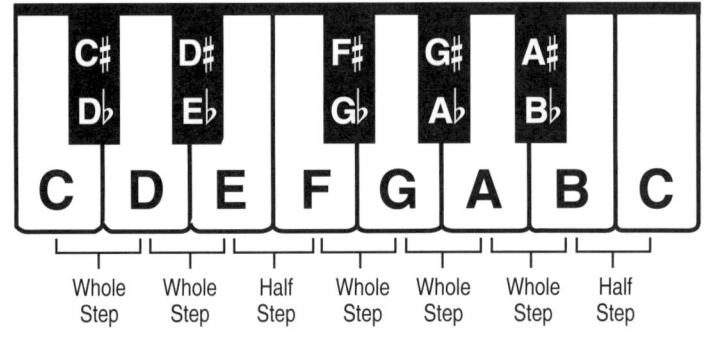

The MAJOR SCALE may be built starting on ANY NOTE—natural, sharp, or flat. Using the pattern we just learned, write a MAJOR SCALE starting on G.

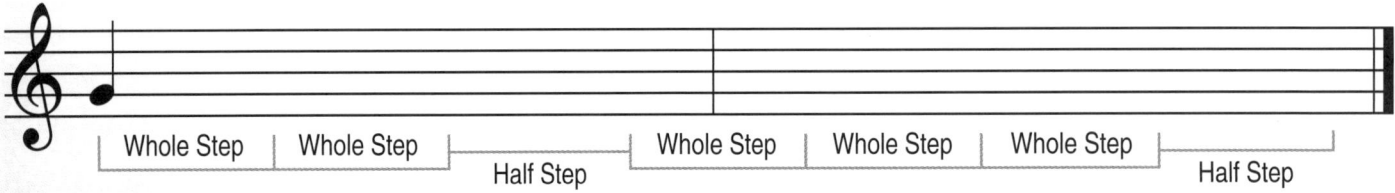

CHECK: Are the notes in alphabetical order? Did you give the 7th note a sharp?

Write a MAJOR SCALE starting on F:

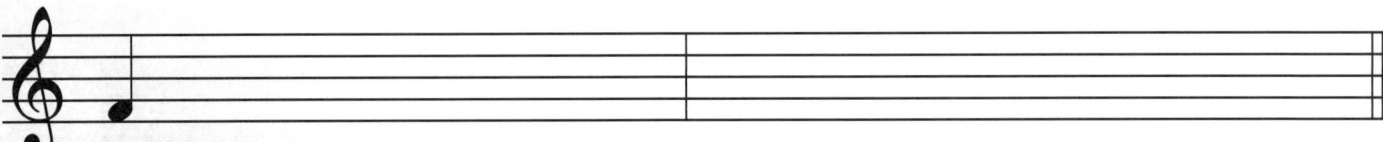

CHECK: Are the notes in alphabetical order? Did you give the 4th note a flat?

KEY SIGNATURES

The Key of C Major
A piece based on the C MAJOR SCALE is in the KEY OF C MAJOR, since there are no sharps or flats in the C scale.

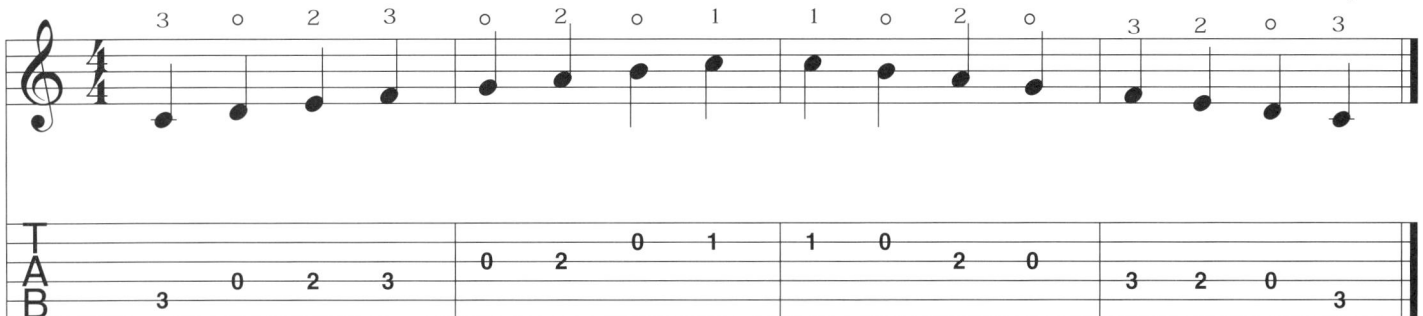

The Key of G Major
A piece based on the G Major scale is in the key of G Major. Since F is sharp in the G scale, every F will be sharp in the key of G Major. Instead of adding a sharp every time an F appears in a piece, the sharp is indicated at the beginning, in the KEY SIGNATURE. Sharps or flats shown in the key signature remain effective throughout the piece.

Key Signature
One Sharp (F♯)

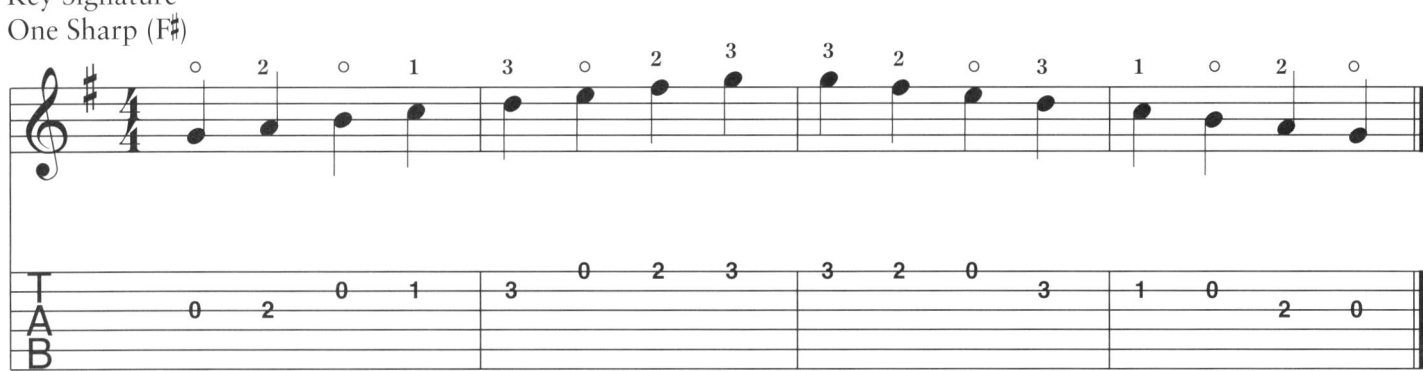

The Key of F Major
A piece based on the F Major scale is in the key of F Major.

Key Signature
One Flat (B♭)

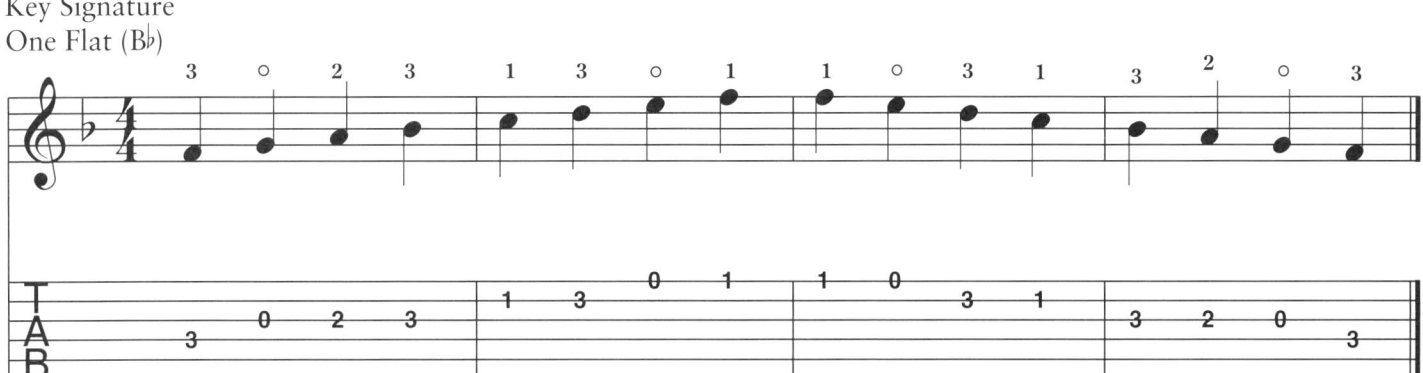

The three scales shown above should be practiced every day. Students who do this should have little difficulty playing selections written in C Major, G Major, and F Major.

46 LED ZEPPELIN GUITAR METHOD
WHAT IS AND WHAT SHOULD NEVER BE (VERSE)
From the album LED ZEPPELIN II

Track 46

No Sharps
No Flats
Signature of
the Key of C

Words and Music by
Jimmy Page, and Robert Plant

Slow Blues

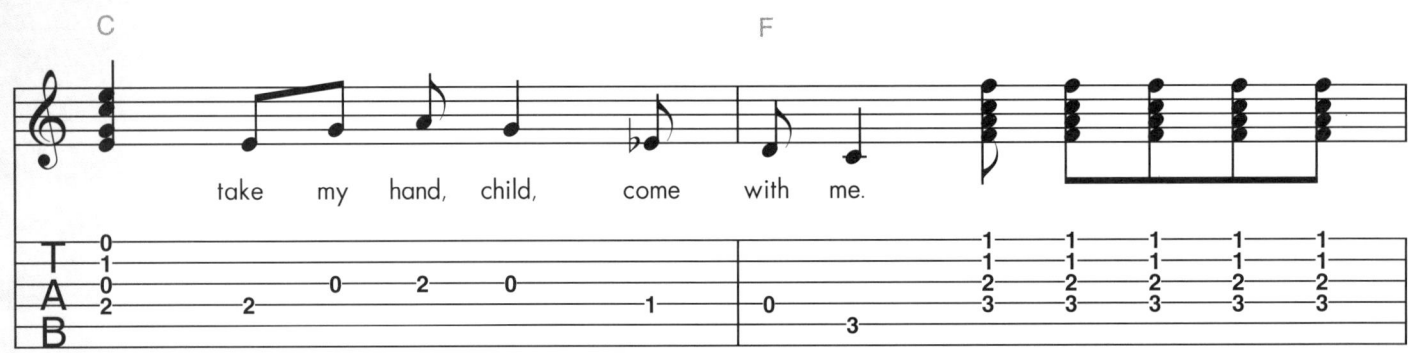

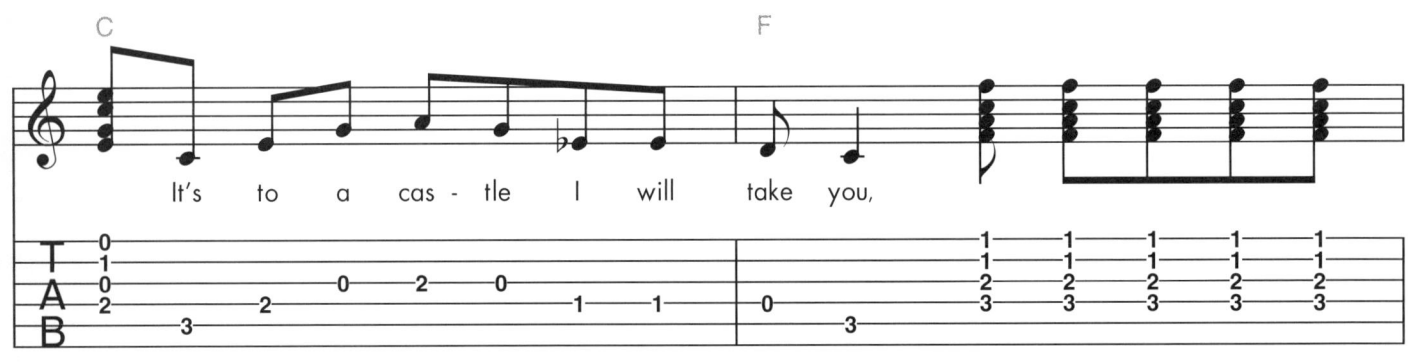

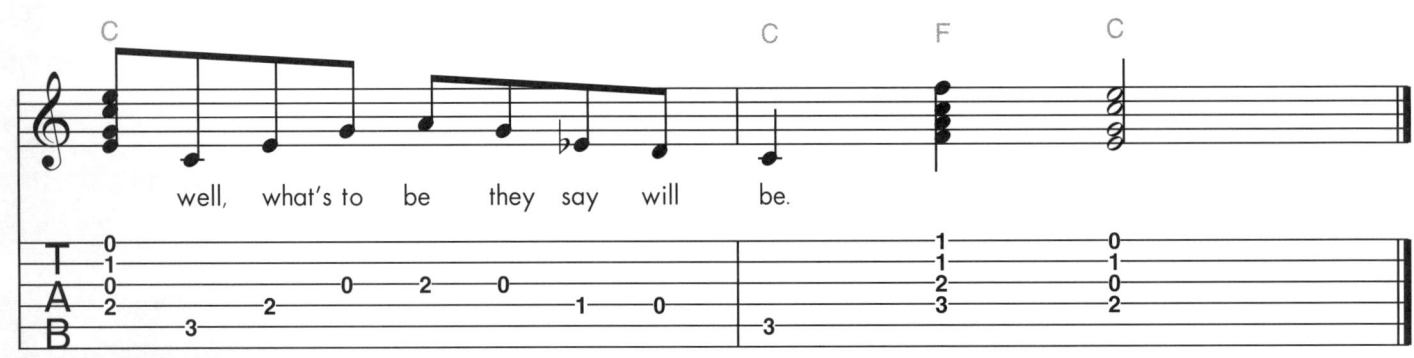

© 1969 (Renewed) FLAMES OF ALBION MUSIC, INC.
All Rights Administered by WB MUSIC CORP.
Exclusive Print Rights for the World Excluding Europe Administered by ALFRED MUSIC PUBLISHING CO., INC.
All Rights Reserved

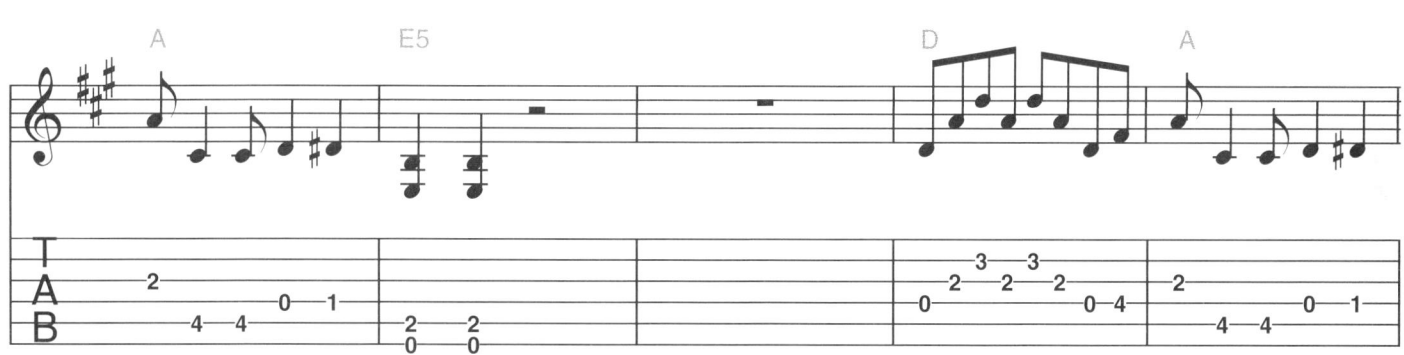
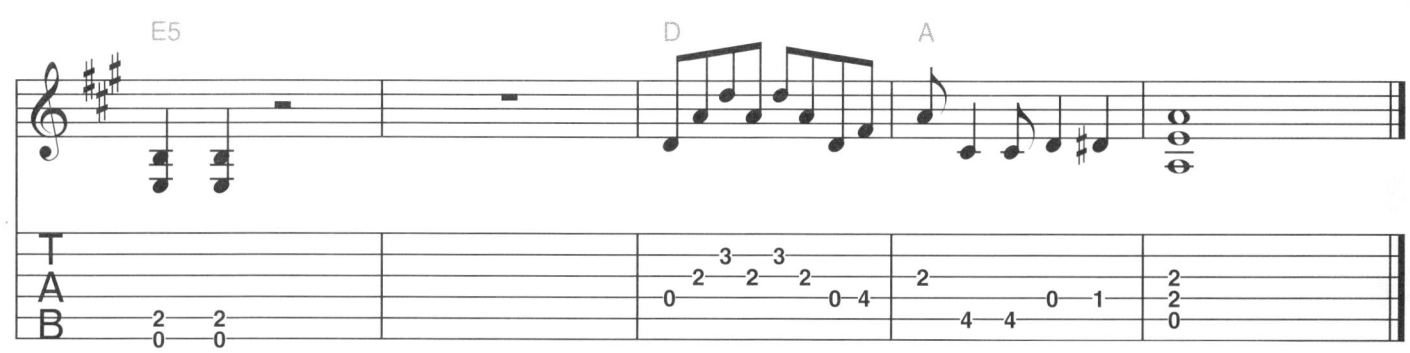

INTRODUCING DOTTED NOTES

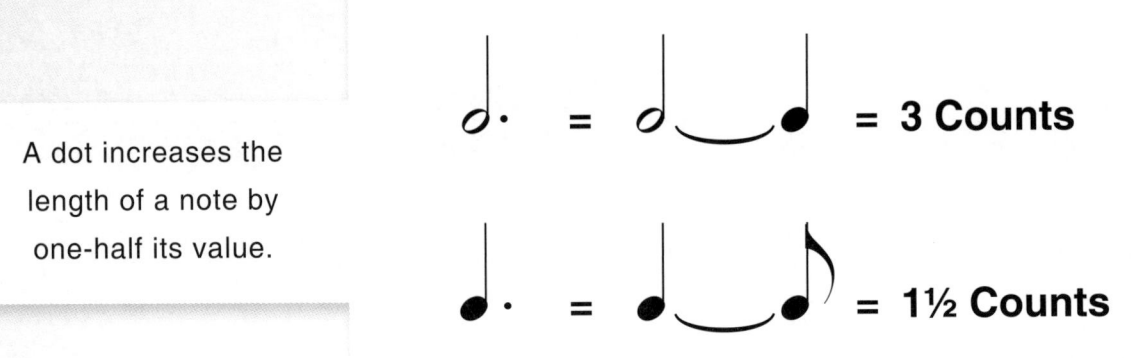

A dot increases the length of a note by one-half its value.

Preparatory Drill

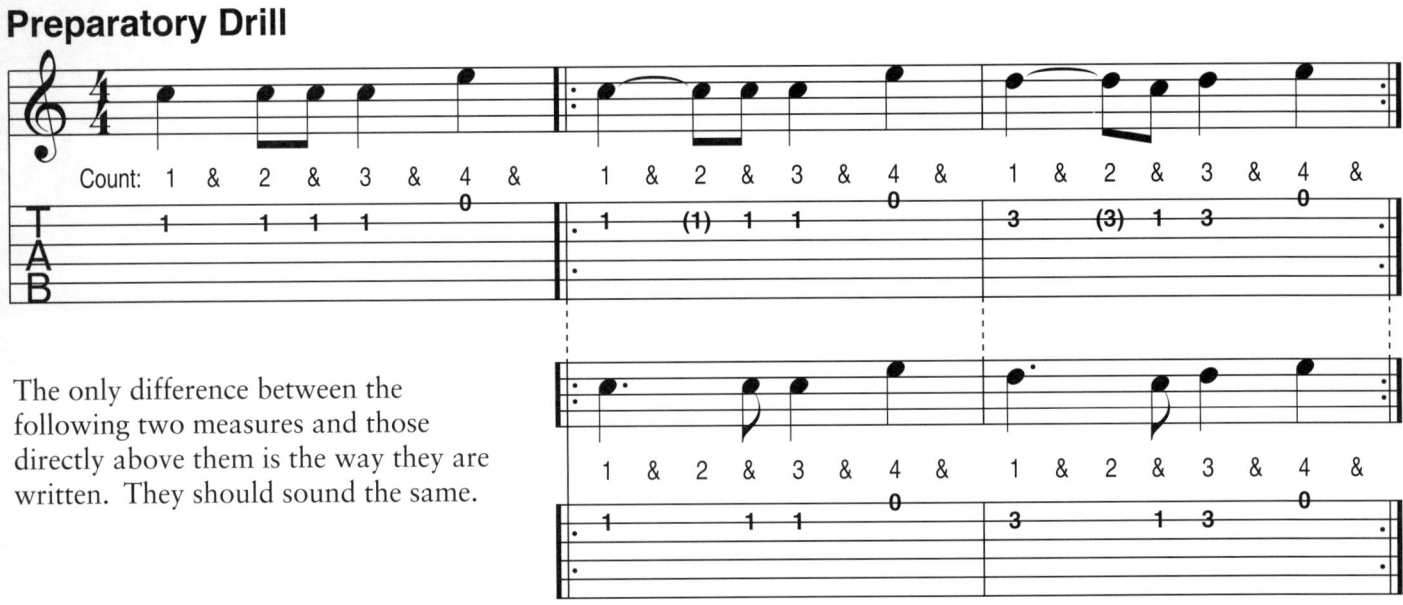

The only difference between the following two measures and those directly above them is the way they are written. They should sound the same.

Since you played this rhythm (♩ ♪ ♩) in "Out on the Tiles," you should have no trouble playing dotted quarter notes.

HEARTBREAKER (RIFF)

From the album Led Zeppelin II

Track 48

Words and Music by
Jimmy Page, Robert Plant,
John Paul Jones, and John Bonham

Slow Rock

Key of A

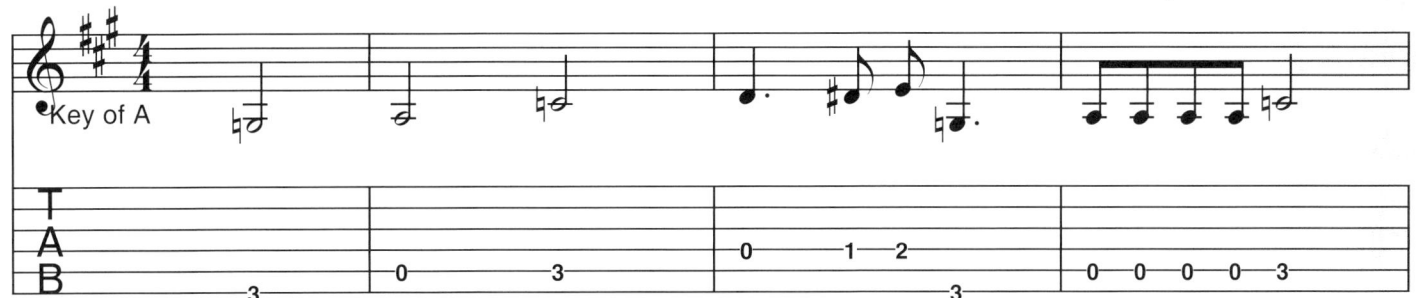
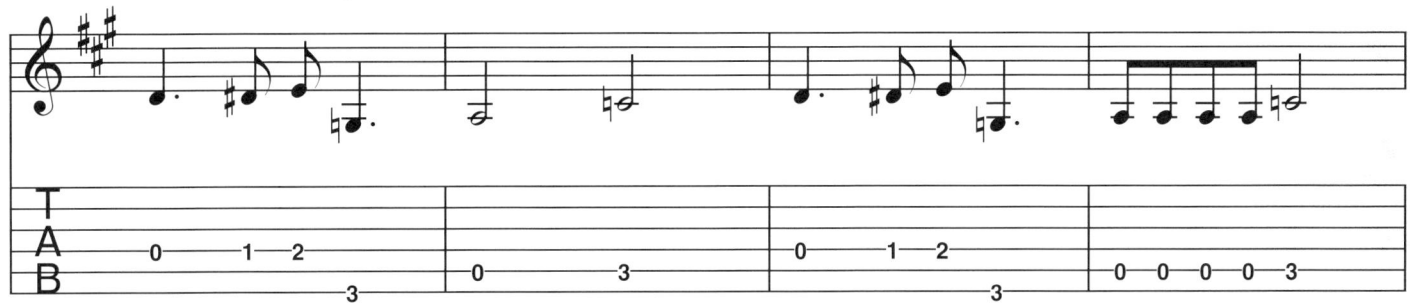

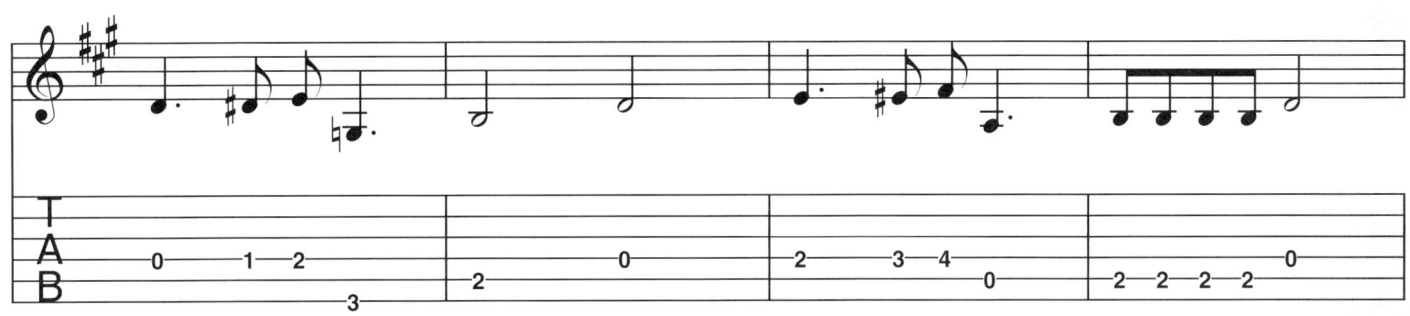
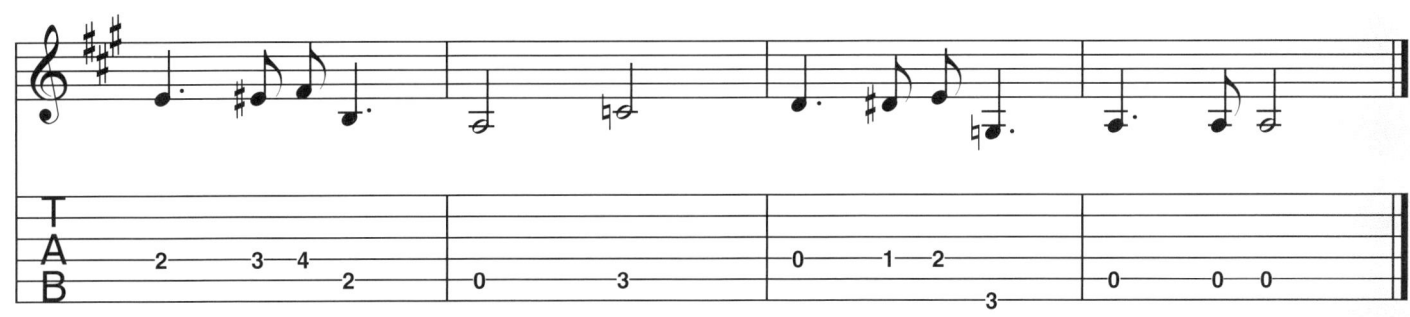

© 1969 (Renewed) FLAMES OF ALBION MUSIC, INC.
All Rights Administered by WB MUSIC CORP.
Exclusive Print Rights for the World Excluding Europe Administered by ALFRED MUSIC PUBLISHING CO., INC.
All Rights Reserved

HOW MANY MORE TIMES
(SOLO, DUET, OR TRIO)

From the album Led Zeppelin

Moderately Fast Blues

Track 49

Words and Music by
Jimmy Page, John Paul
Jones, and John Bonham

© 1969 (Renewed) FLAMES OF ALBION MUSIC, INC.
All Rights Administered by WB MUSIC CORP.
Exclusive Print Rights for the World Excluding Europe Administered by ALFRED MUSIC PUBLISHING CO., INC.
All Rights Reserved

* This note is B-flat, played on the 1st string at the 6th fret.

THE THREE PRINCIPAL CHORDS

(These pages are a study of musical theory and are not to be played.)
Every key has three chords with which any melody can be satisfactorily harmonized.
They are called the three principal chords; their technical names are:

Tonic, Sub-Dominant, and Dominant

If we number the notes of the scale with Roman numerals, the tonic is the I, sub-dominant is the IV, and the dominant is the V.

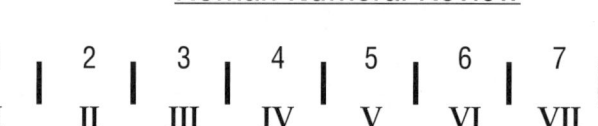

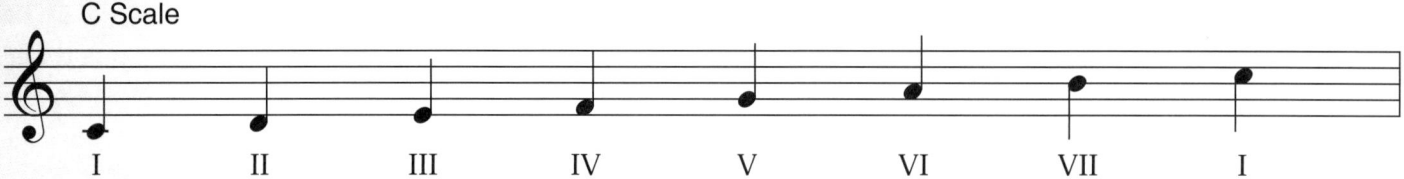

Tonic (I)

The tonic chord is built on the first note of the scale (the tonic, or key-note).
The fundamental construction of tonic chords is the 1st, 3rd, and 5th notes of the scale.
The 1st note of a chord is called the root (R).

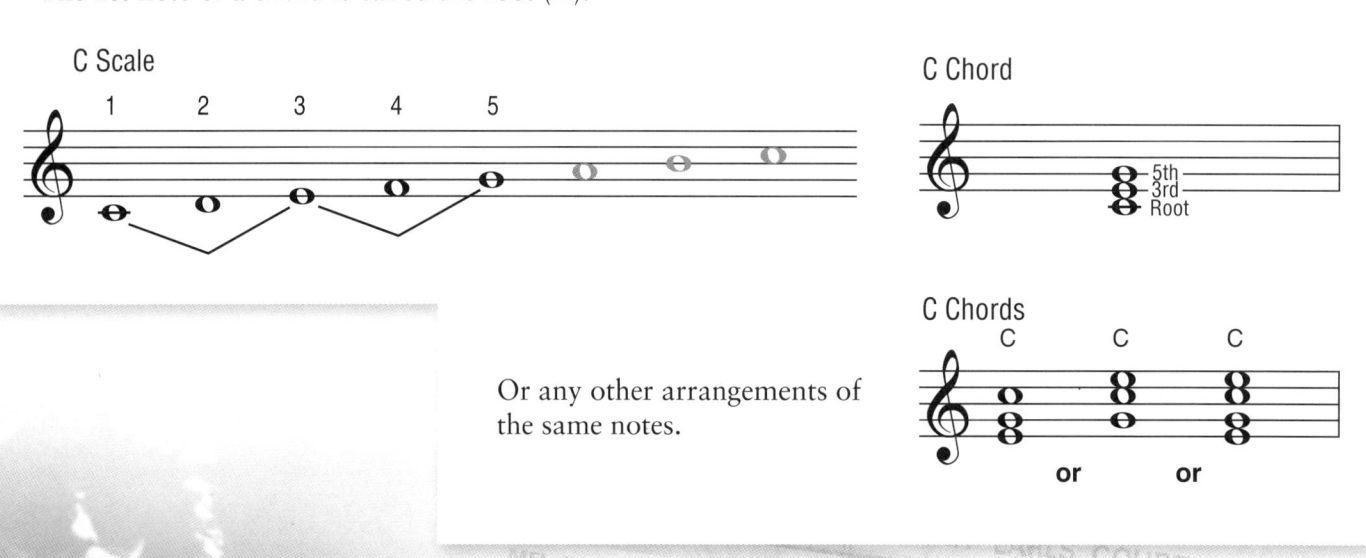

Or any other arrangements of the same notes.

Sub-Dominant (IV)

The sub-dominant chord is built on the 4th step of the scale.

The sub-dominant chord is constructed of a root, 3rd, and 5th with the root being the 4th step of the scale.

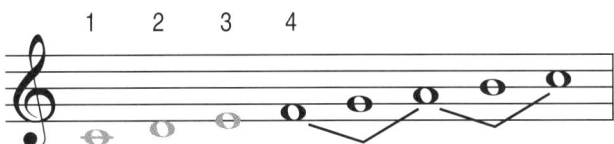

F Chord

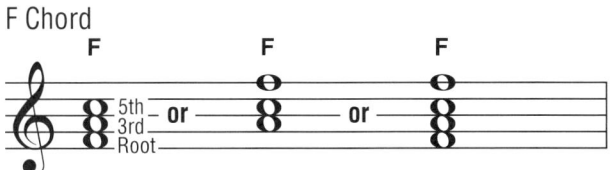

Dominant (V)

The dominant chord is built on the 5th step of the scale.

The dominant chord is constructed of a root, 3rd, and 5th with the root being the 5th step of the scale.

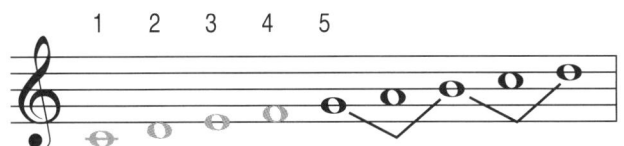

G Chord

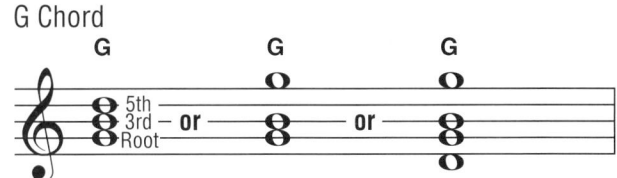

On the dominant chord, it is common to add the 7th above the root; the chord is then called the dominant 7th, marked G7.

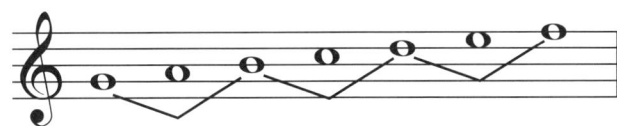

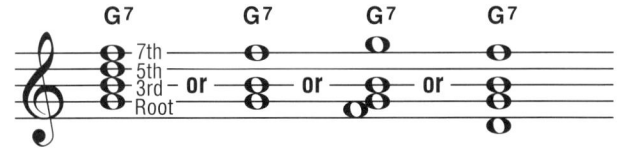

THE THREE PRINCIPAL CHORDS IN THE KEY OF C MAJOR

Track 50

THE FIVE-STRING C CHORD

THE FOUR-STRING F CHORD

THE SIX-STRING G7 CHORD

RHYTHM PATTERNS USING THE THREE PRINCIPAL CHORDS IN C MAJOR

Track 51

The chord progressions on this page were made popular by songs, including "Twist and Shout," "La Bamba," "Peggy Sue," and countless others.

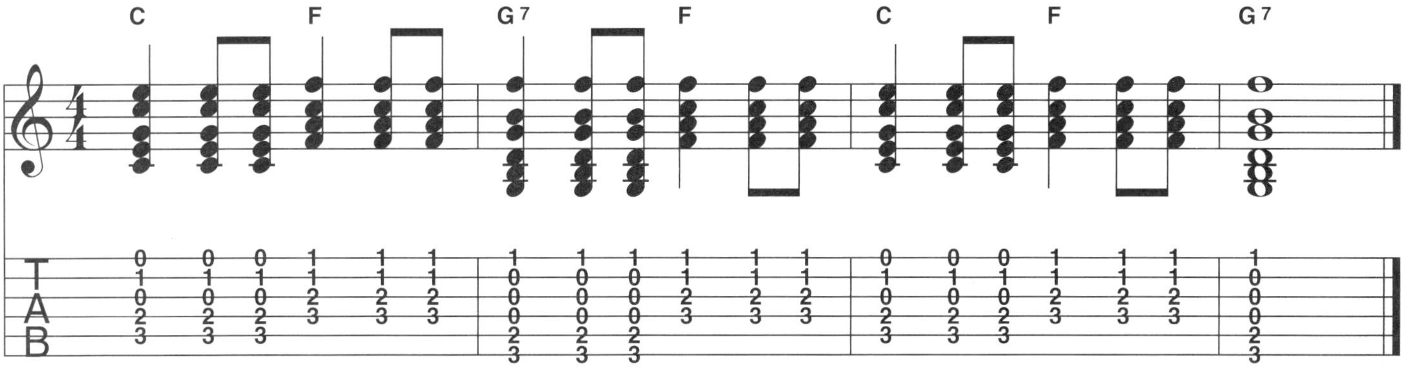

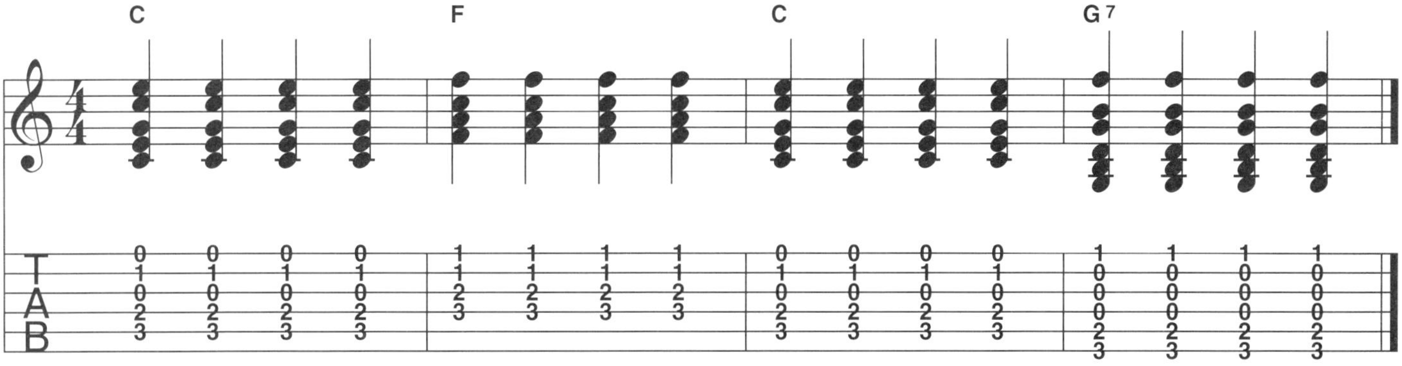

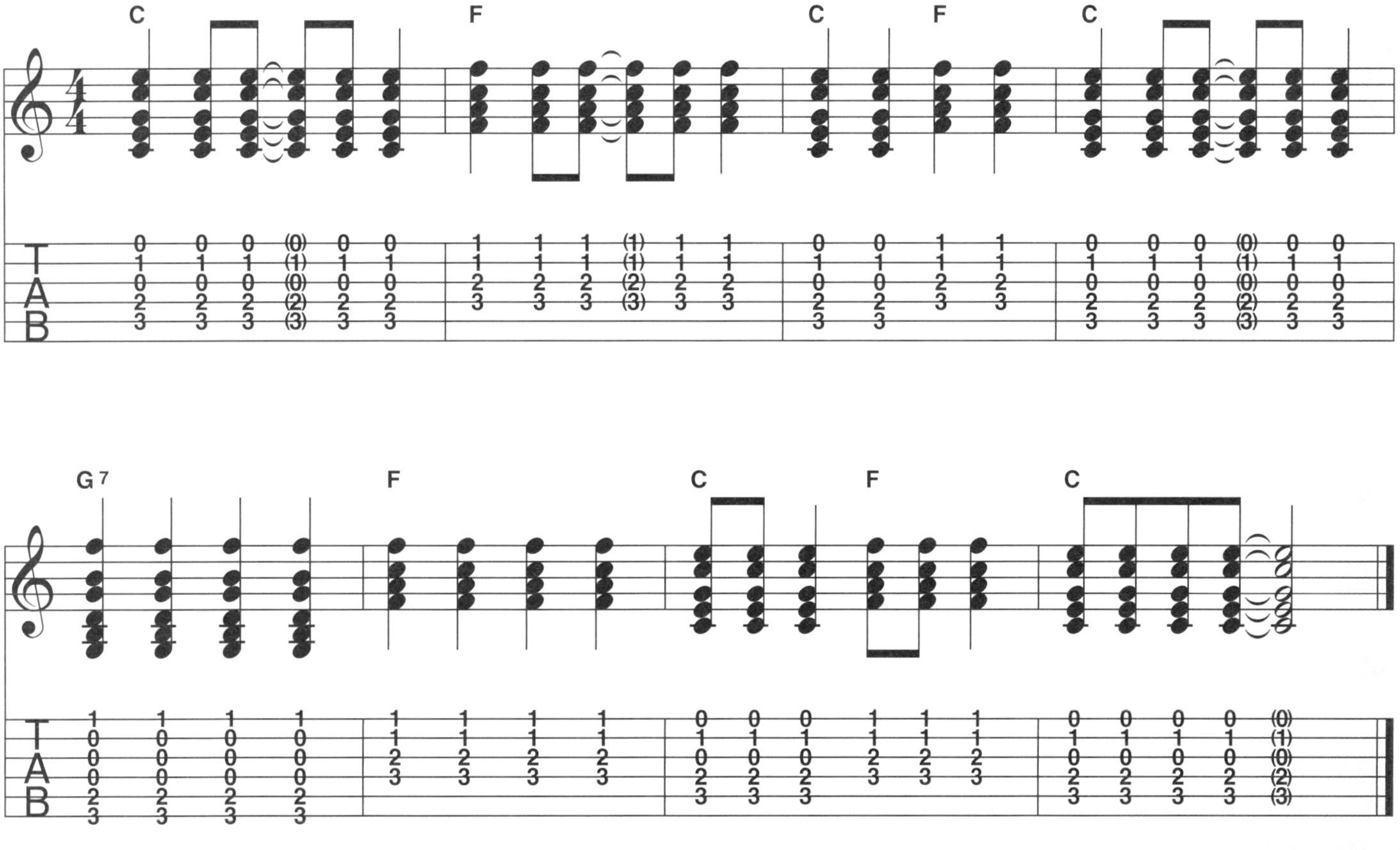

INTRODUCING TRIPLETS 🎵 Track 52

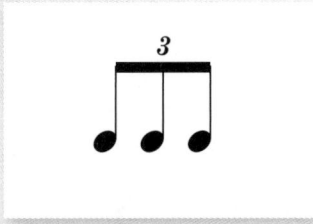

When three notes are grouped together with the figure "3" above or below the notes, the group is called a TRIPLET. The rhythmic value of the triplet is equal to the value given to two of the same kind of note.
In 3/4 or 4/4 time, two eighth notes get one count, so an eighth note triplet will also get one count.

In the following exercise, play the three notes of each triplet in one count.

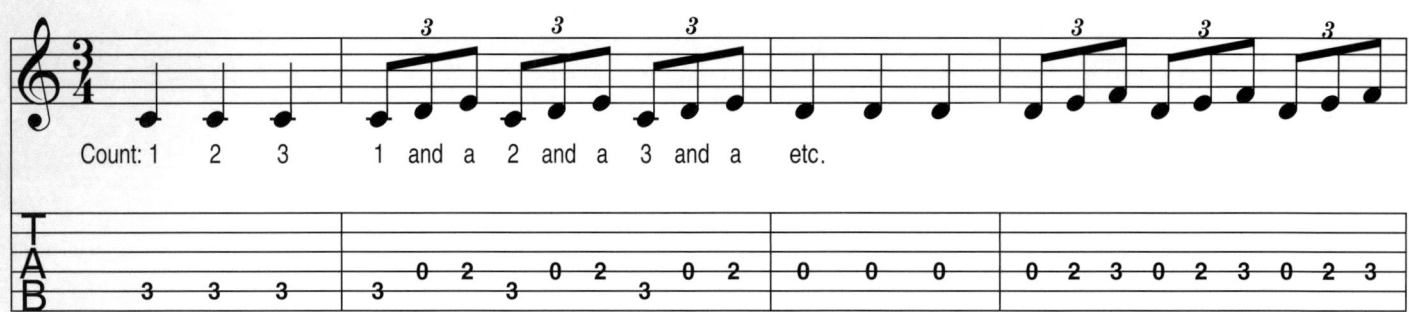

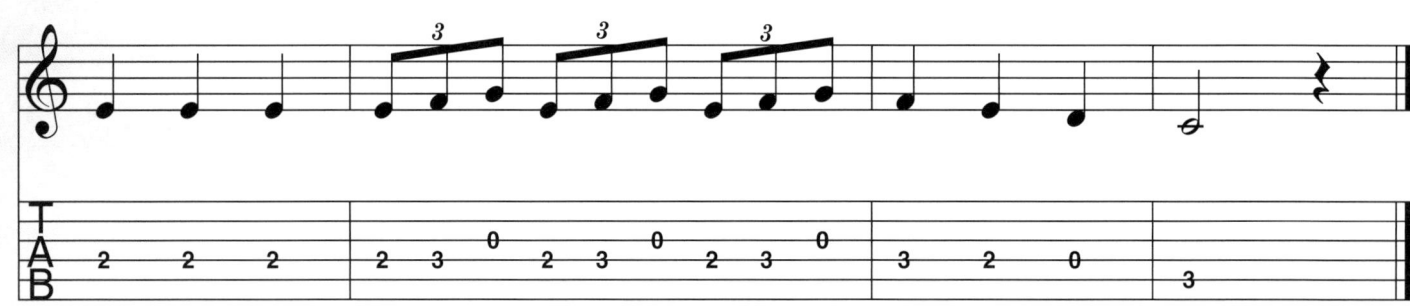

YOU SHOOK ME 🎵 Track 53

From the album LED ZEPPELIN

Slow Blues

Words and Music by
Wille Dixon and J.B. Lenoir

1, 3. You know you shook me, you shook me all night long.
2. bird that whis-tles, and I have birds that sing.

* *Segno* Sign. See bottom of page 57.

© 1962 (Renewed) HOOCHIE COOCHIE MUSIC and ARC MUSIC CORP.
All Rights for HOOCHIE COOCHIE MUSIC Administered by BUG MUSIC
All Rights Reserved   Used by Permission

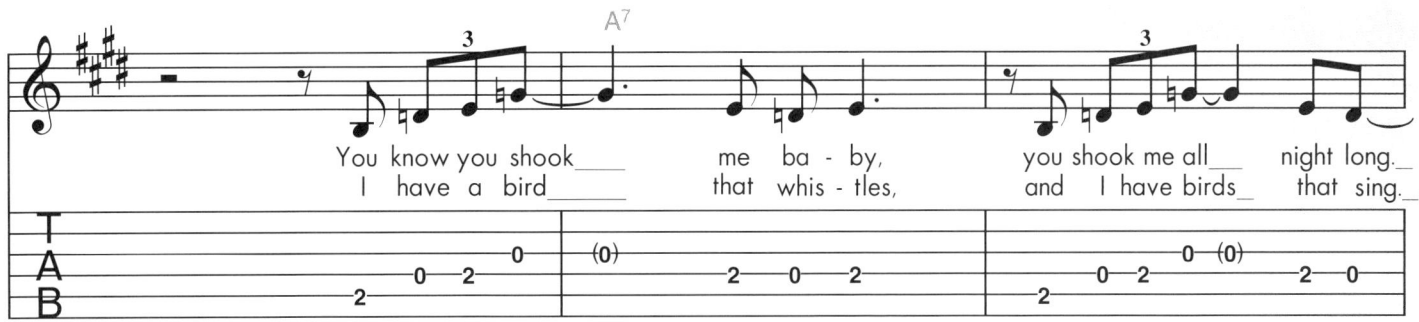
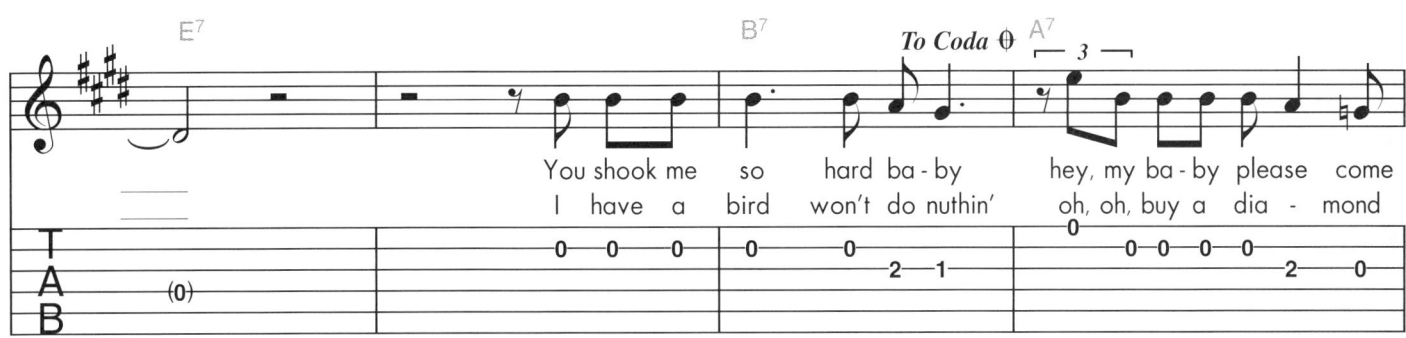

* del Segno al Coda. Go back to the sign 𝄋, play up to the Coda sign ⊕, then skip to the Coda (ending section), and play to the end.

KEY OF A MINOR

For every major key, there is a minor key with the same key signature called the RELATIVE MINOR KEY. The keys of A Minor and C Major are relative keys because they have the same key signature (no sharps, no flats). The relative minor scale is built on the 6th tone of the relative major scale, and its 7th step is raised a half step to form a harmonic minor scale. Chords in a minor key are built using the notes of this harmonic minor scale.

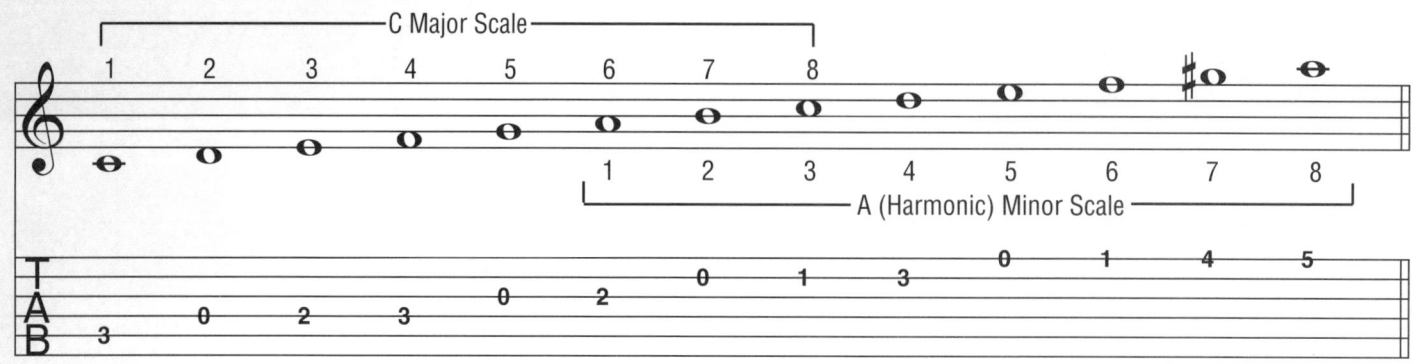

The Two-Octave A (Harmonic) Minor Scale

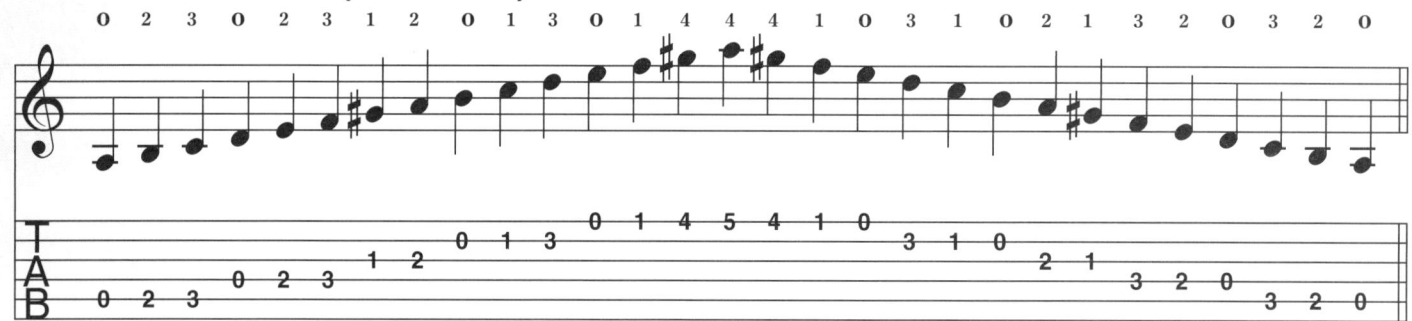

THE THREE PRINCIPAL CHORDS IN THE KEY OF A MINOR

Track 54

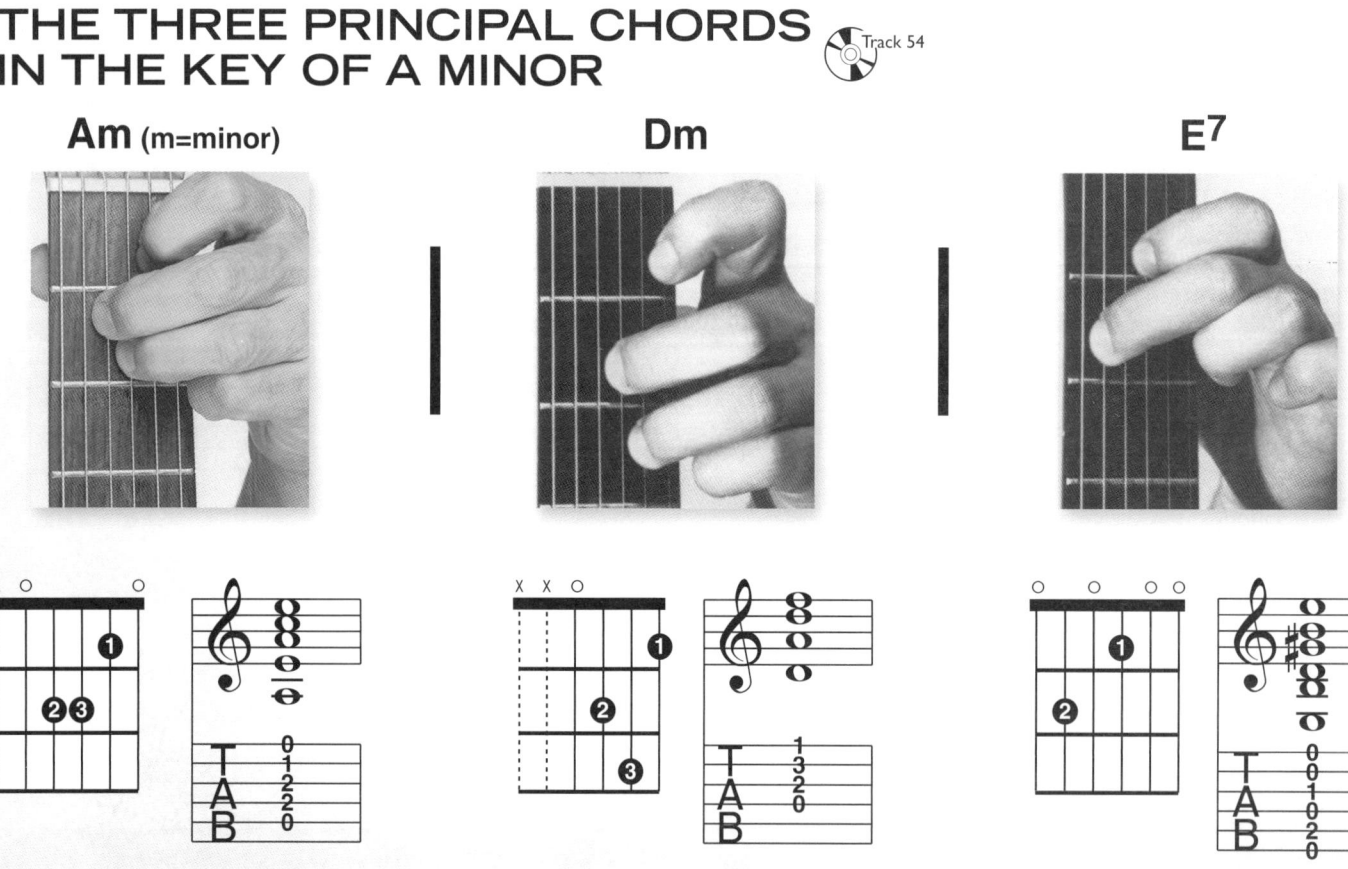

LED ZEPPELIN GUITAR METHOD

1.

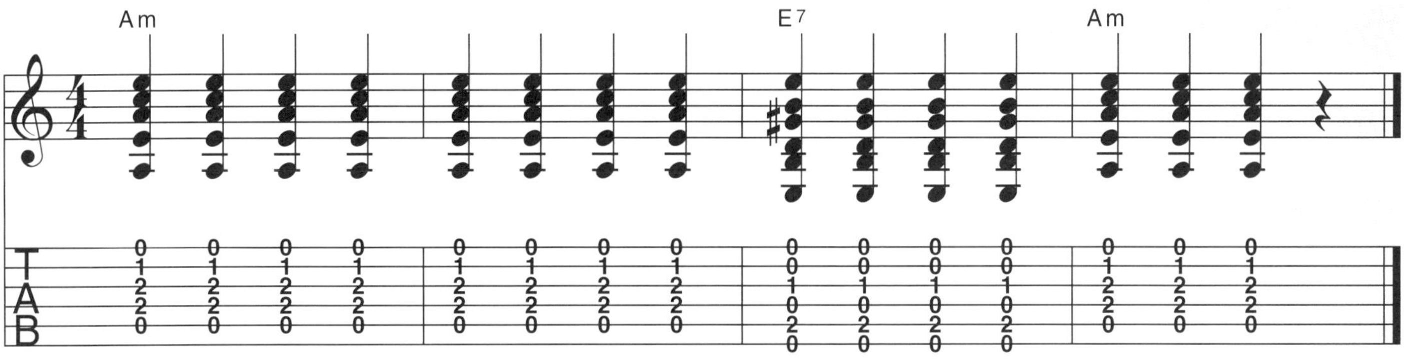

2.

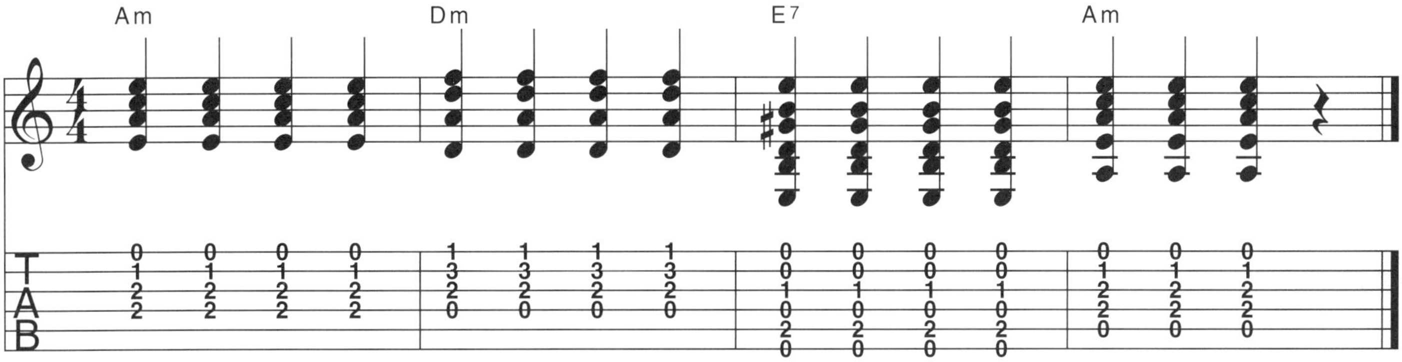

3.

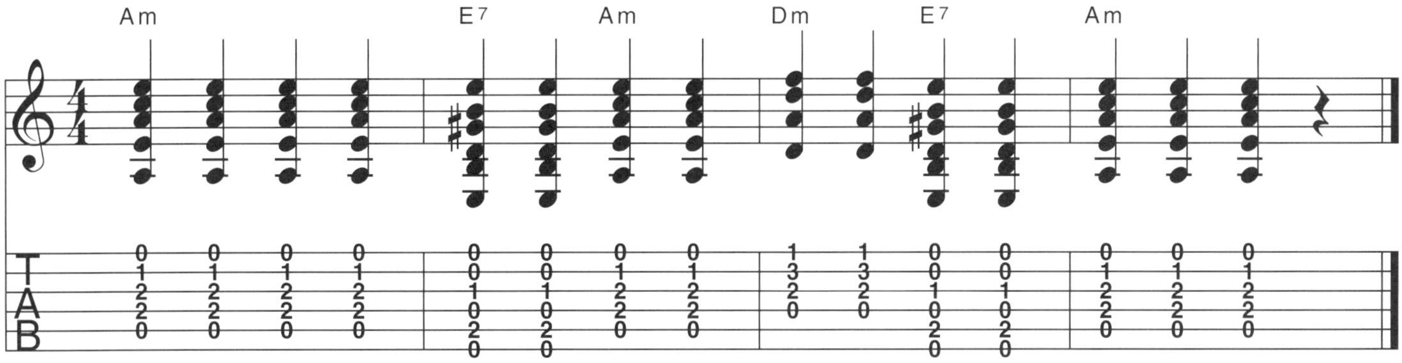

THE FOUR-STRING D7 CHORD 🎵 Track 55

Much of Led Zeppelin's output is heavily influenced by the blues. Some of their most popular songs were written by iconic blues figures such as Willie Dixon ("You Shook Me," "Bring It on Home"). Seventh chords, like D7, are an important part of what gives the blues its distinctive sound.

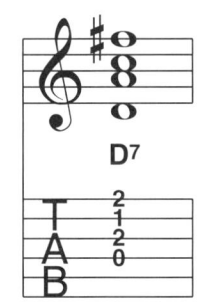
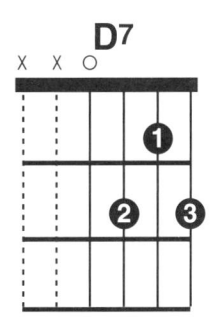

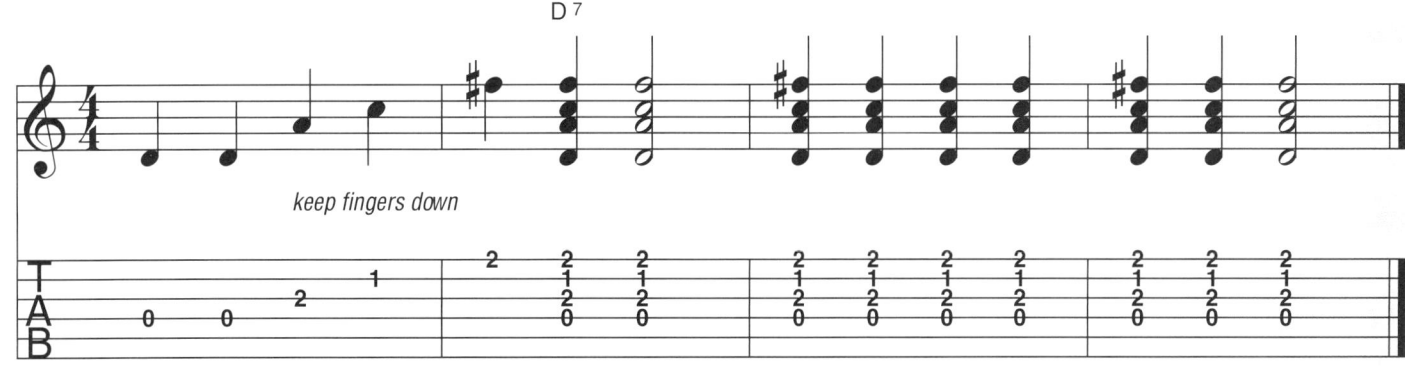

keep fingers down

60 LED ZEPPELIN GUITAR METHOD

8th FRET

1st string, 8th fret

The high C on the 1st string (shown on the left) is introduced in this song.

Triplet rhythms can appear in a number of ways. It is possible to have a quarter note within a triplet, which is the same as a tie between two of the eighth notes. The quarter-eighth triplet rhythm is particularly popular in much blues and jazz, and is often called swing feel, or shuffle. Led Zeppelin used both quarter-eighth and eight-quarter triplets in their blues-based tunes.

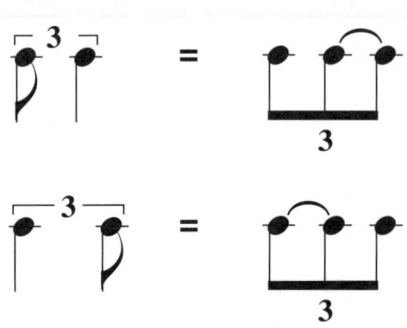

Bring It On Home
(SOLO, DUET, OR TRIO)
From the album LED ZEPPELIN II

Track 56

Words and Music by
Wille Dixon

Moderate Blues

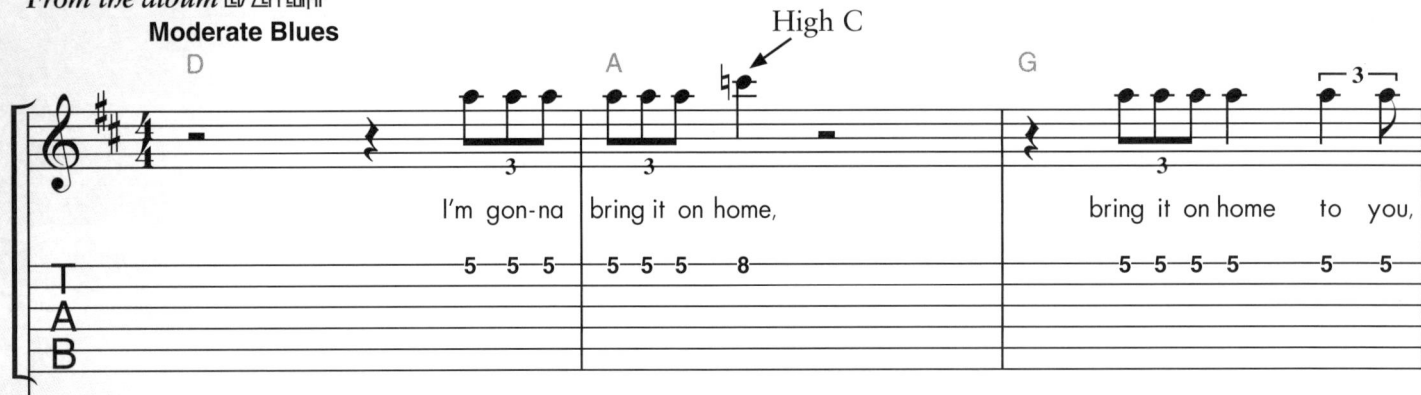

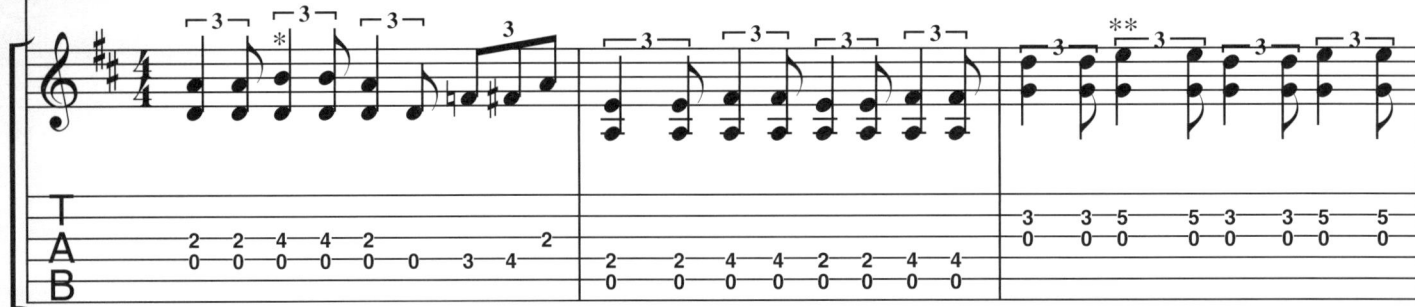

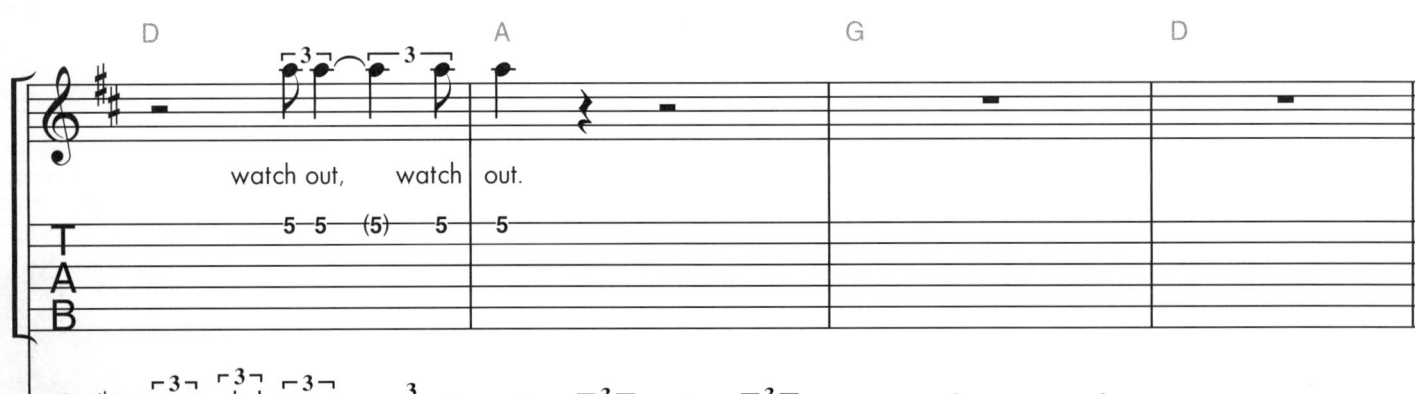

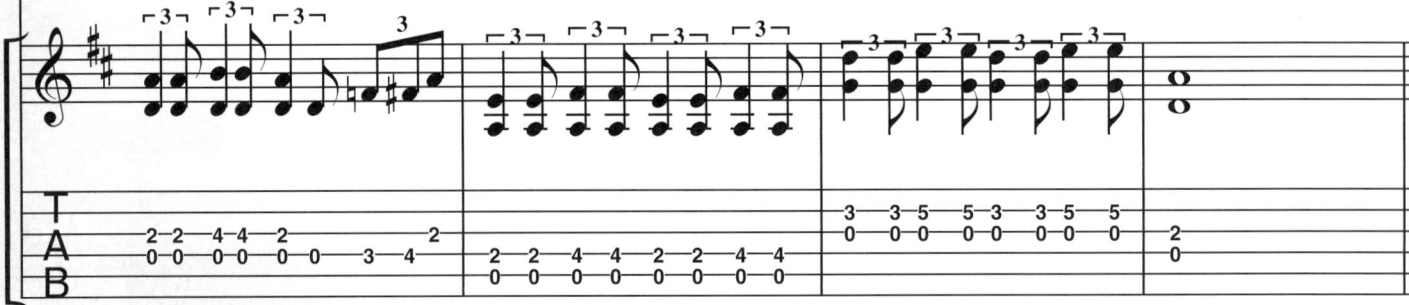

* This B note, usually played on the open 2nd string, can also be played at the 4th fret of the 3rd string.
** This E note, usually played on the open 1st string, can also be played at the 5th fret of the 2nd string.

© 1964 (Renewed) HOOCHIE COOCHIE MUSIC
All Rights Administered by BUG MUSIC
All Rights Reserved   Used by Permission

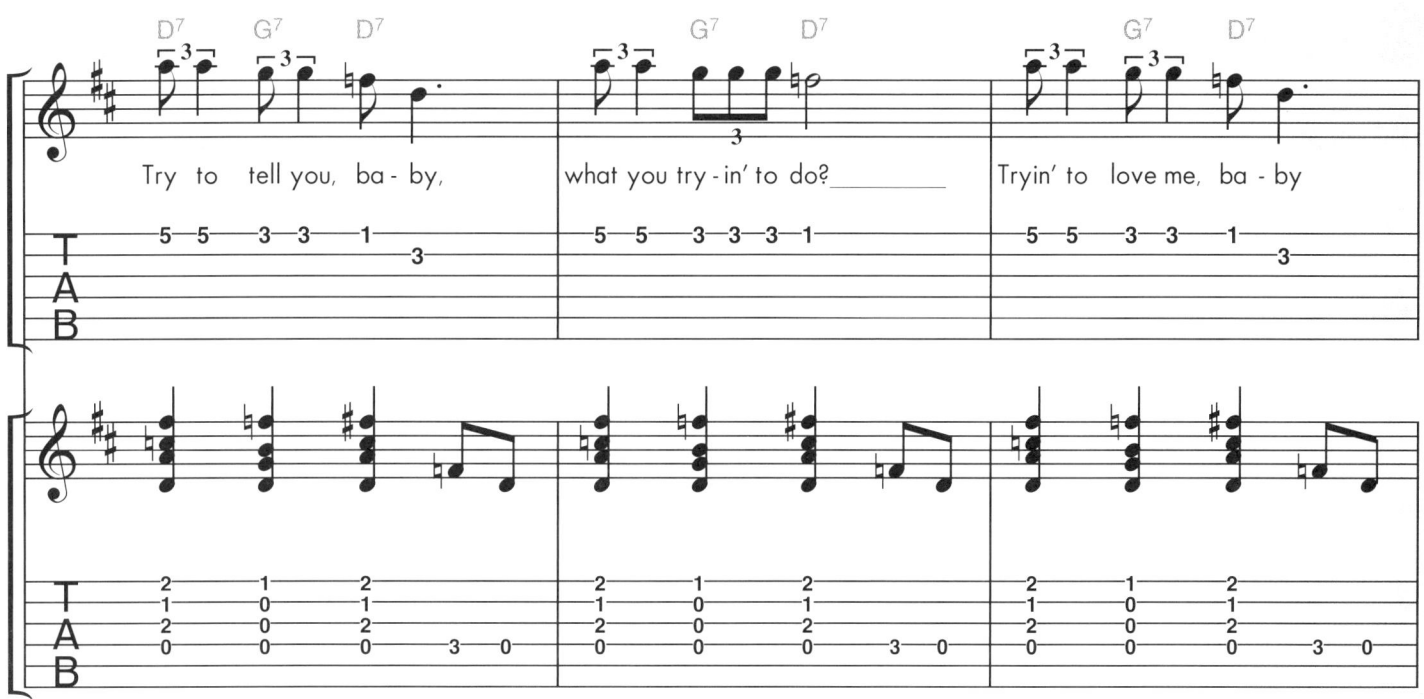
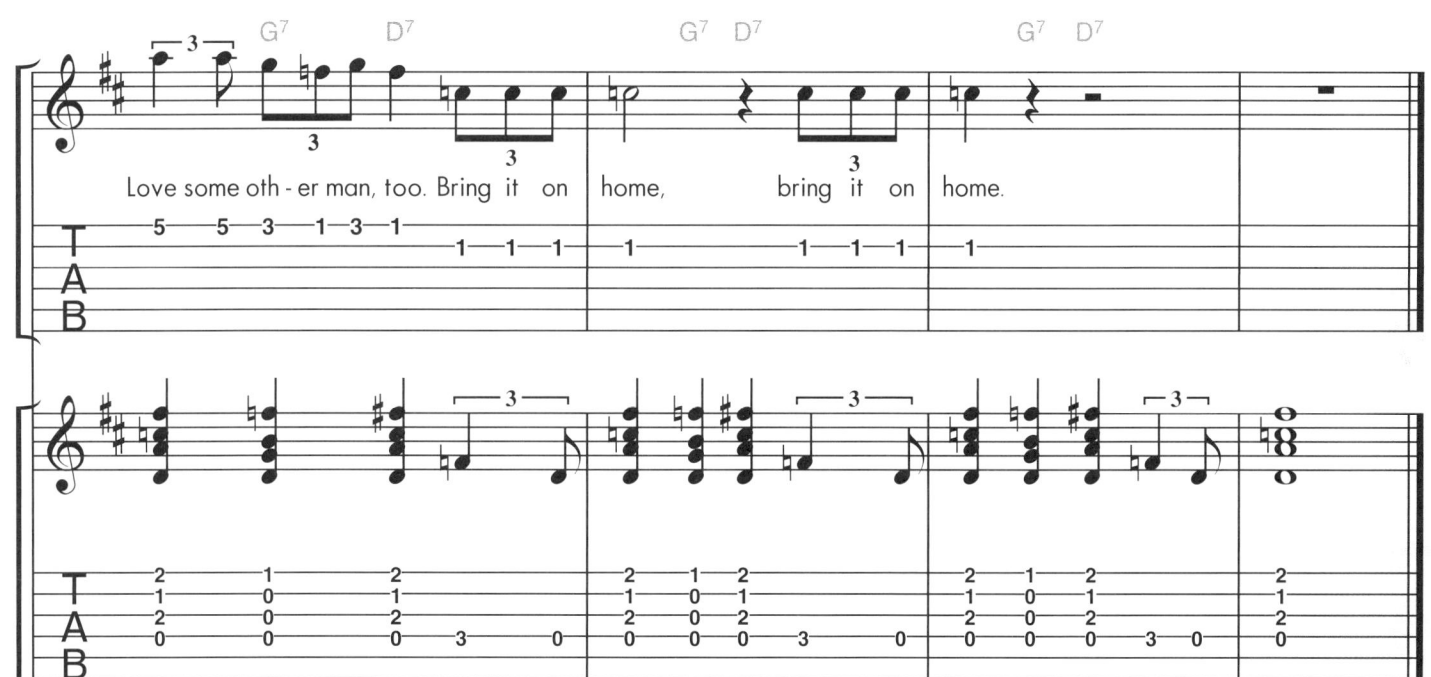

LED ZEPPELIN GUITAR METHOD 63

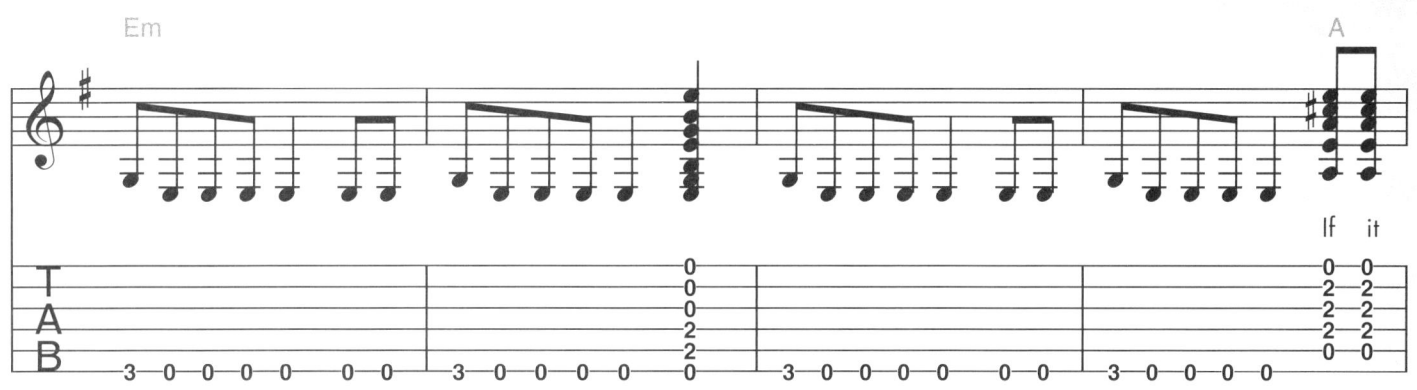

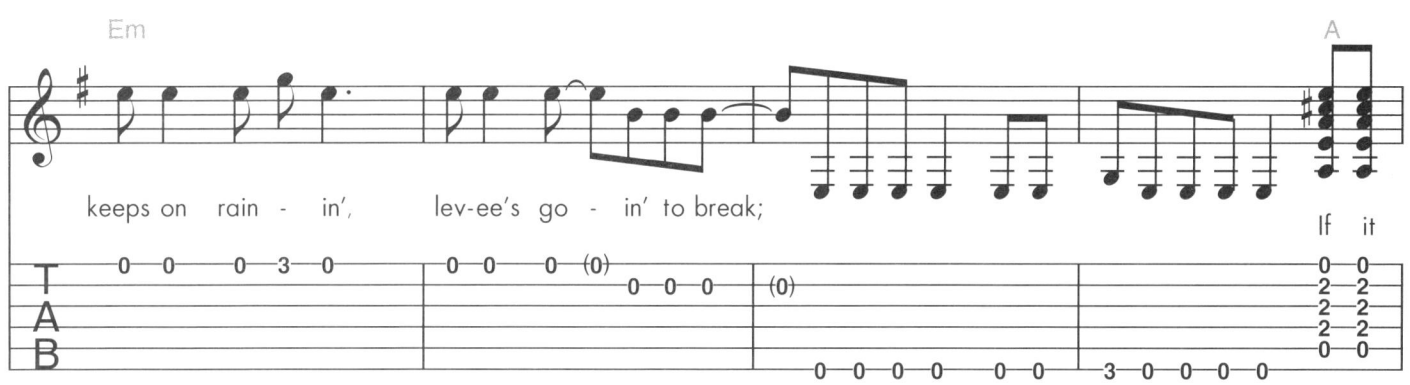

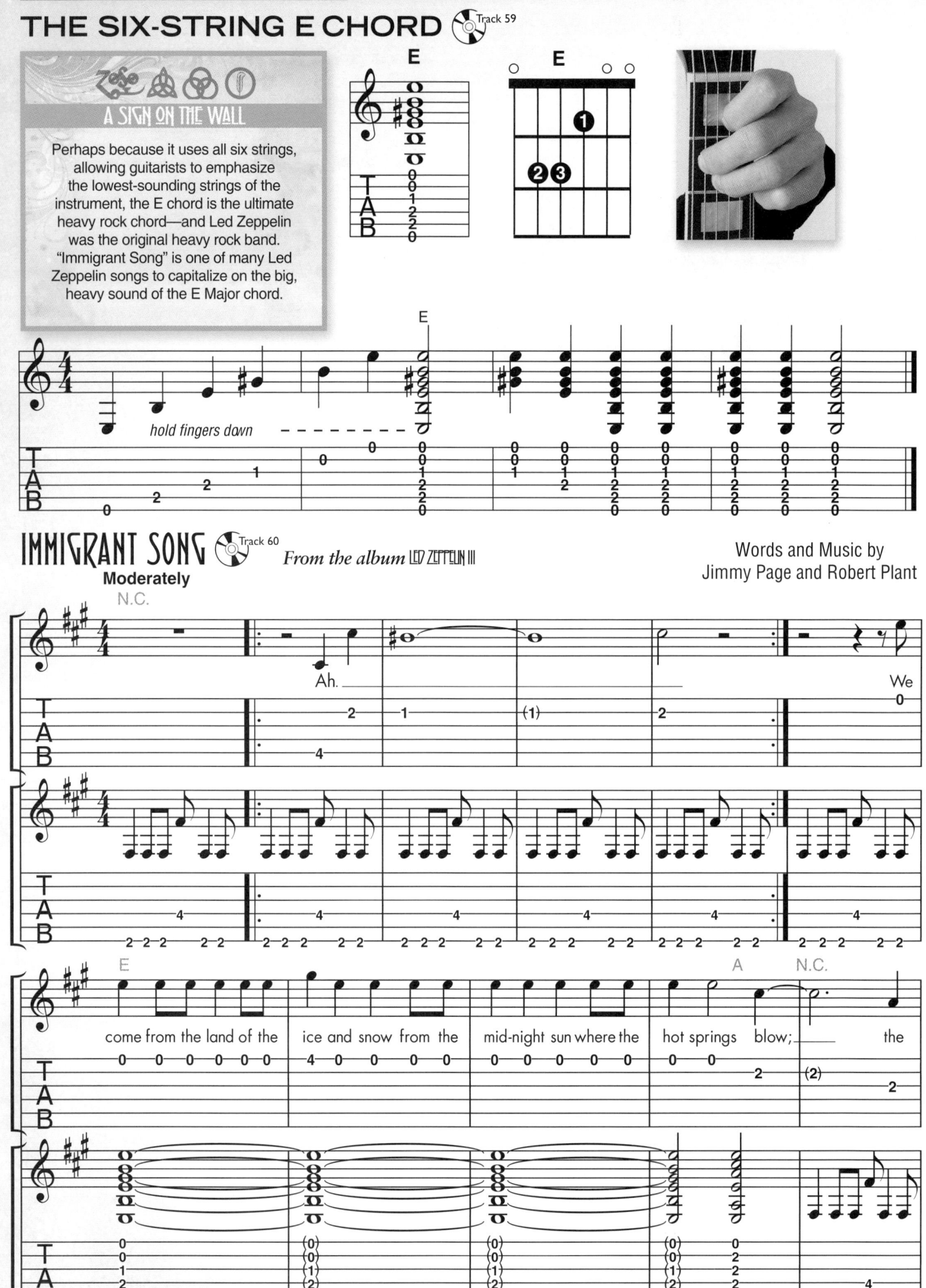

THE THREE PRINCIPAL CHORDS IN THE KEY OF G MAJOR

Track 62

THE SIX-STRING G CHORD

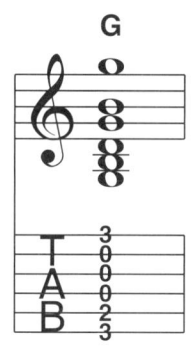 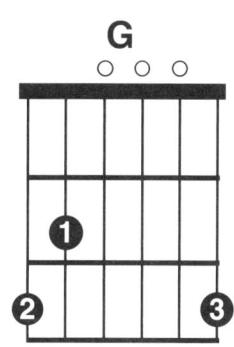 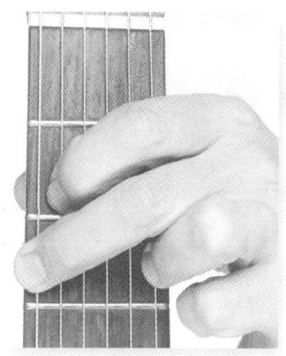

THE FIVE-STRING C CHORD

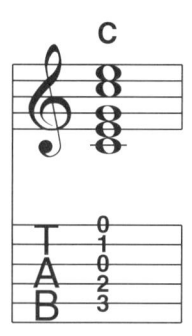 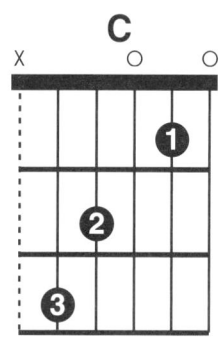 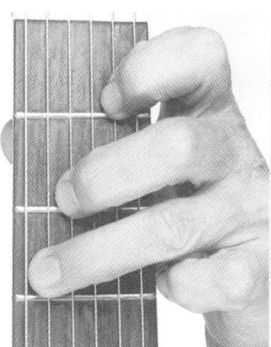

THE FOUR-STRING D7 CHORD

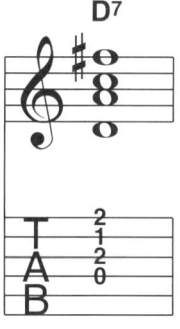 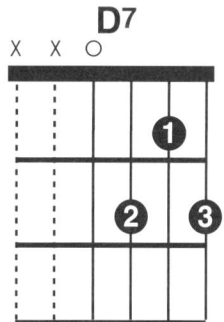 

Chord Progression in G

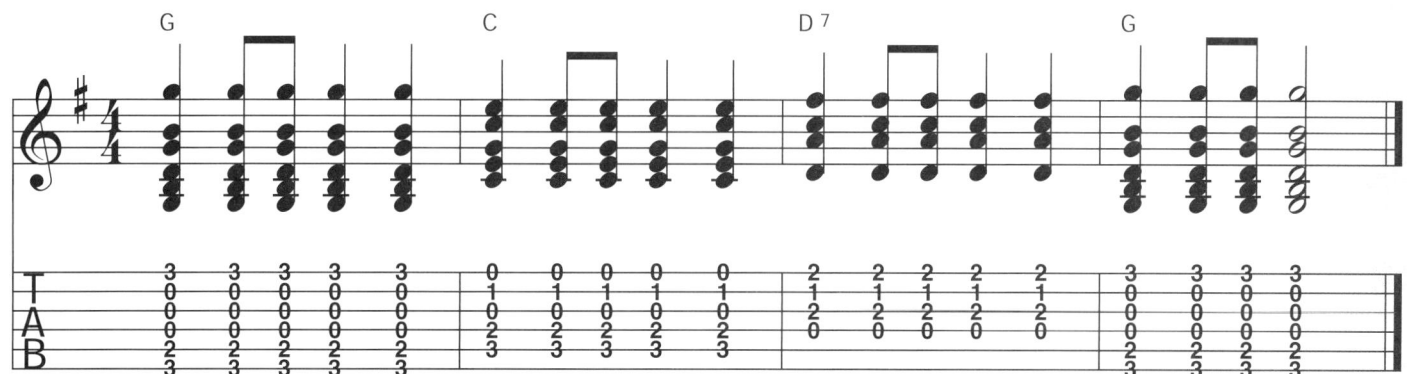

68 LED ZEPPELIN GUITAR METHOD

This song gives you an excellent chance to practice the three principal chords in the key of G Major. If you know the melody, the words are provided so that you can sing to your own accompaniment. If you don't know the melody, play the chords anyway, keeping as steady and even a beat as possible.

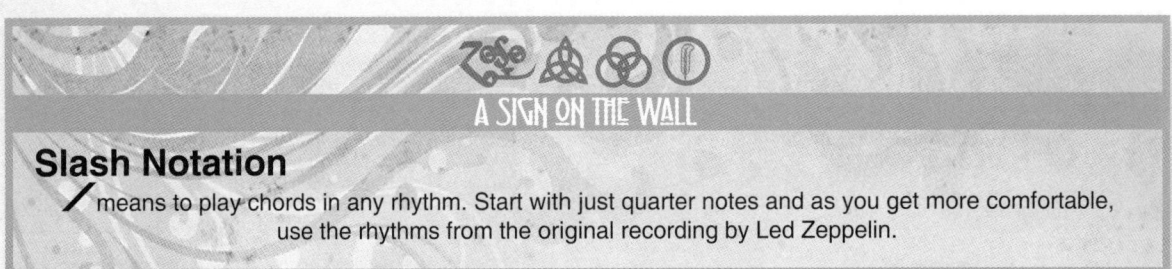

A Sign On The Wall

Slash Notation

/ means to play chords in any rhythm. Start with just quarter notes and as you get more comfortable, use the rhythms from the original recording by Led Zeppelin.

ROCK AND ROLL
Fast Rock Beat
From the album [symbols]

Track 63

Words and Music by
Jimmy Page, Robert Plant, John Paul Jones, and John Bonham

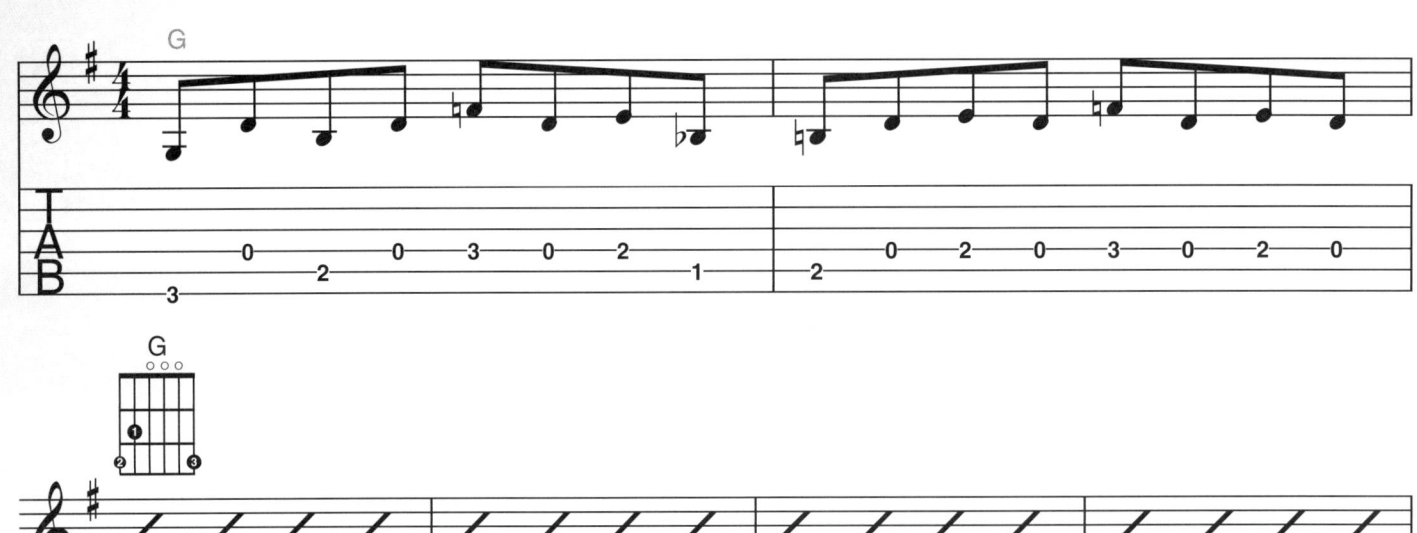

It's been a long time since I rock and rolled.

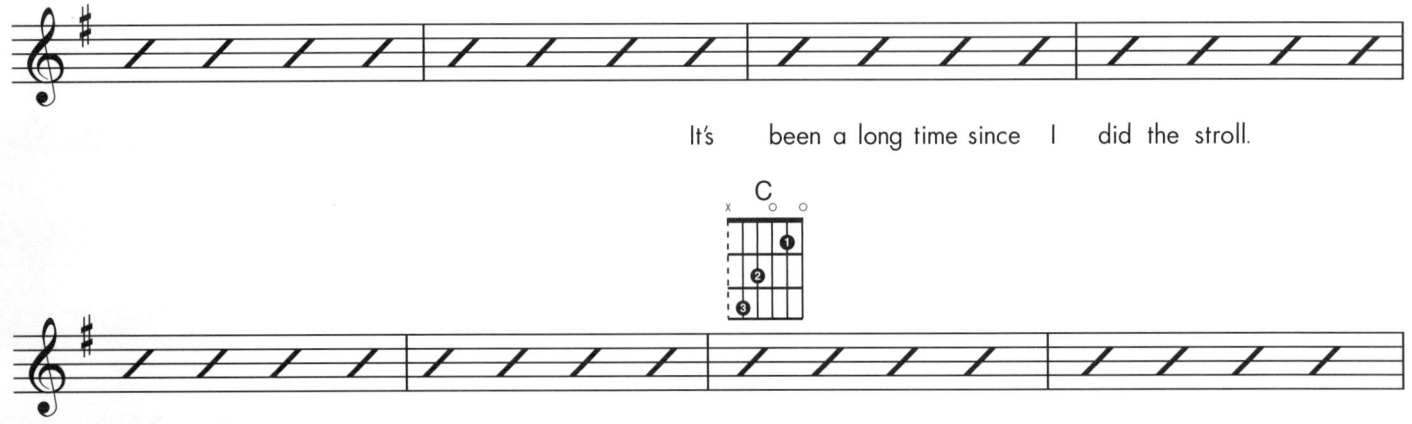

It's been a long time since I did the stroll.

Let me get it back, let me get it back, let me get it

© 1972 (Renewed) FLAMES OF ALBION MUSIC, INC.
All Rights Administered by WB MUSIC CORP.
Exclusive Print Rights for the World Excluding Europe Administered by ALFRED MUSIC PUBLISHING
All Rights Reserved

THE DOMINANT MAJOR CHORD

You should remember that the chord built on the fifth tone of the scale is called the dominant chord (see page 52).

Many composers of popular music use the seventh chord as the dominant chord. Led Zeppelin often use a major chord instead of a seventh to give the harmony a more straightforward, simple sound.

On page 28, you learned to play a very simple version of part of the melody of "Thank You." To play a more complete version, using melody and chords, you must first learn to play the D Major chord, which is used in this song as the dominant chord in the key of G Major.

THE FOUR-STRING D MAJOR CHORD 🎵 Track 64

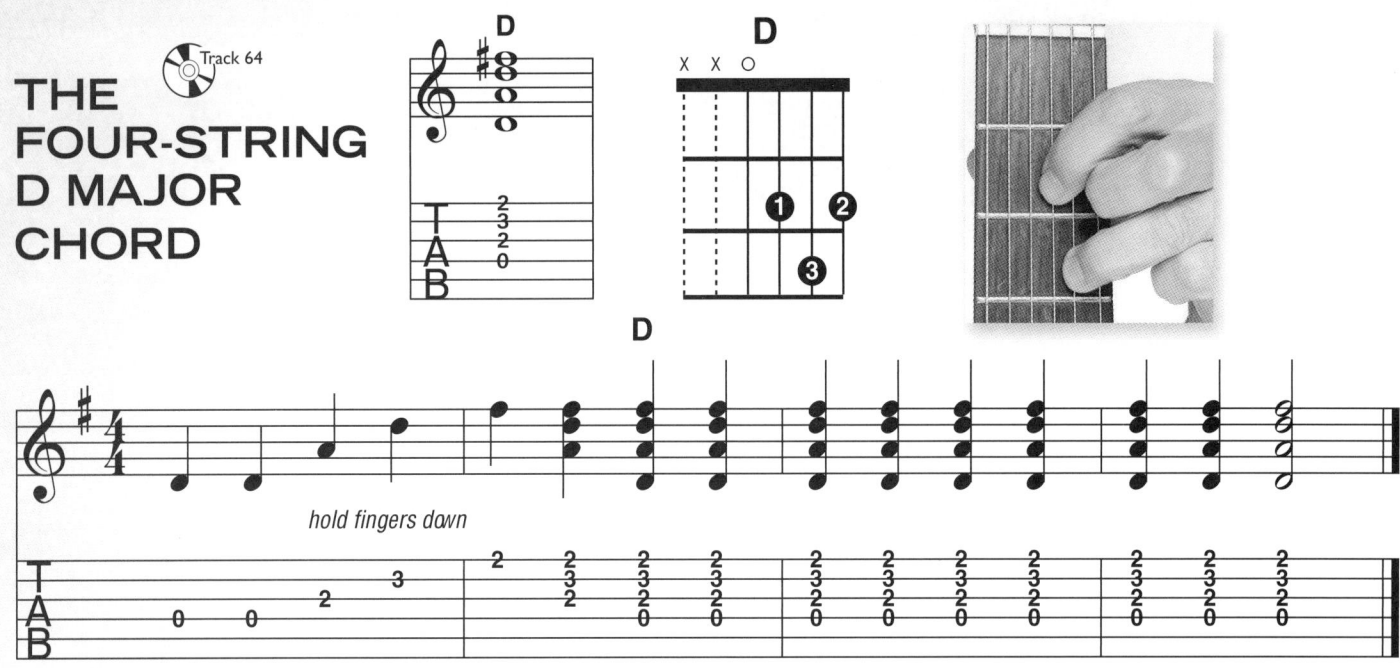

THANK YOU 🎵 Track 65
From the album LED ZEPPELIN II

Words and Music by Jimmy Page and Robert Plant

Moderately Slow

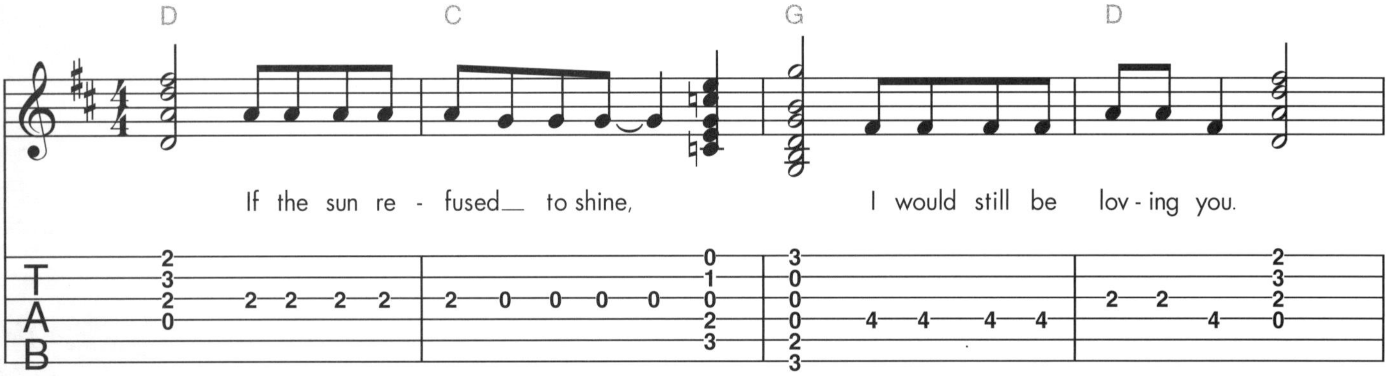

If the sun re-fused to shine, I would still be lov-ing you.

When moun-tains crum-ble to the sea, there would still be you and me.

© 1969 (Renewed) FLAMES OF ALBION MUSIC, INC.
All Rights Administered by WB MUSIC CORP.
Exclusive Print Rights for the World Excluding Europe Administered by ALFRED MUSIC PUBLISHING CO., INC.
All Rights Reserved

KEY OF E MINOR

E Minor and G Major are relative keys. They both have the key signature of one sharp (F#). Like the A Minor scale to the C Major scale, the E Minor scale is built on the 6th tone of the relative (G) major.

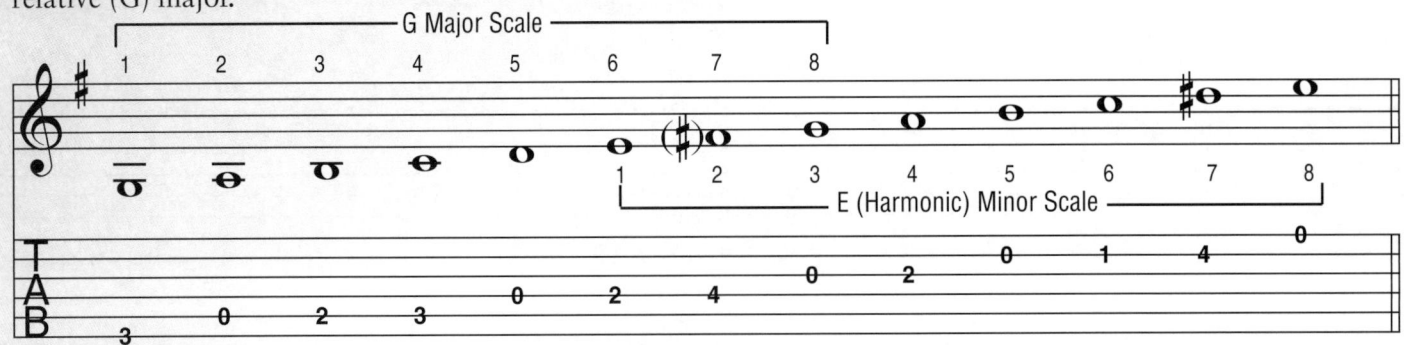

The Two-Octave E (Harmonic) Minor Scale

THE THREE PRINCIPAL CHORDS IN THE KEY OF E MINOR

Track 66

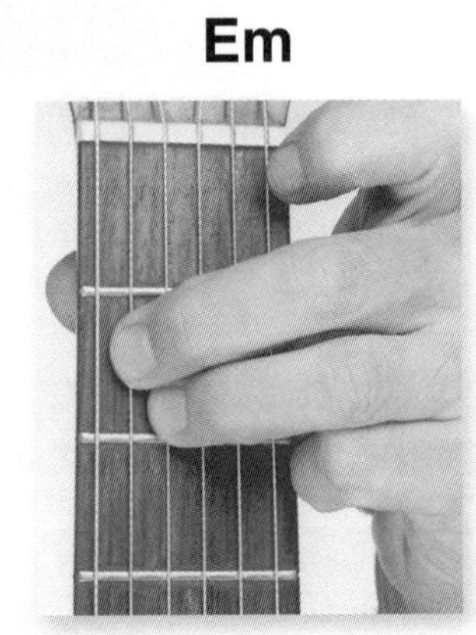

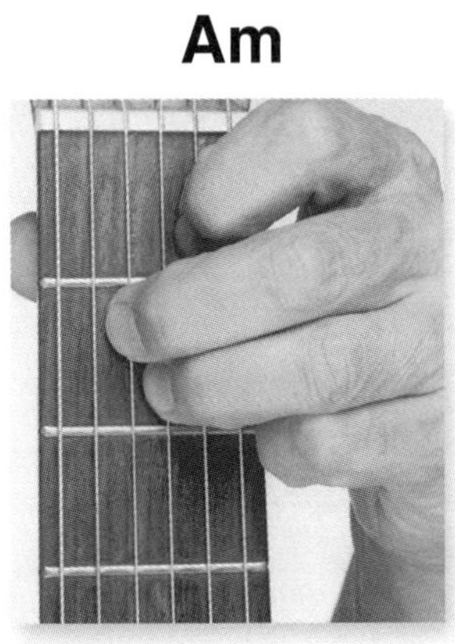

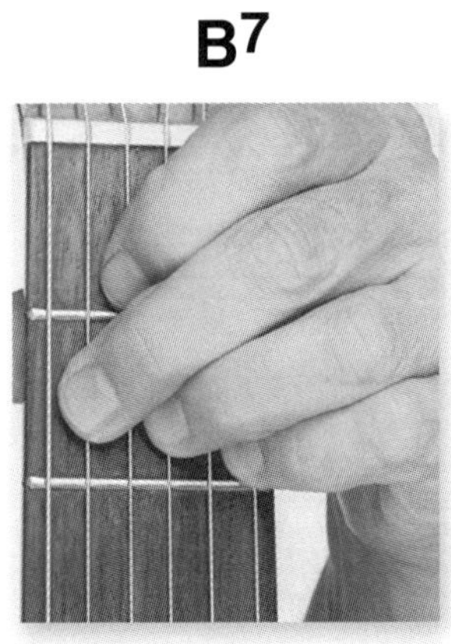

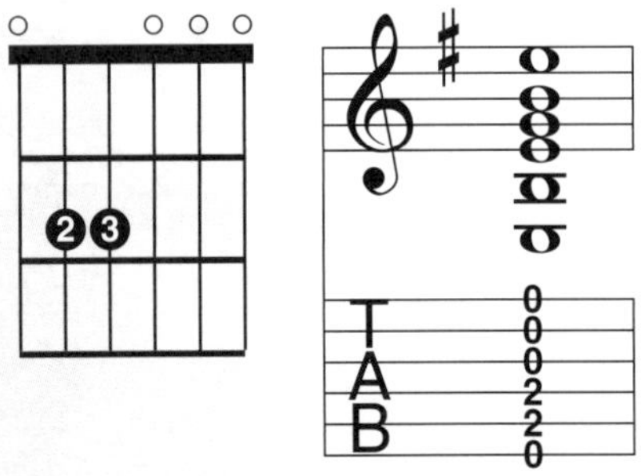

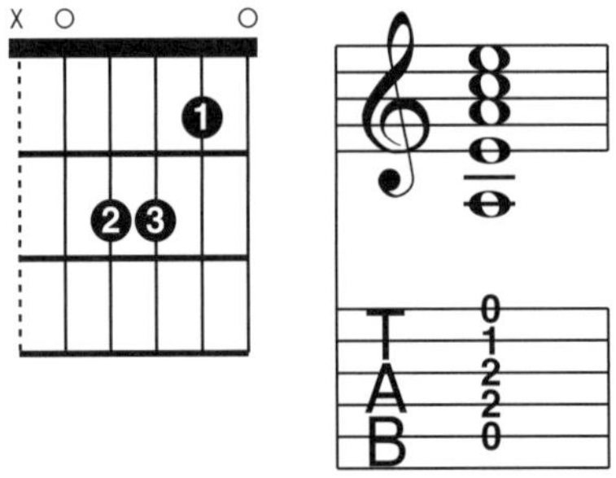

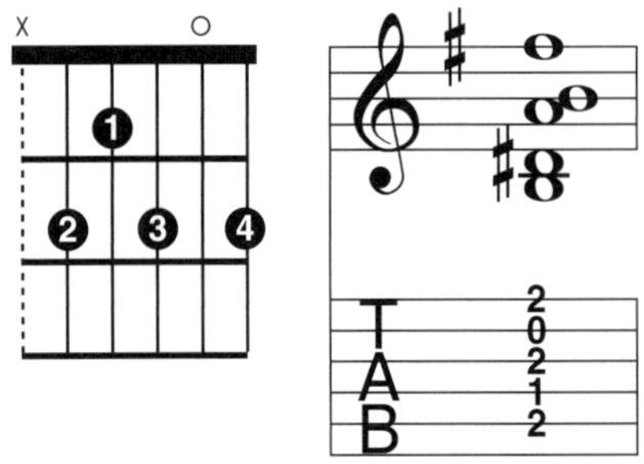

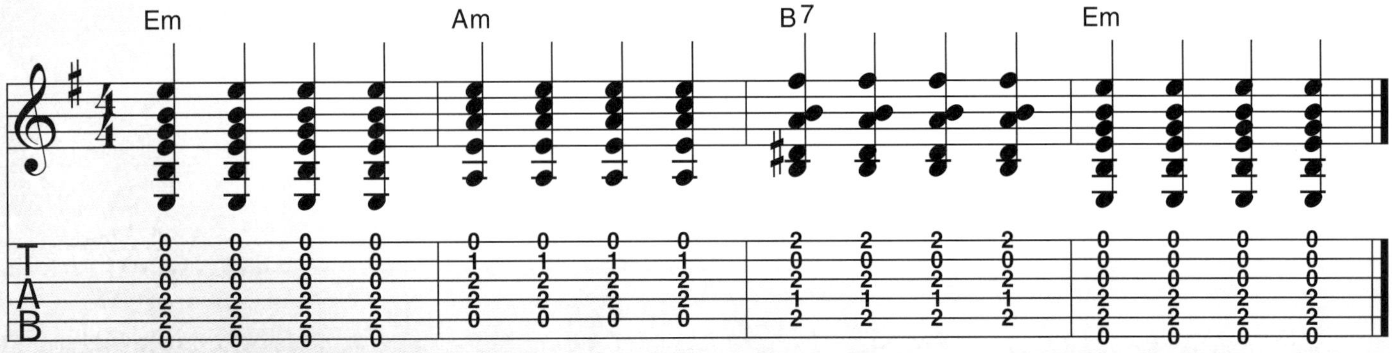

House of the Rising Sun Track 67

Traditional

Moderately slow

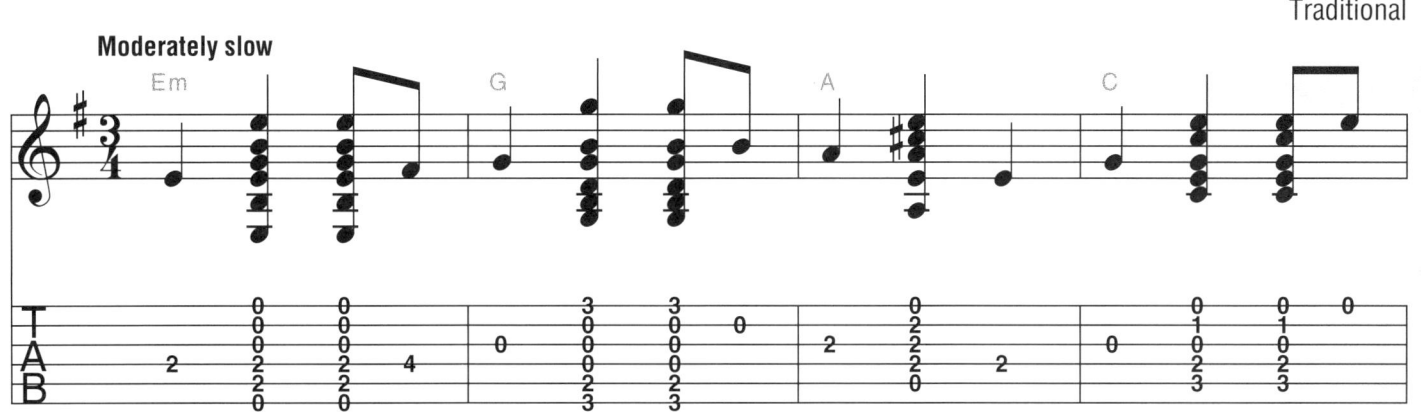
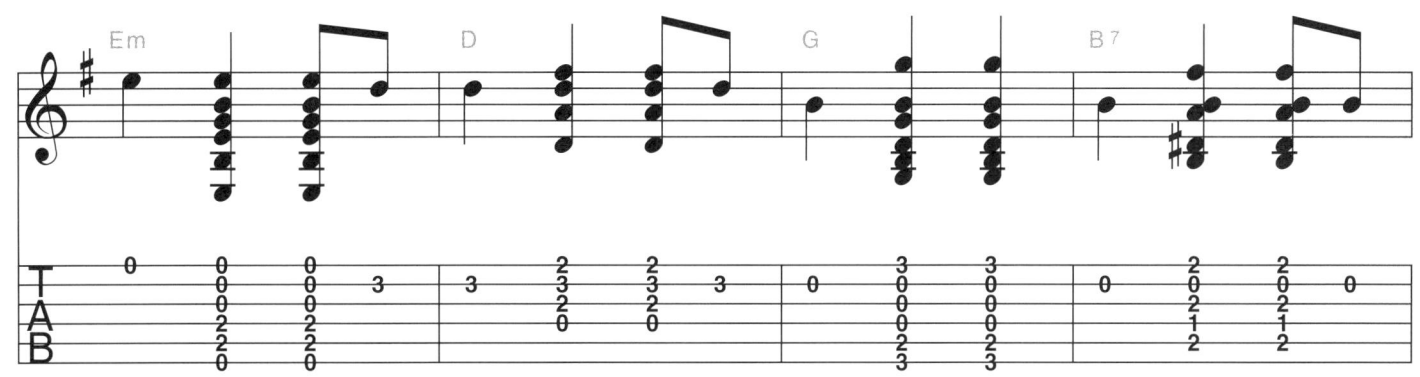
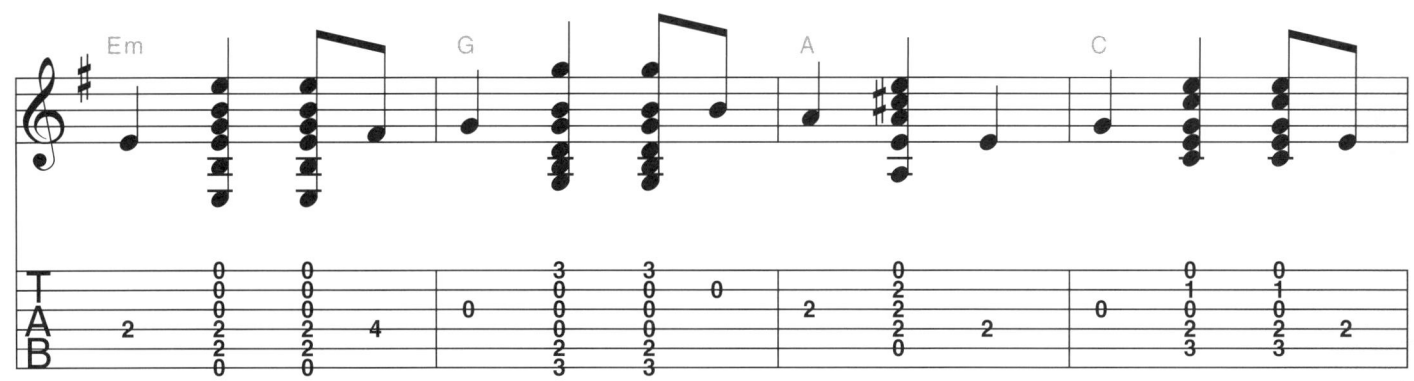
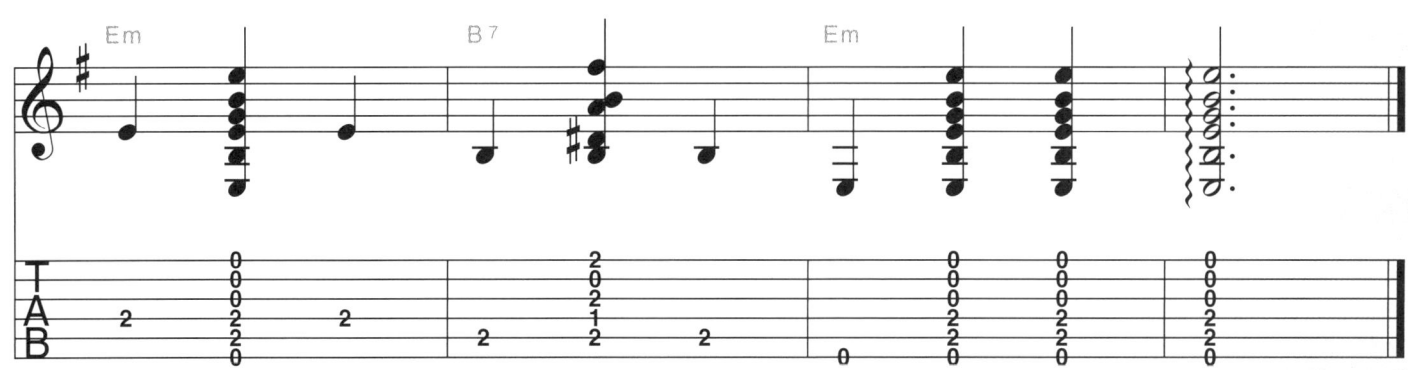

POWER CHORDS

As you know, a major chord is made using the first, third, and fifth notes of the major scale. The first and lowest note of the chord is called the root.

A C Major chord uses all these notes, but the C power chord only uses the root and the fifth. A power chord is indicated by the chord name followed by a 5 (C5).

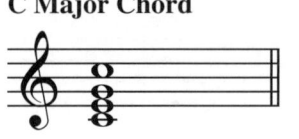
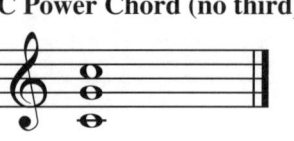

"Misty Mountain Hop" uses a few different fingerings for power chords. There is one power chord fingering you can move up and down the neck in your own songs. In the following example, the power chord is movable except when open E is used.

You can use this same fingering with the root played on the A string. Experiment with power chords when you practice.

Words and Music by Jimmy Page, Robert Plant, and John Paul Jones

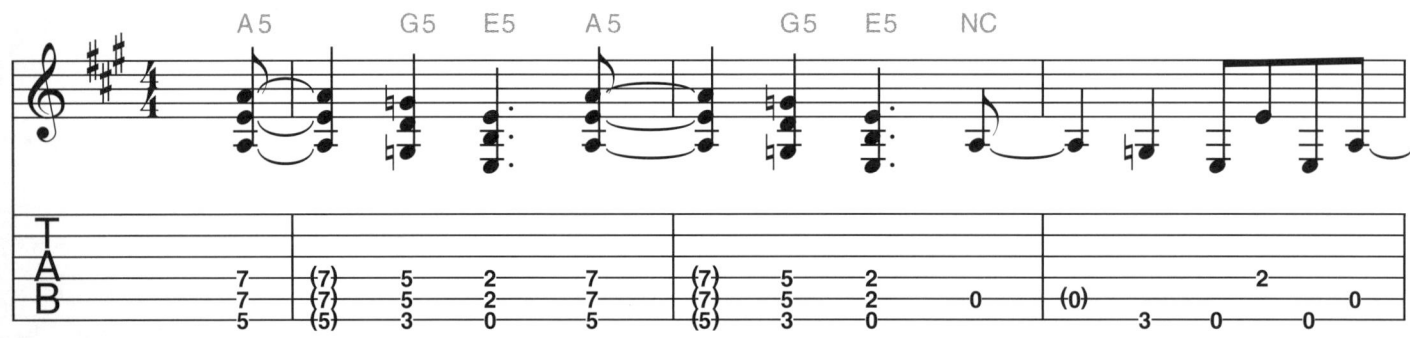

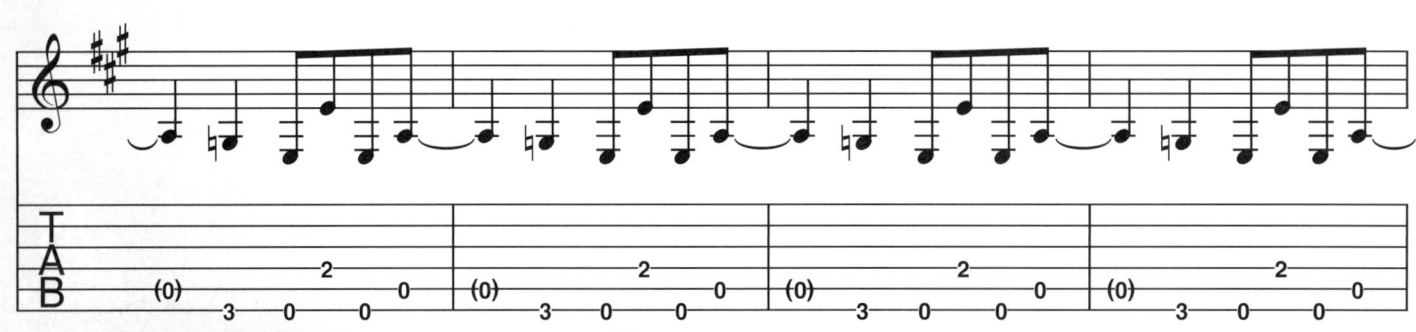

© 1972 (Renewed) FLAMES OF ALBION MUSIC, INC.
All Rights Administered by WB MUSIC CORP.
Exclusive Print Rights for the World Excluding Europe Administered by ALFRED MUSIC PUBLISHING
All Rights Reserved

PREPARATION FOR BARRE CHORDS

By this time you should be ready to play BARRE CHORDS. These are very important in playing rock music.

Barre chords that eliminate open strings can be moved to any position on the fingerboard. At each of the first 12 fret positions, such chords have a different letter name. Thus each barre chord you learn is the equivalent of 12 different chords, one for each note of the chromatic scale.

Begin by barring across all six strings with the first finger. Start up the neck a little, at the 3rd fret. The strings are easier to depress as you move closer to the middle of the fingerboard.

By observing the following points, playing the barre will be easier:

1. The tip of the finger should extend beyond the edge of the fingerboard.

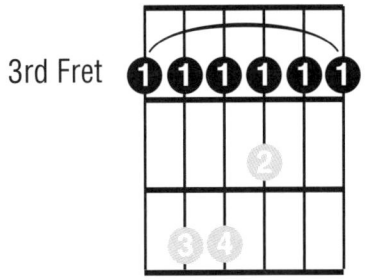

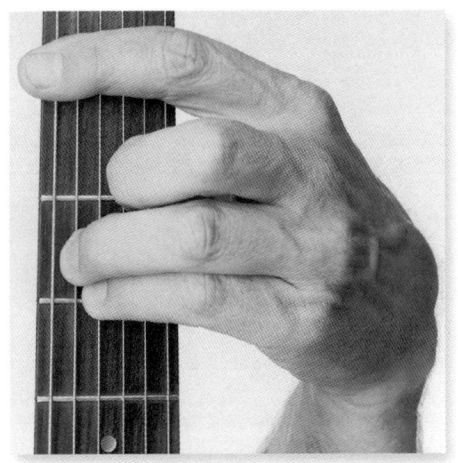

2. Apply pressure to the first finger on its SIDE NEAREST THE THUMB.

3. Bend the left wrist slightly, away from the body.

4. The LEFT THUMB should be entirely behind the neck of the guitar and should also apply pressure when the barre is formed.

5. The LEFT ELBOW should be held very close to the body.

After you have formed the barre, strike all the strings with one downstroke of the pick. Do this several times, listening for a clear sound. Then strike the strings one at a time, beginning with the 6th string. Listen for a clear tone from each string. If a string does not sound, be sure you are pressing that string down. Avoid excessive pressure, however. Press the strings just hard enough to produce a clear tone.

After you have succeeded in getting a clear tone from each string, form the barre at the 1st fret and repeat the above process. When you can produce a clear tone at the 1st fret you will be ready to play the barre chords shown on the following page.

THE THREE PRINCIPAL CHORDS
IN THE KEY OF F MAJOR

F

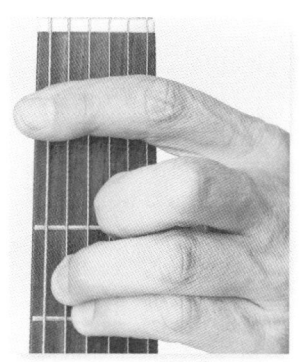

B♭

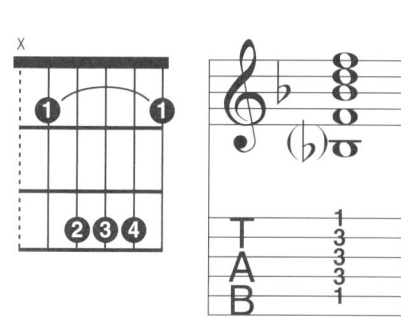

C7

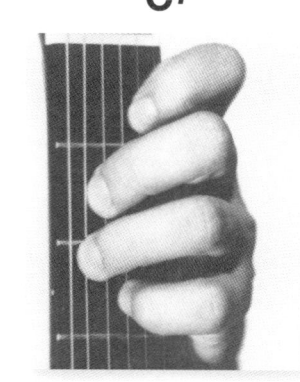

Before playing each of the following lines, form the proper chord first.
Hold the chord throughout the entire line of music.

F Barre Chord

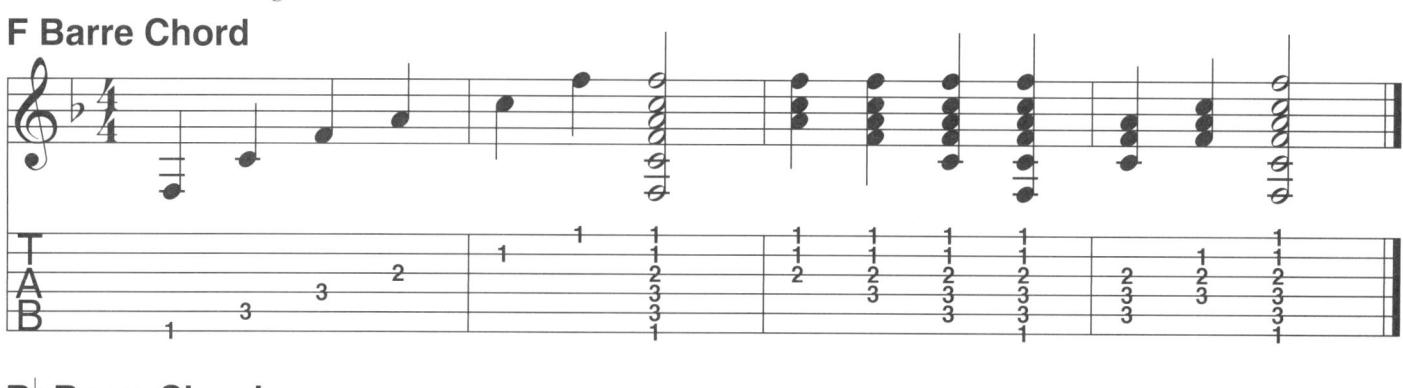

B♭ Barre Chord

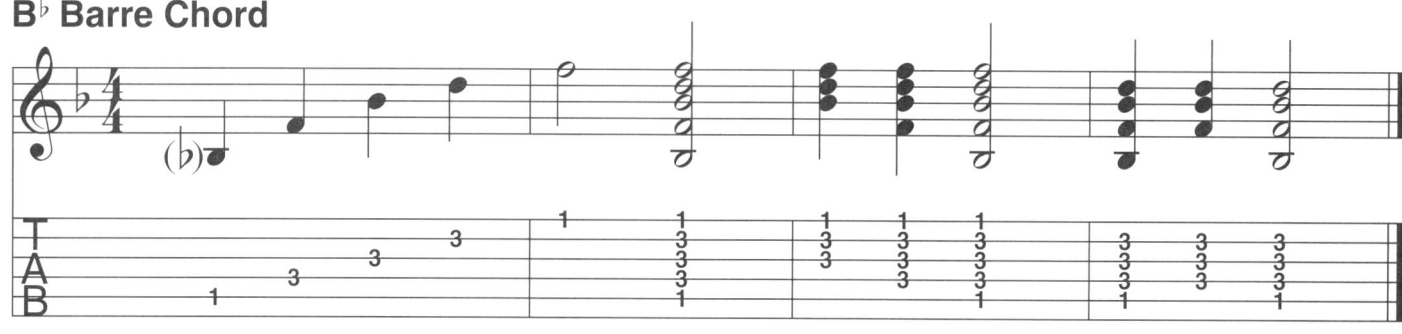

Five-String C7 Chord

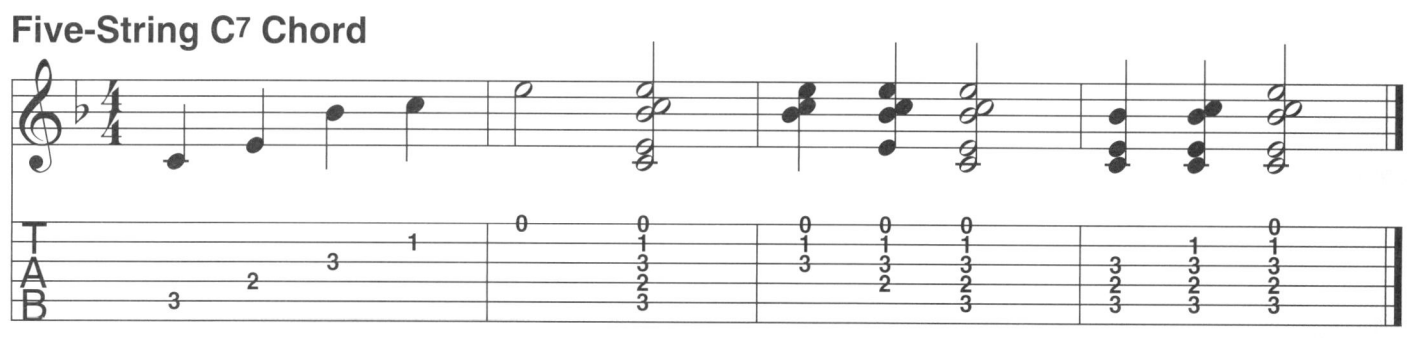

IMPORTANT OPEN CHORDS

The most frequently used BARRE CHORDS are derived from the open forms of the E and A chords. For example, if you play an E Major chord and move each finger of the left hand one fret higher and to a full barre at the first fret, you have an F Major chord. If you play an A Major chord and move each finger one fret higher and add a full barre, you have a B♭ Major chord. To add the barre, you will have to substitute different fingers for the chord notes to free the first finger to make the barre, but this is simple once you understand the principle involved.

The chords on this page are the most frequently used E and A chord forms. They are very useful themselves, as open chords. The most frequently used barre chords are formed from these chords, as you will see on the following page.

E Chords

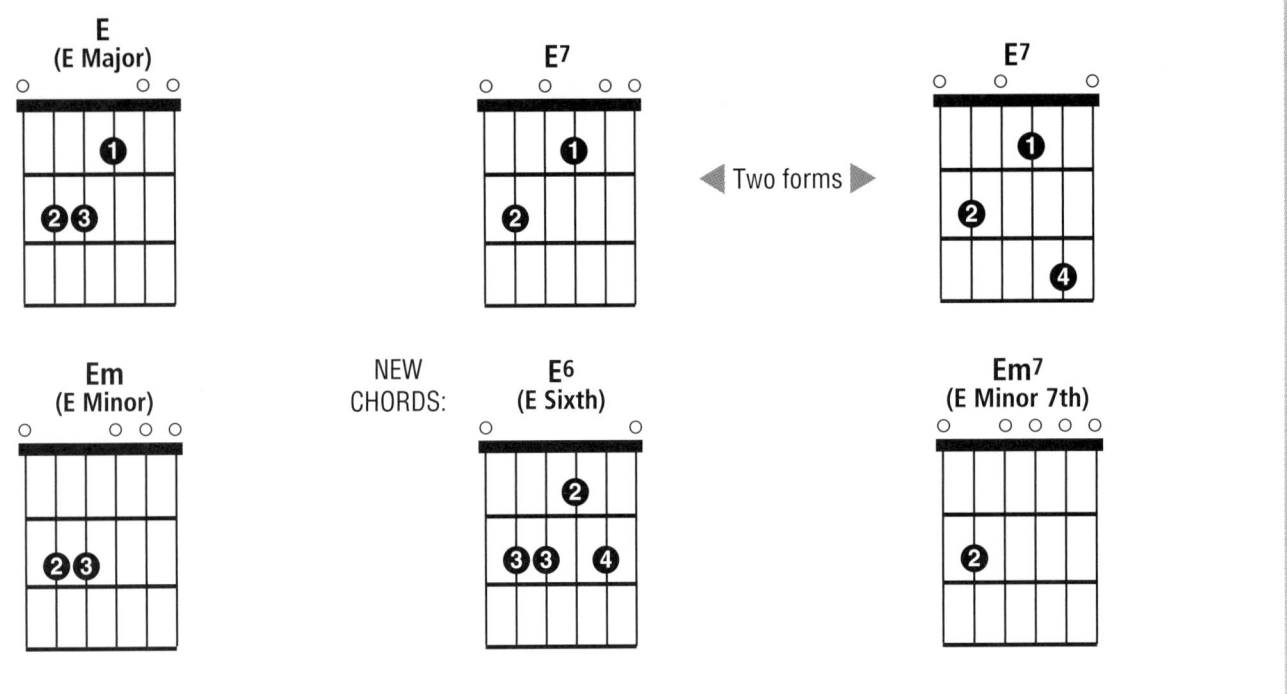

A Chords

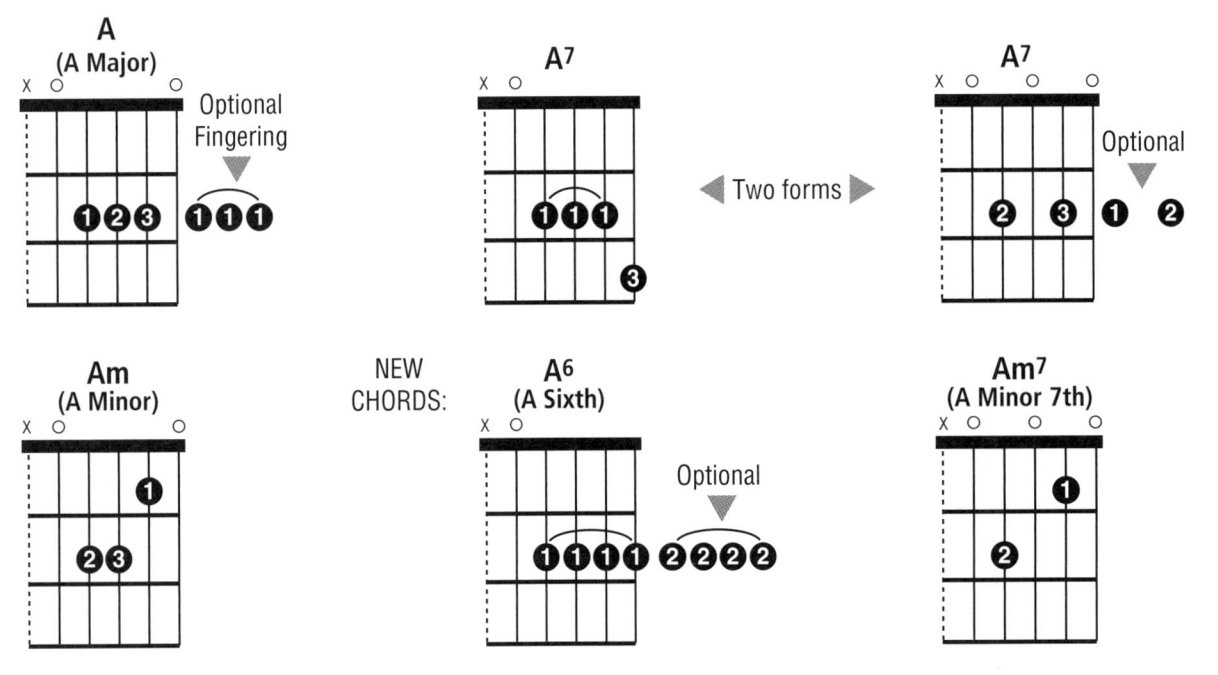

MOST COMMONLY USED BARRE CHORDS

The following chords are derived from the OPEN E CHORDS. They are shown in the F position (with the barre at the 1st fret).

Each of these chords may be moved to any position on the fingerboard and will have names corresponding to the letters shown in the fingerboard diagram on the right. For example, the minor chord, formed at the 2nd fret, will be F♯ Minor. At the 3rd fret, it will be G Minor, etc. The name of the chord is determined by the fret position of the barre.

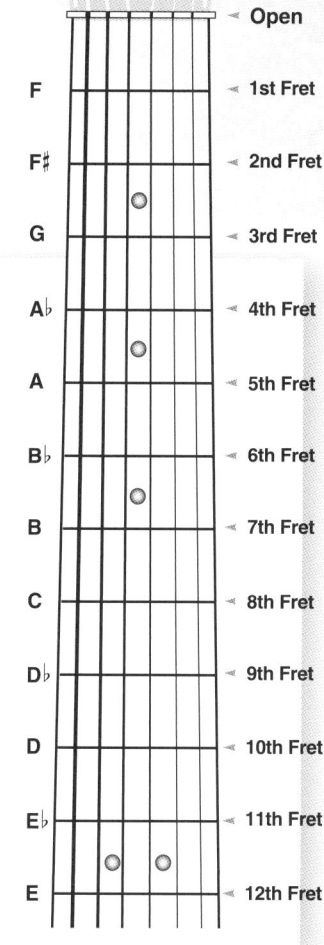

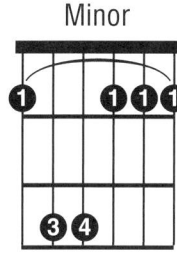
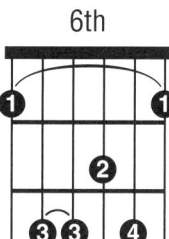
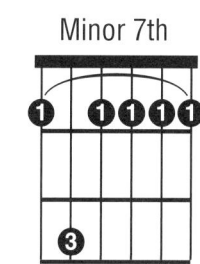

Type 1
E-Type Chords

The following chords are derived from the OPEN A CHORDS. They are shown in the B♭ position (with the barre at the first fret). (The 6th string may be played if the barre is extended to include it.)

Each of these chords, when moved to other positions on the fingerboard, will have names corresponding to the letters shown in the diagram on the right. For example, the minor chord, formed at the 2nd fret will be B Minor. At the 3rd fret, it will be C Minor, etc. The name of the chord is determined by the fret position of the barre.

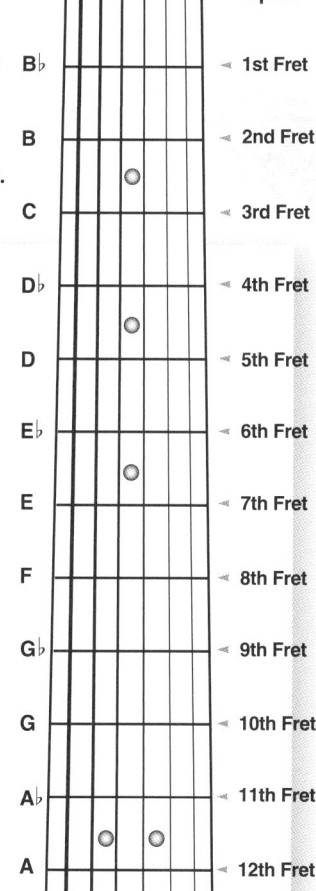

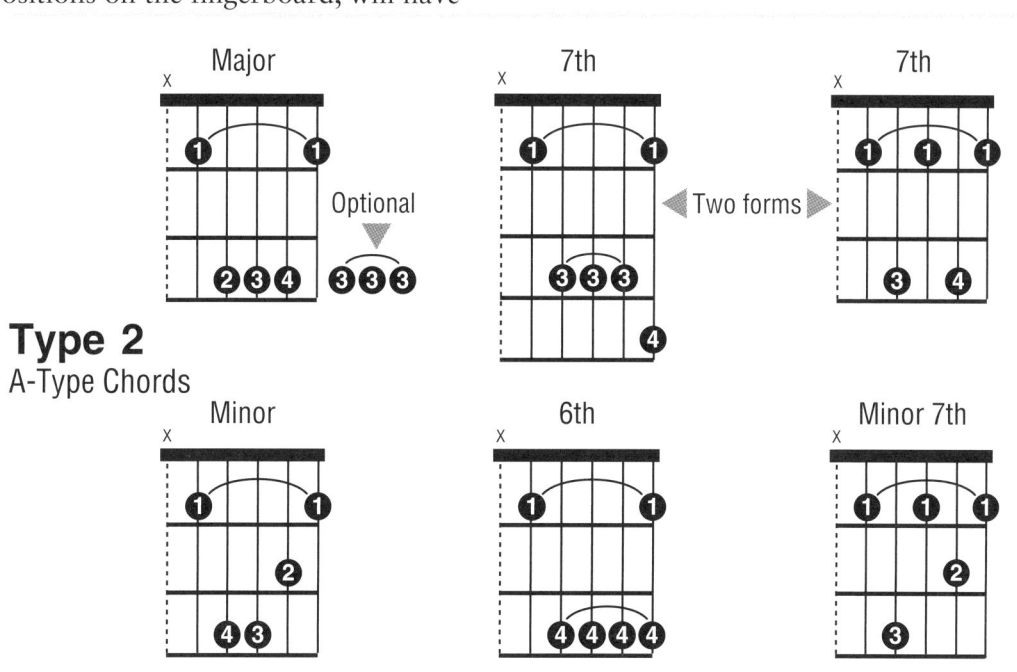

Type 2
A-Type Chords

82 LED ZEPPELIN GUITAR METHOD

The ending section of "Stairway to Heaven" gives you an excellent chance to practice barre chords. If you know the melody, the words are provided so that you can sing to your own accompaniment. If you don't know the melody, play the chords anyway, trying to match the rhythm on the original album.

STAIRWAY TO HEAVEN
(ENDING SECTION)

From the album

Words and Music by
Jimmy Page and Robert Plant

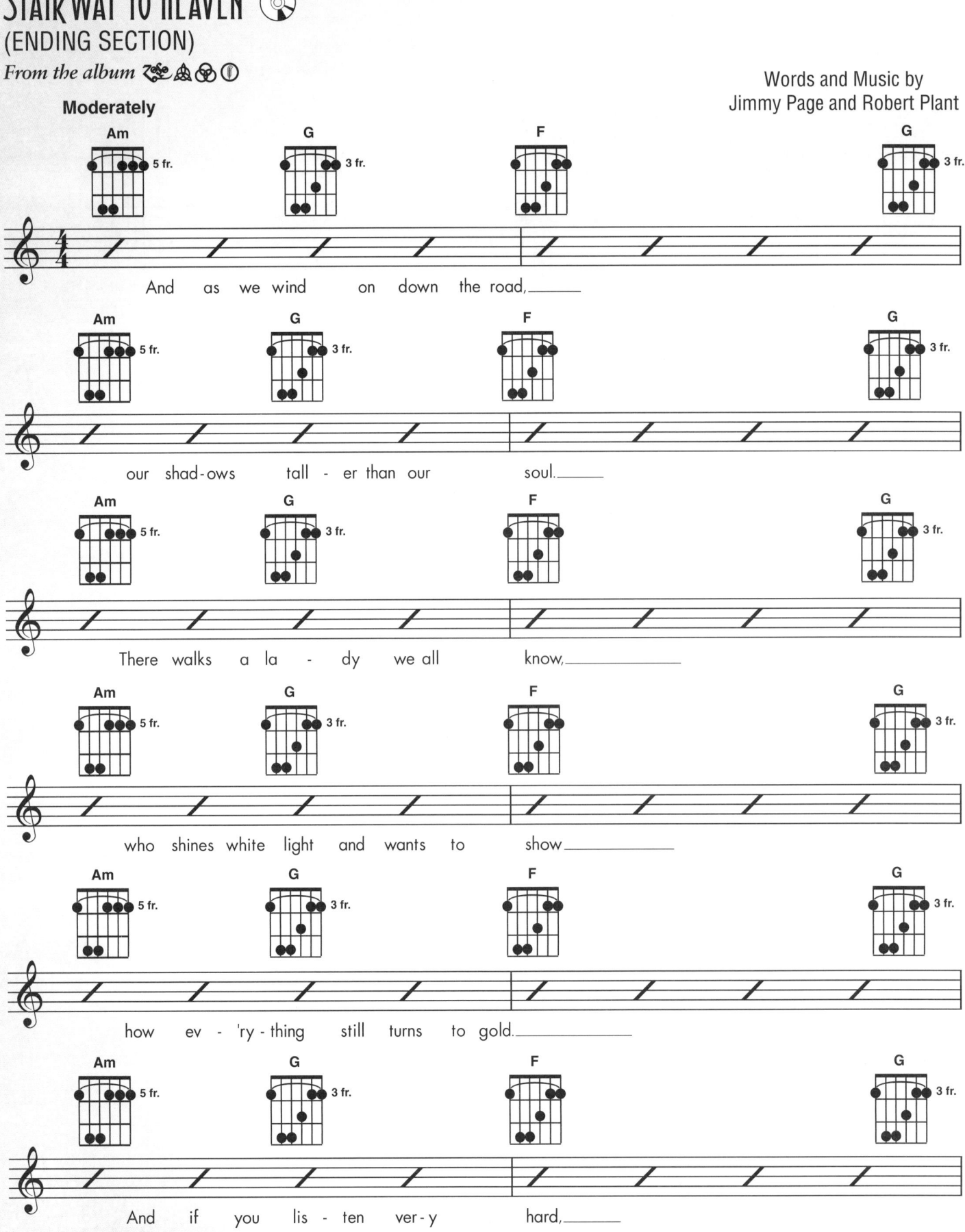

Lyrics:
And as we wind on down the road,
our shad-ows tall-er than our soul.
There walks a la-dy we all know,
who shines white light and wants to show
how ev-'ry-thing still turns to gold.
And if you lis-ten ver-y hard,

© 1972 (Renewed) FLAMES OF ALBION MUSIC, INC.
All Rights Administered by WB MUSIC CORP.
Exclusive Print Rights for the World Excluding Europe Administered by ALFRED MUSIC PUBLISHING
All Rights Reserved

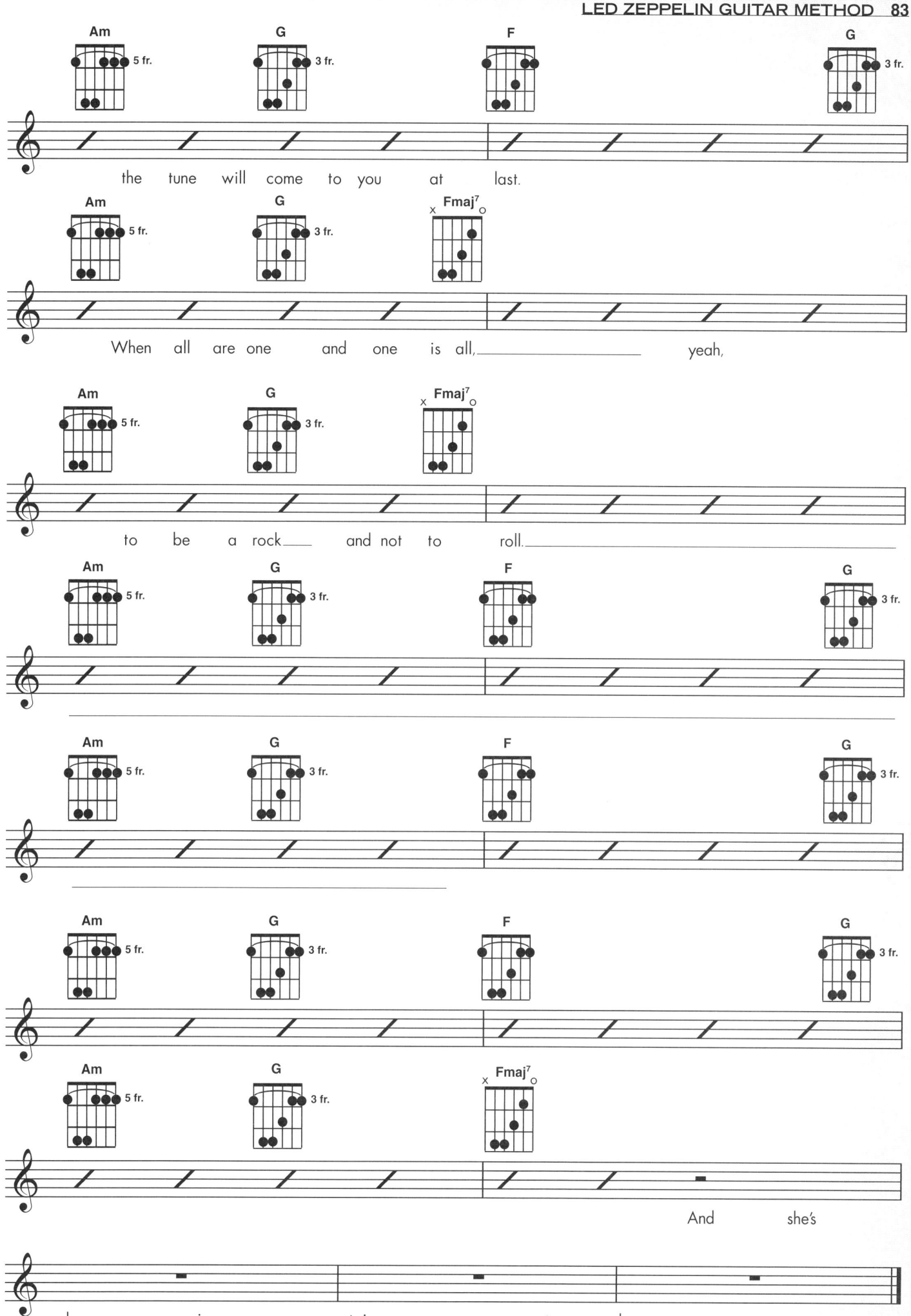

SIXTEENTH NOTES

These are SIXTEENTH NOTES:

When one sixteenth note is written alone, it looks like this:

When two or more sixteenth notes are written together, they look like this:

A sixteenth rest looks like this:

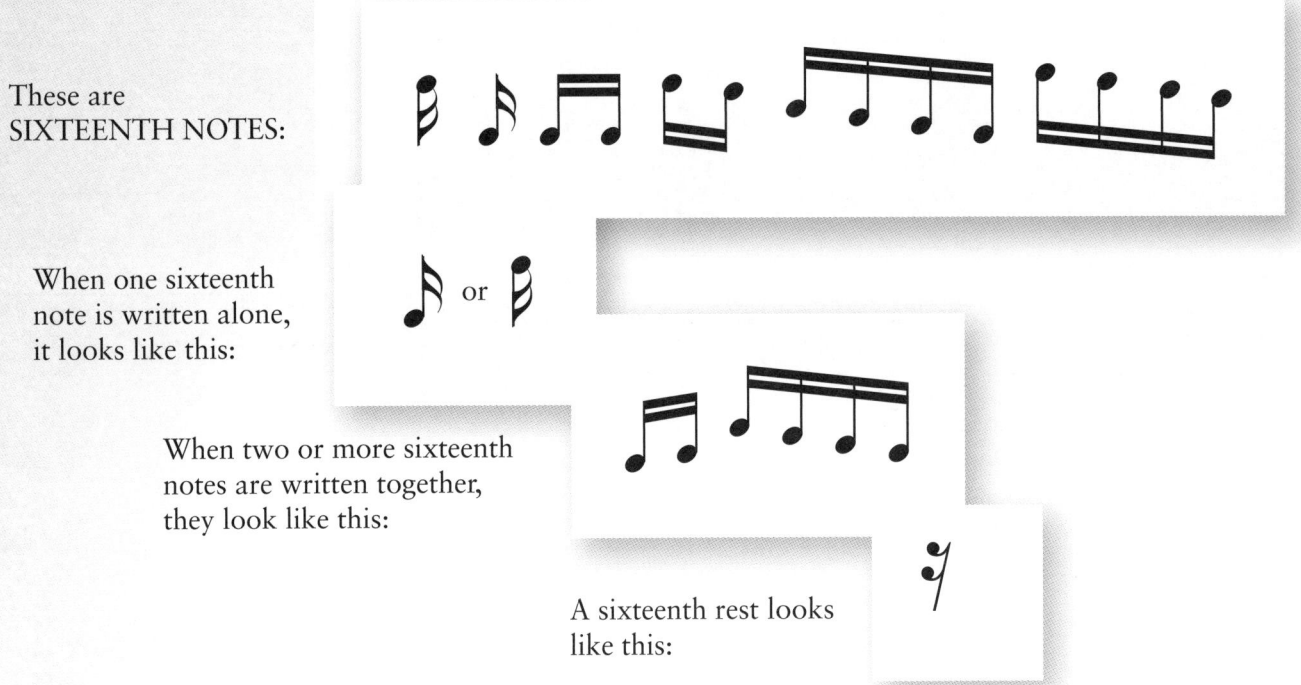

Four sixteenth notes are equal to one quarter note.

Exercise in Sixteenths  Track 72.1

(Review: ⊓ = downstroke of pick. V = upstroke.)

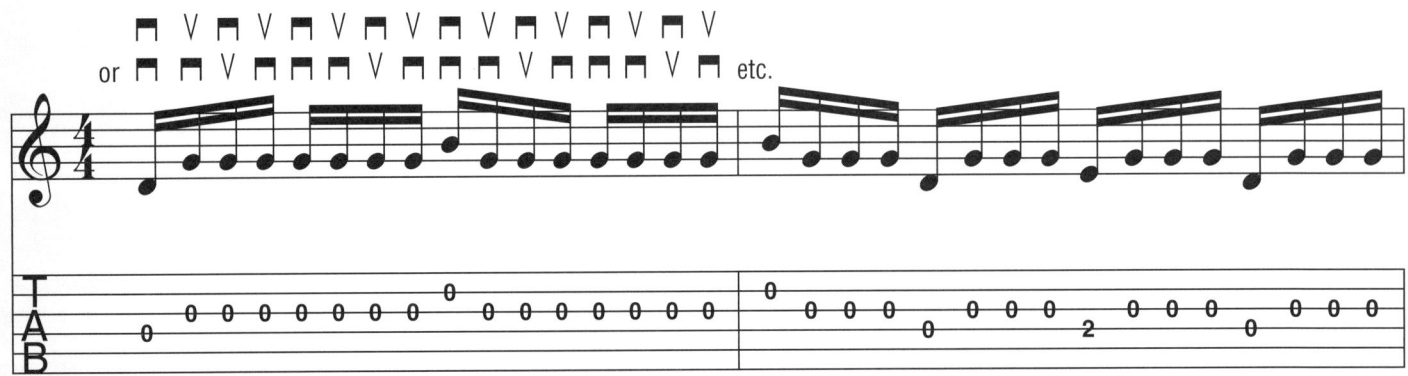

DOTTED EIGHTH AND SIXTEENTH NOTES

A DOTTED EIGHTH note has the same value as an eighth note tied to a sixteenth note.

This example should sound exactly like the one above. The only difference is the way they are written. Note that a dotted eighth rest ᨎ· is equal to the same duration as a dotted eighth note.

SIXTEENTH-NOTE TRIPLETS

SIXTEENTH NOTE TRIPLETS occur in several Led Zeppelin songs. The three notes of the triplet are played evenly, in the time usually occupied by two sixteenth notes. The three sixteenth notes of the triplet are therefore equivalent in value to one eighth note.

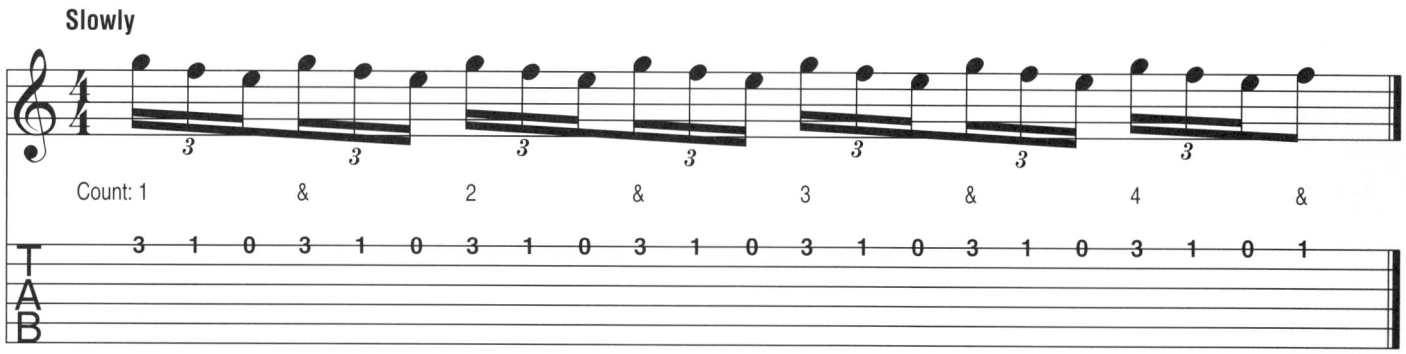

HAMMER-ONS AND PULL-OFFS

In the music so far in this book, every note was picked with the right hand. Incorporating other techniques will add more dimension to your solos.

HAMMER-ONS and PULL-OFFS are two important techniques for any guitarist. They are examples of legato playing, where the right hand does not pick every note. A hammer-on is when you pick the first note, then "hammer" onto a higher fret on the same string with another finger to sound a second note without picking a second time. A pull-off is just the opposite; you fret a note and, after picking it, pull off to a lower note on the same string. Look at the notation and tablature TO THE RIGHT.

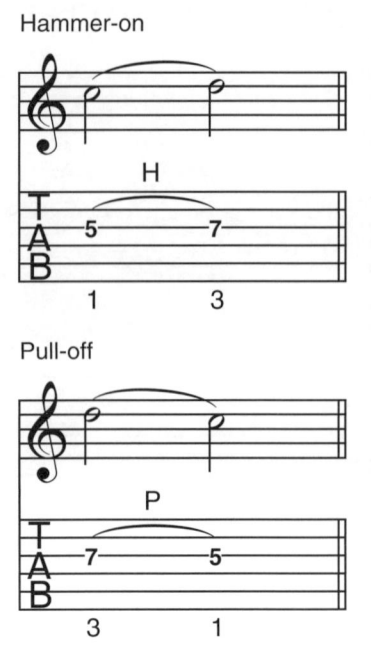

$\underset{\frown}{H}$ = Hammer-on

$\underset{\frown}{P}$ = Pull-off

This arrangement of some of the great guitar licks in "Over the Hills and Far Away" will give you great practice with sixteenth notes, sixteenth-note triplets, and hammer-ons and pull-offs. Have fun.

OVER THE HILLS AND FAR AWAY
From the album HOUSES OF THE HOLY

Track 73

Words and Music by Jimmy Page and Robert Plant

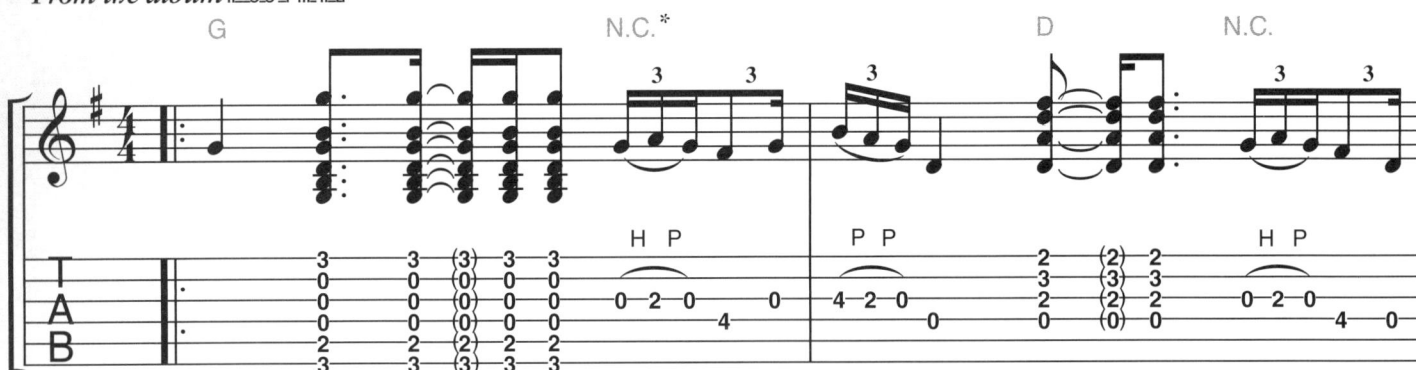

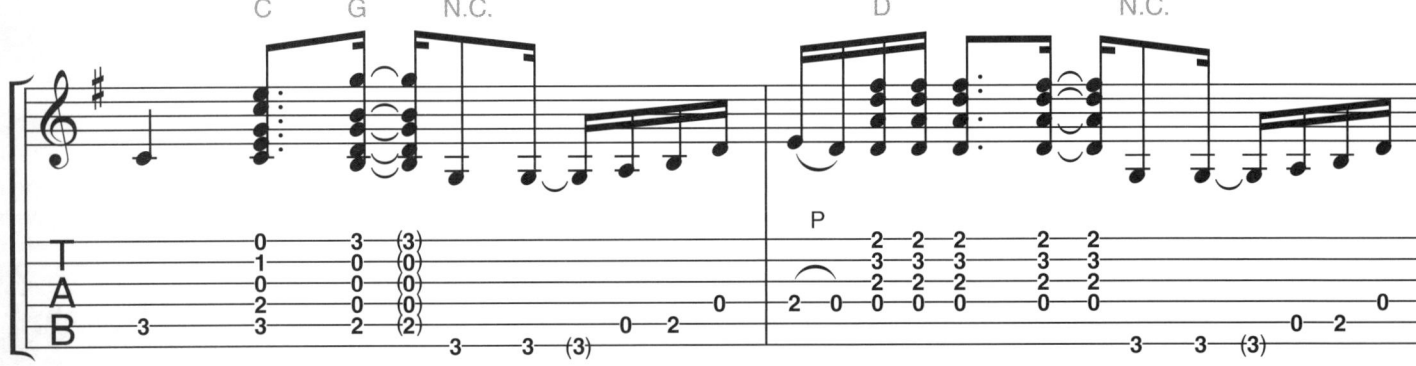

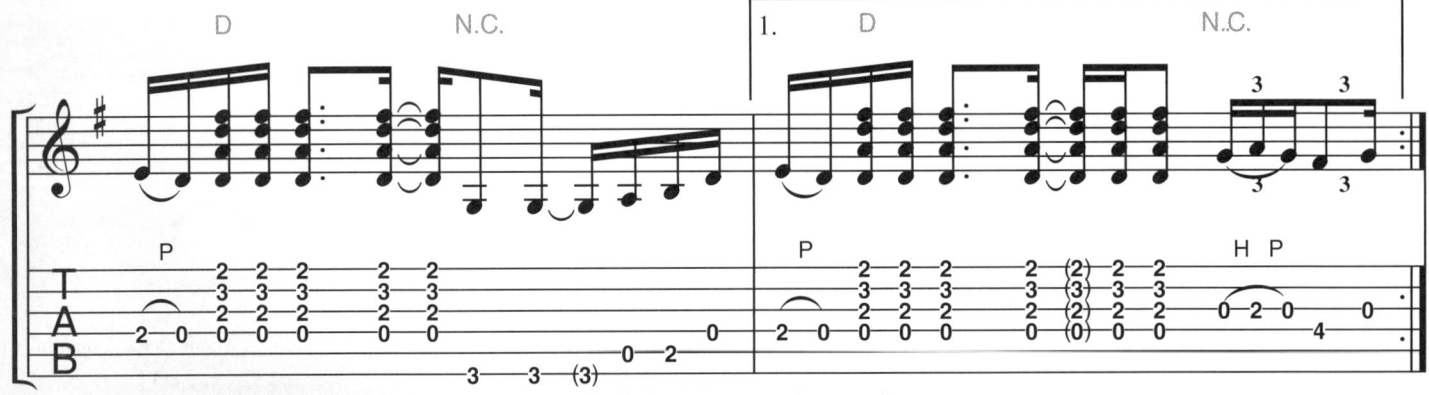

* N.C. = No chord

© 1973 (Renewed) FLAMES OF ALBION MUSIC, INC.
All Rights Administered by WB MUSIC CORP.
Exclusive Print Rights for the World Excluding Europe Administered by ALFRED MUSIC PUBLISHING
All Rights Reserved

FINGERSTYLE

FINGERSTYLE is the art of sounding the strings with the fingers of the right hand instead of a pick. Jimmy Page included many fingerstyle passages in Led Zeppelin songs, including "Babe, I'm Gonna Leave You" and "Stairway to Heaven." The information and exercises on this page will help prepare you to learn to play those songs.

Right-Hand Fingers

The most common method for naming the fingers of the right hand comes from the classical guitar tradition, which uses the Spanish names for the fingers (*pulgar* = thumb, *indice* = index, *medio* = middle, *anular* = ring). All you have to memorize is the first letter of each.

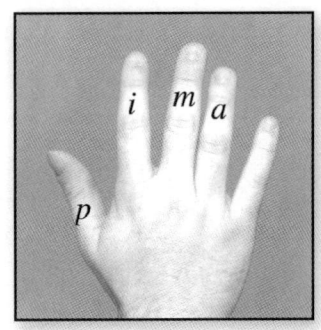

Basic Position

Contemporary acoustic and folk fingerstyle playing is based on a basic position:

> *p*.....mostly plays the 4th, 5th, and 6th strings
> *i*......mostly plays the 3rd string
> *m*....mostly plays the 2nd string
> *a*.....mostly plays the 1st string

Fingerstyle technique is often used to play ARPEGGIOS (the notes of a chord played one at a time, or "broken chords").

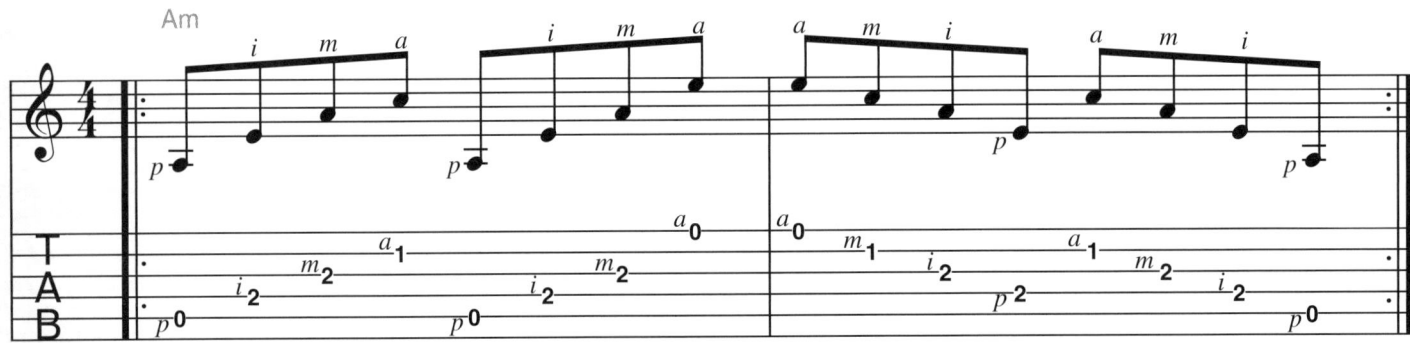

The PINCH, playing two notes at the same time, often separated by one or more strings, is a common fingerstyle technique.

LED ZEPPELIN GUITAR METHOD   89

A SIGN ON THE WALL

Jimmy begins to play this famous piece by J. S. Bach about 4:40 into "Heartbreaker" on the Led Zeppelin live album *How the West Was Won*.

BOURÉE IN E MINOR Track 74

Johann Sebastian Bach

Allegro

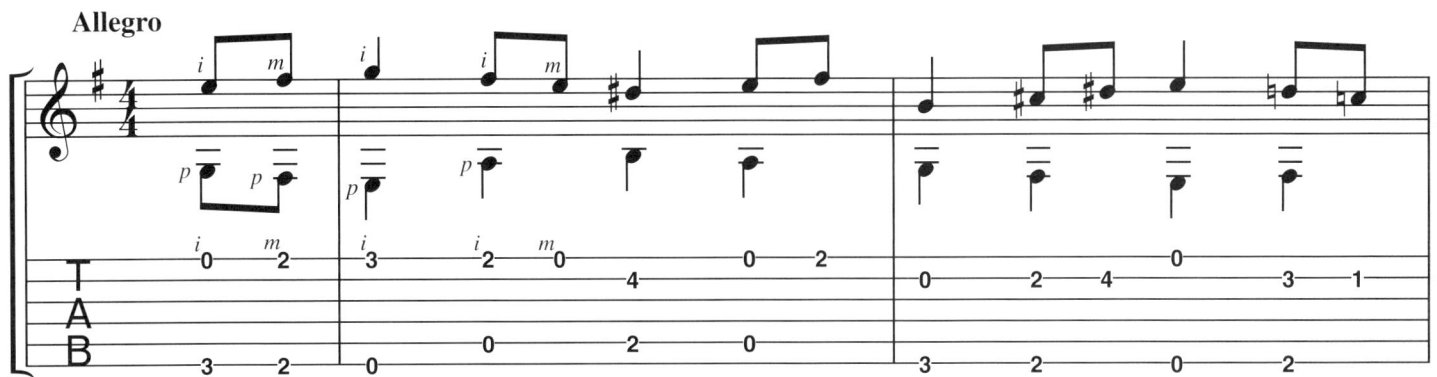
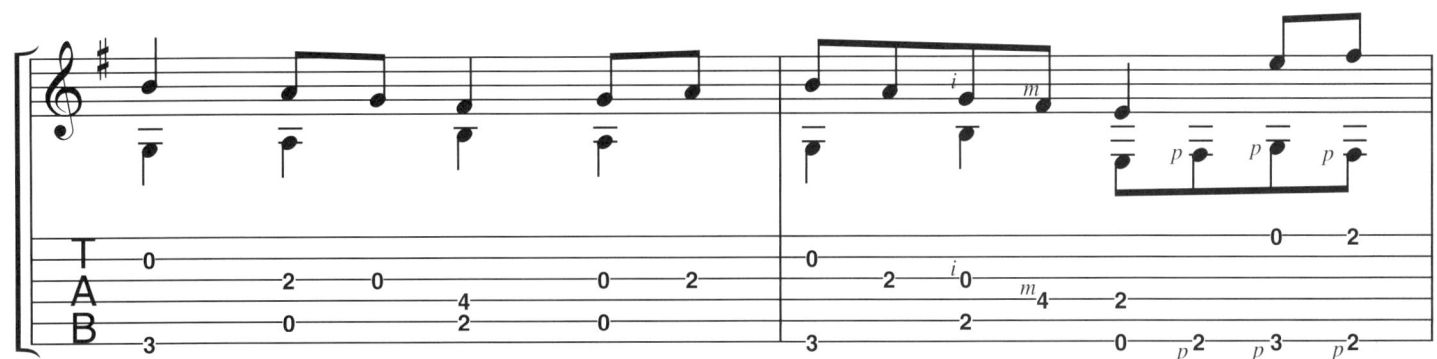
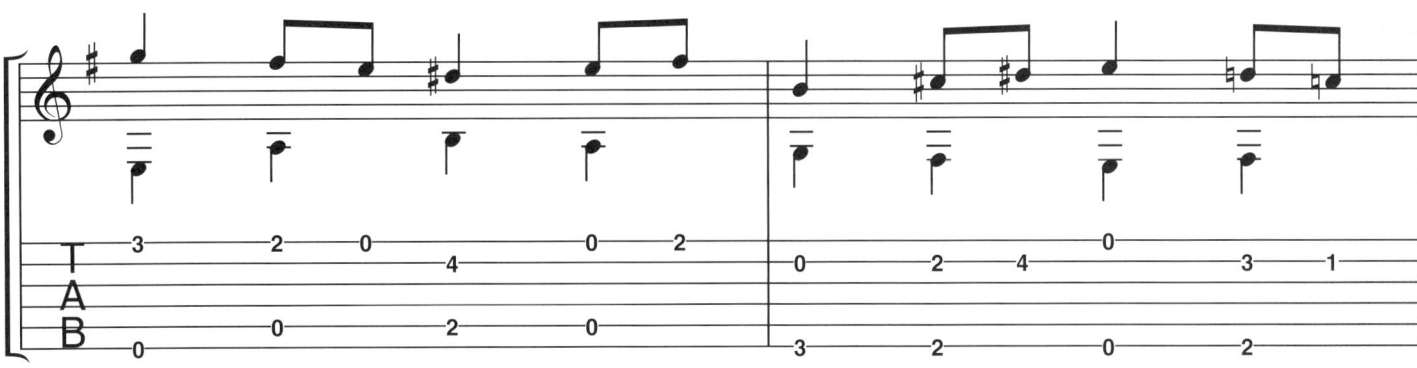

90 LED ZEPPELIN GUITAR METHOD

Fingerstyle technique creates opportunities for many new chord shapes. Chord diagrams showing the basic shapes being used are provided for this song. Often, an additional note is added with the fourth finger (pinky). Use the diagrams together with the music and TAB. Hold down every left-hand finger until it is necessary to lift it, allowing the notes to ring into each other.

BABE I'M GONNA LEAVE YOU (INTRO)
From the album LED ZEPPELIN

Track 75

Words and Music by
Anne Bredon, Jimmy Page,
and Robert Plant

© 1969 (Renewed) FLAMES OF ALBION MUSIC, INC. and UNIVERSAL-SONGS OF POLYGRAM INTERNATIONAL, INC. All Rights
for FLAMES OF ALBION MUSIC, INC. Administered by WB MUSIC CORP.
Exclusive Print Rights for FLAMES OF ALBION MUSIC, INC. for the World Excluding Europe
Administered by ALFRED MUSIC PUBLISHING CO., INC.
All Rights Reserved

IMPORTANT SMALL BARRE CHORDS

The small barre chords illustrated below are useful for playing solos. If only the first three strings are played, the chord is movable. The three positions shown are the most frequently used. The barre may be formed with the first, second, or third finger, whichever is most convenient. This often depends upon the notes or chord preceding or following it.

If the barre is extended to include the 4th string, it becomes a minor 7th chord. The letter name may be determined by the note sounding on the 1st string. This may also be considered a 6th chord, in which case the letter name is determined by the note sounding on the 3rd string. (A 6th chord adds the 6th note of the scale to the triad.)

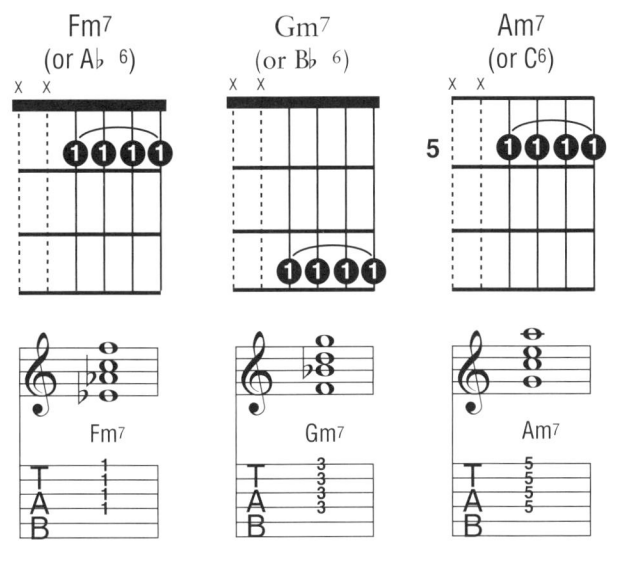

Preparation for "Stairway to Heaven" Intro

Practice the following chord sequence, fingering each chord as indicated on the diagram above it:

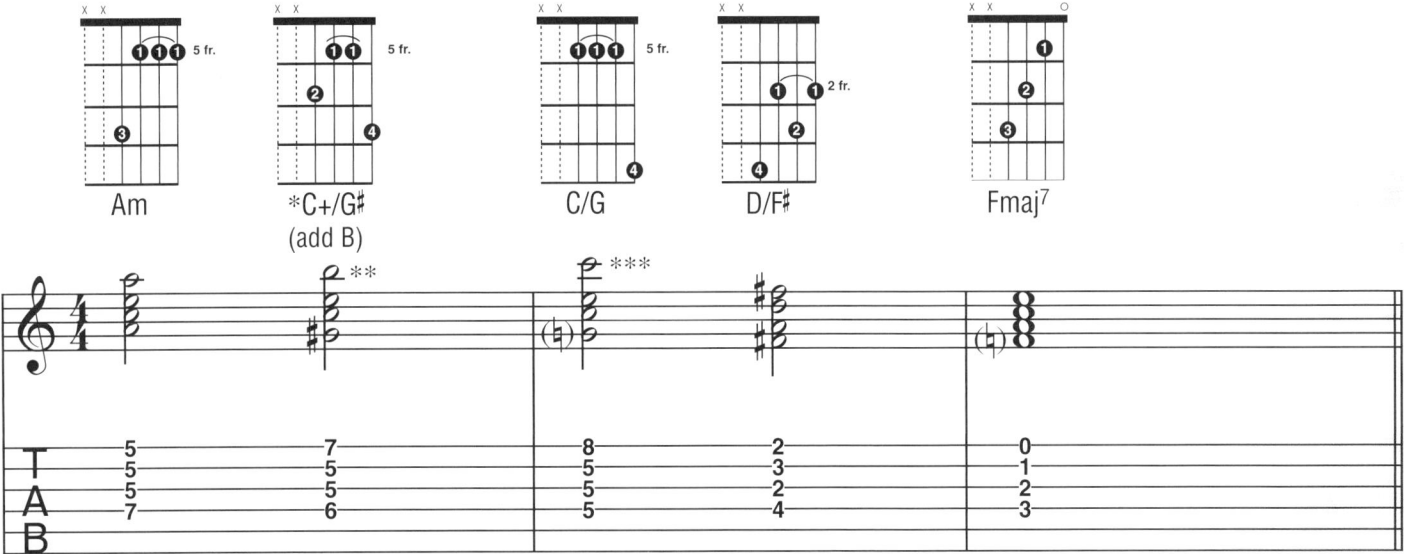

Finger the chords exactly as shown above, but play the individual notes as indicated:

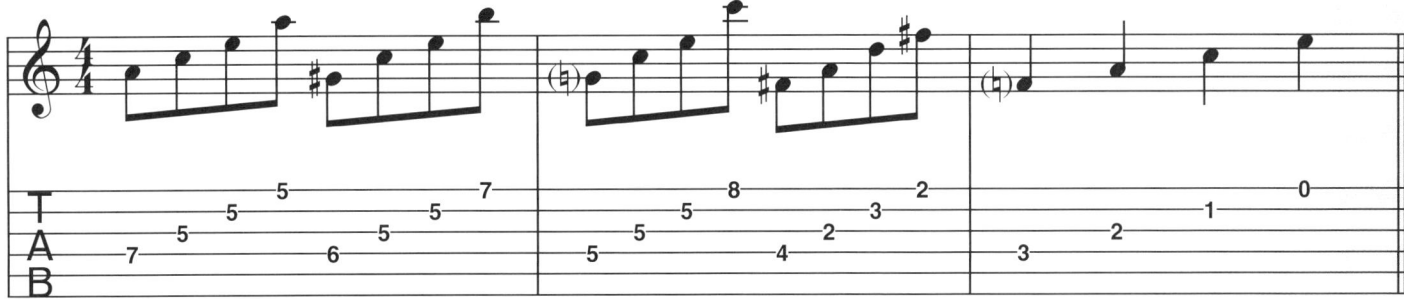

* An augmented + chord is a major triad with the 5th raised a half step.

** High B is fingered on the 1st string at the 7th fret   *** High C is fingered on the 1st string at the 8th fret.

STAIRWAY TO HEAVEN
(INTRO)

From the album

Words and Music by
Jimmy Page and Robert Plant

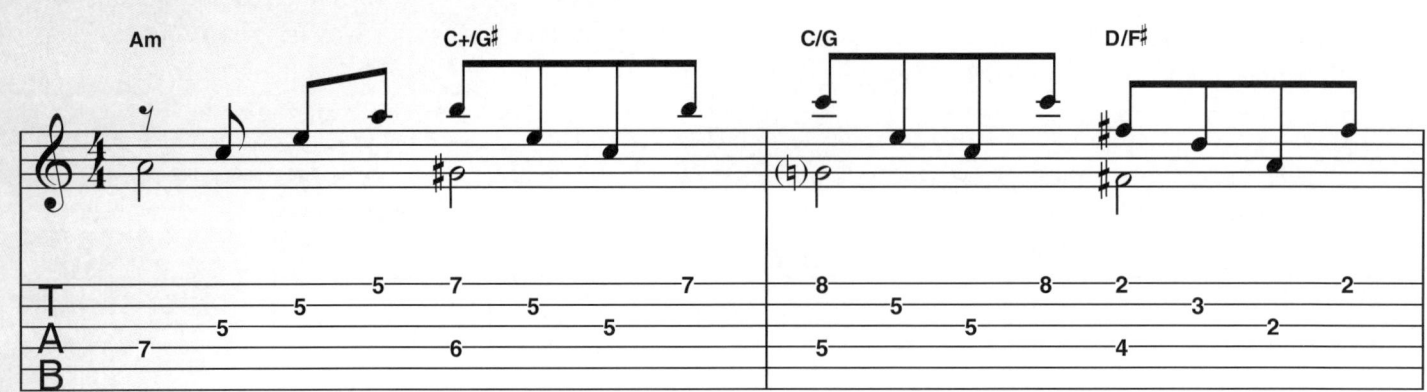
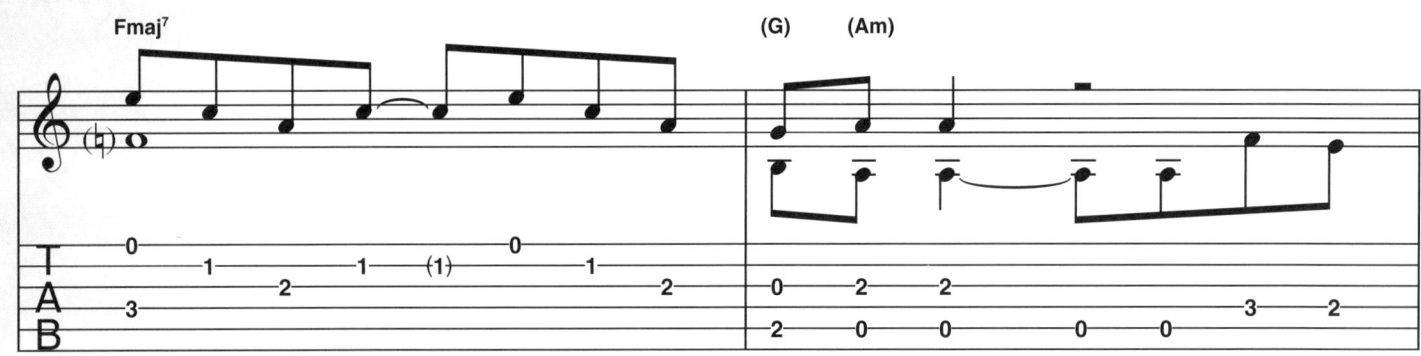
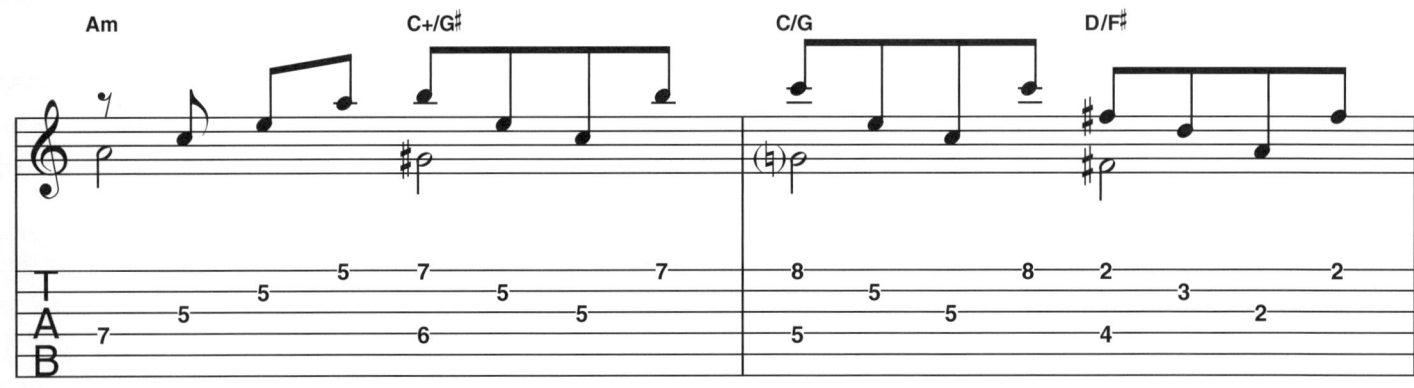
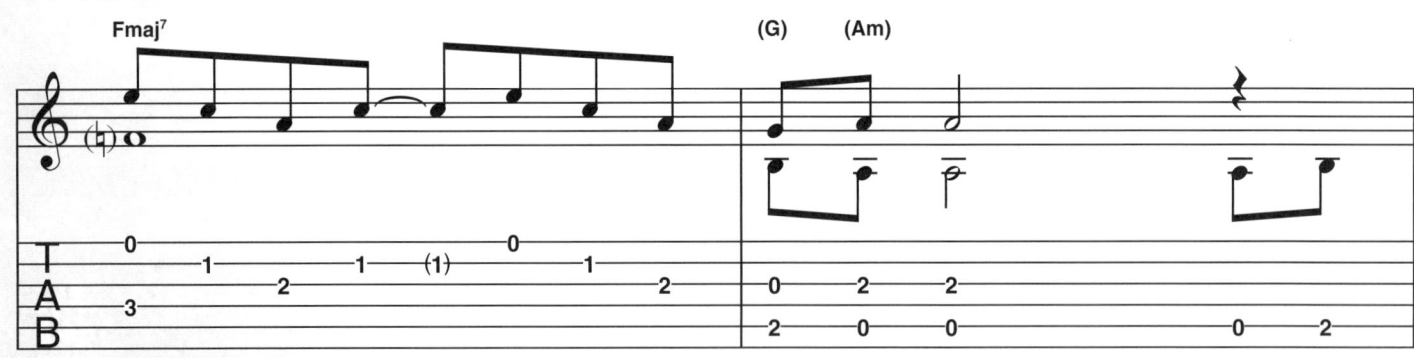

© 1972 (Renewed) FLAMES OF ALBION MUSIC, INC.
All Rights Administered by WB MUSIC CORP.
Exclusive Print Rights for the World Excluding Europe Administered by ALFRED MUSIC PUBLISHING
All Rights Reserved

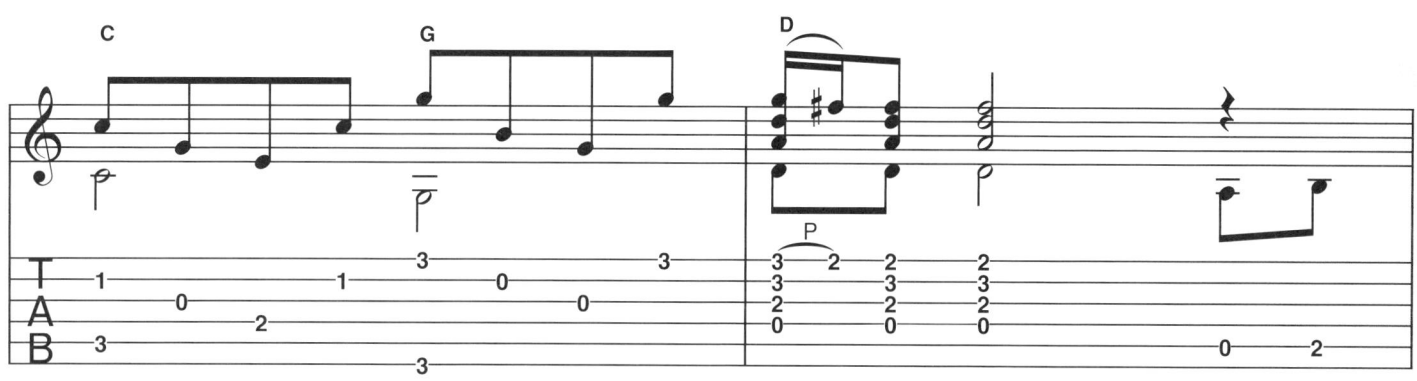
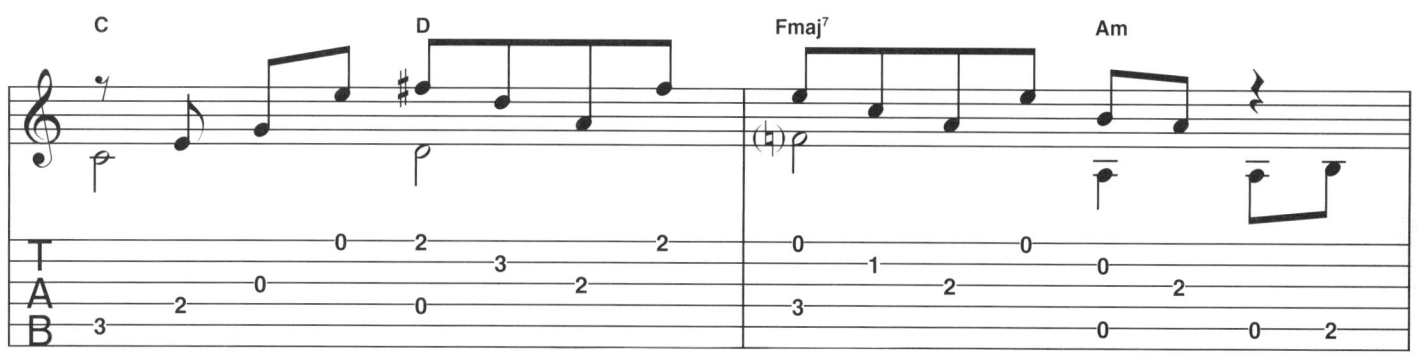
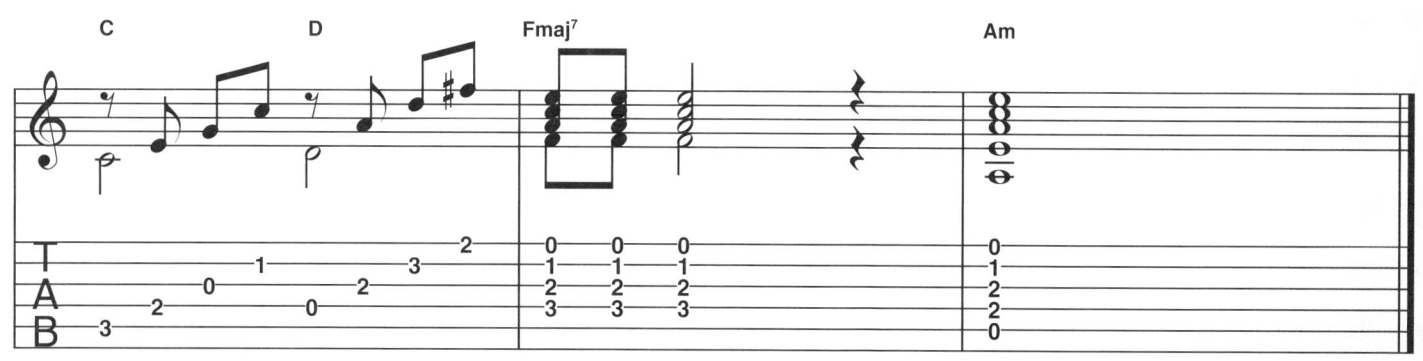

CHORD CHART

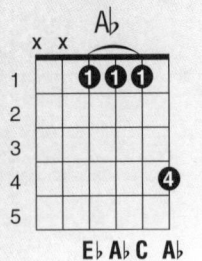 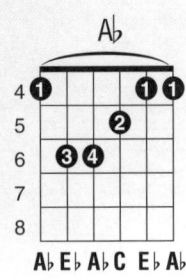 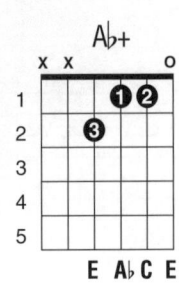 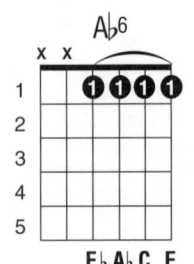 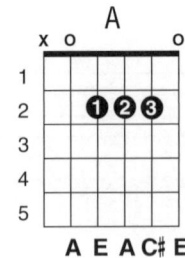 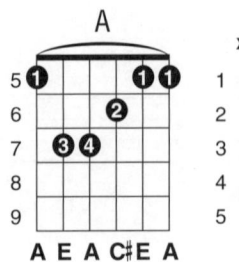 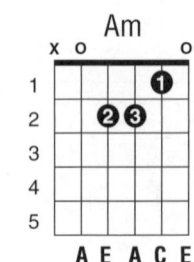

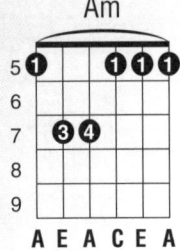 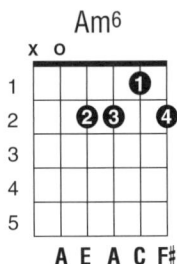 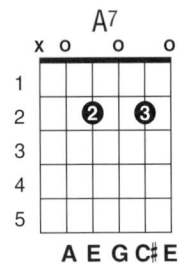 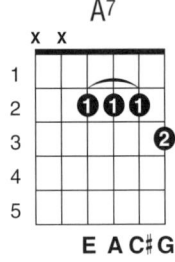 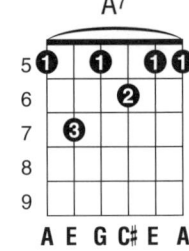 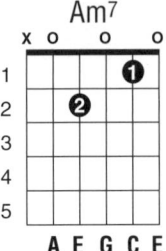 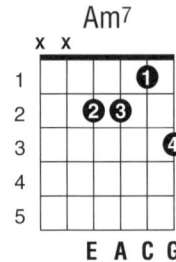

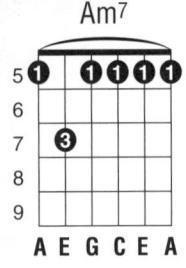 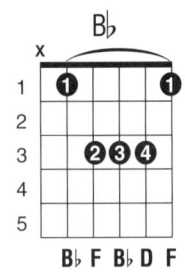 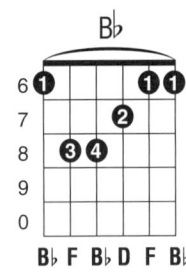 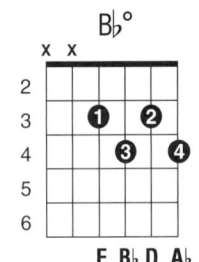 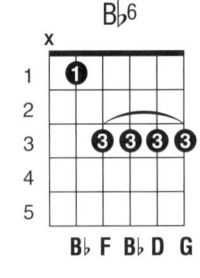 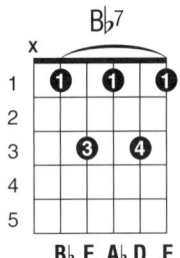 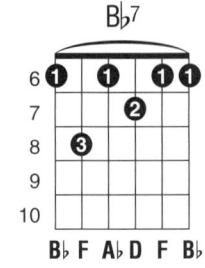

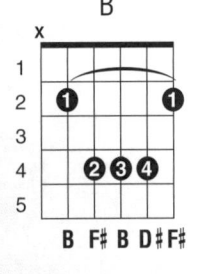 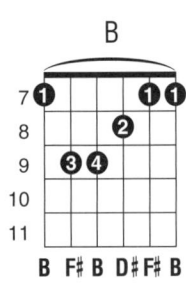 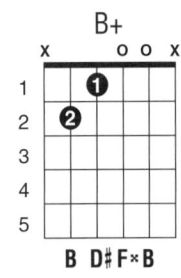 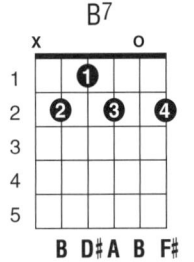 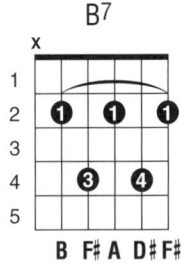 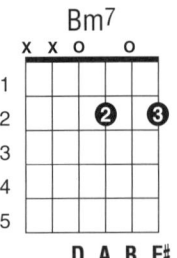 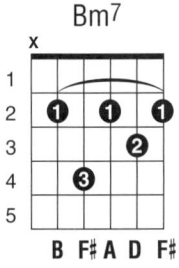

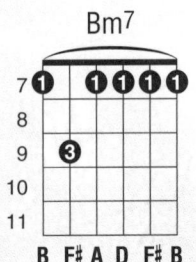 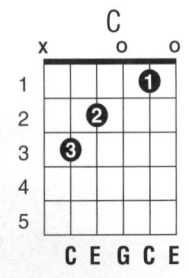 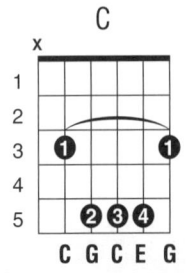 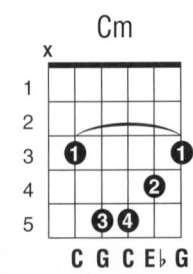 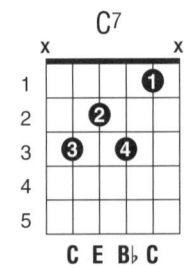 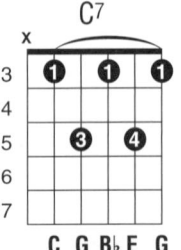 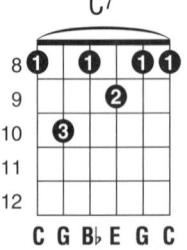

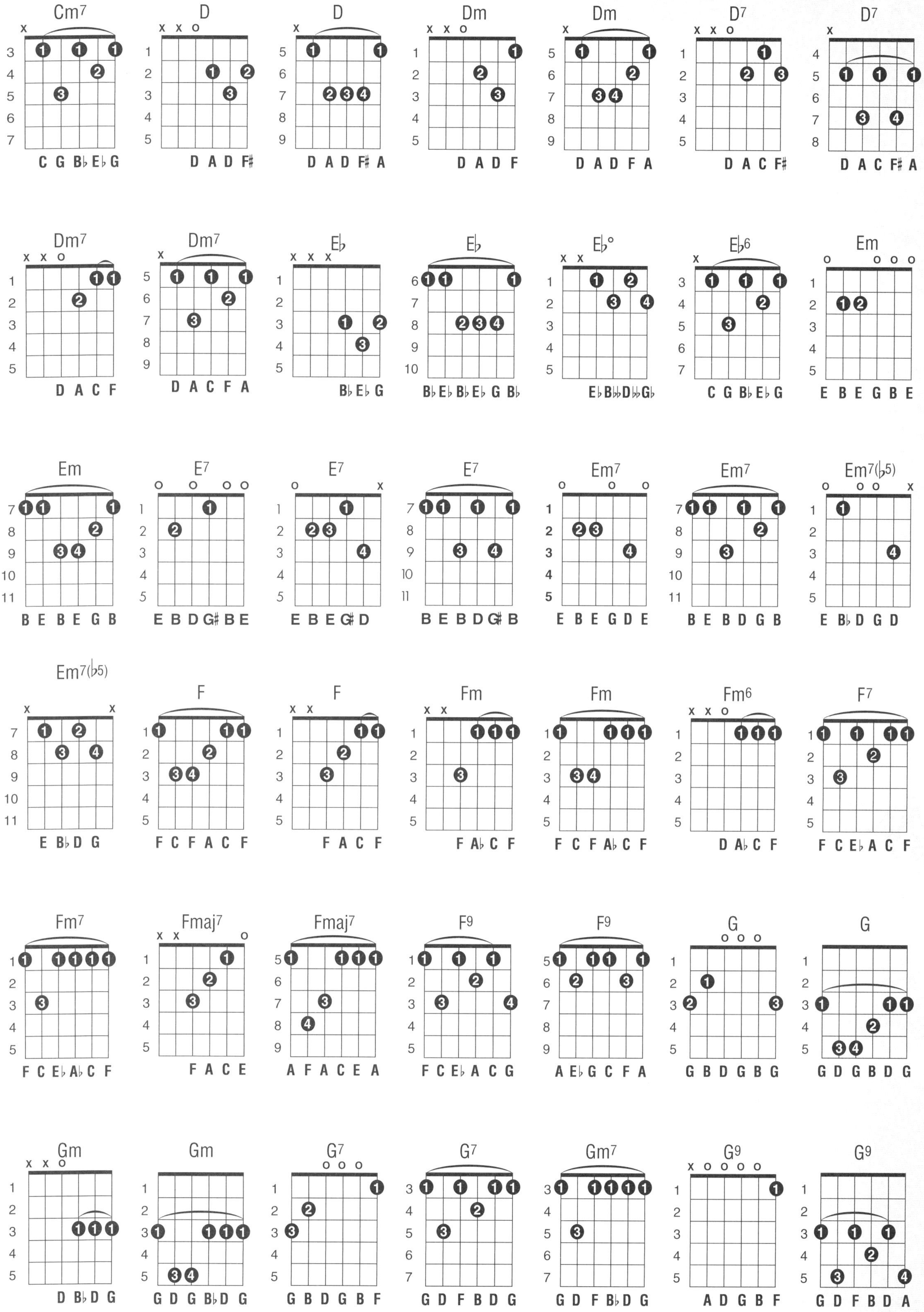

LED ZEPPELIN GUITAR METHOD 95

Guitar Fingerboard Chart

Frets 1–12